The Family Flamboyant

SUNY series in Feminist Criticism and Theory
Michelle A. Massé, Editor

The Family Flamboyant

Race Politics, Queer Families, Jewish Lives

Marla Brettschneider

STATE UNIVERSITY OF NEW YORK PRESS

Published by
State University of New York Press, Albany

© 2006 State University of New York

For information, address State University of New York Press
194 Washington Avenue, Suite 305, Albany, NY 12210-2384

Production by Kelli Williams
Marketing by Susan M. Petrie

Library of Congress Cataloging-in-Publication Data

Brettschneider, Marla.
    The family flamboyant : race politics, queer families, Jewish lives / Marla
Brettschneider.
        p. cm.— (SUNY series in feminist criticism and theory)
    Includes bibliographical references and index.
    ISBN-13: 978-0-7914-6893-7 (hardcover : alk. paper)
    ISBN-10: 0-7914-6893-3 (hardcover : alk. paper)
    ISBN-13: 978-0-7914-6894-4 (pbk. : alk. paper)
    ISBN-10: 0-7914-6894-1 (pbk. : alk. paper)
    1. Gay and lesbian studies.   2. Jewish lesbians—Family relationships.
3. Jewish families.   4. Monogamous relationships.   5. Jews—Identity.   6. Race
awareness.   7. Group identity.   8. Identity (Psychology)   I. Title.   II. Series.

HQ75.15.B74 2006
306.84'8089924—dc22   2005036235

10 9 8 7 6 5 4 3 2 1

For Dawn

Contents

Acknowledgments

We flutter out the door on our way to a party. The neighbors sneer, "Why must they be so flamboyant?" Our friends at the party think we're fabulous.

I come out as "Jewish" in a Women's Studies class and assign one book by a Jewish author. A student writes on the end of semester evaluation: "This class was too Jewish." Another writes: "Does she have to flaunt the Jewish thing so much?" These, they think, are criticisms.

At the end of a public lecture on adoption in which I've talked about my family, I get a short stack of cards with comments and questions to respond to. On the first one is written: "Your discussion of your family addresses just about every issue I am working on these days, thank you." On the second is written: "Are you purposely trying to flout *every* convention?"

Flamboyance is in the eye of the beholder. What I find most interesting is the politics of what is called flamboyant, whether the beholder thinks this is good or bad, and why. Welcome to *The Family Flamboyant: Race Politics, Queer Families, Jewish Lives.*

This book has been many years in the making, with many changes in our lives, policy, and the world along the way. Although I, alone, am responsible for all its shortcomings, this book could not have been written without the involvement and sustenance of many individuals, institutions, and organizations.

At the University of New Hampshire, Vickie, Holly, Marcie and the whole of Political Science, Women's Studies, Queer Studies, and the College of Liberal Arts have each been a source of much appreciated support. I extend thanks to the many students who worked with me over the years on this project: Katrina Royce-Malmgren, Shiju Cui, Caroline Leyva, Kate Bedford, Amanda Smith, Annie Medeiros, Peter Joseph, and Ashley Jane Kneeland.

Pat Moynagh and Lori Marso have remained steadfast friends and supportive colleagues. Sarah and H. Mark Roelofs have made so very much possible.

The following people generously gave of their time and expertise to read and comment on drafts of the manuscript: Lori Marso, Danielle Gougon, Martha Ackelsberg, Sean Cahill, Molly Shanley, Jane Litman, Bill Krisel, Rebecca Alpert, Carol Conaway, and Martin Kavka. I am humbled by their engagement. Many reviewers remain anonymous and I would like to thank each of them for their thoughtful and occasionally all too necessarily searing responses.

I am grateful for the feedback from, and connections with, Marie Fritz, Clare Kinberg, Alan Soble, Caryn Aviv and David Shneer, and to Tobin Belzer for acting as shadchanit. James Peltz at State University of New York has been a great editor, I am lucky to have worked with him and with Randi Dubrick and everyone at SUNY.

Deep thanks to Deborah Greniman, Shulamit Reinhardz, the additional editors and all the writers for the special issue of *Nashim* (2004): 8; Elizabeth Schussler Fiorenza, Kwok Pui-lan and the writers for the special issue of the *Journal of Feminist Studies in Religion* 19, no. 1 (Spring 2003); Jean Belkhir and the writers for the special issue of *Race, Gender, and Class* 6, no. 4 (1999); Susan Berrin and the writers for the special issue of *Shma* 33 (June 2003): 602. Let us continue to create space so that more may lift their voices into communal conversation.

A special thank you is needed for Melanie Kaye/Kantrowitz. Her life, work, friendship, and commitments over a lifetime have simply made possible the kind of Jewed racial analysis found throughout this work.

Warm thanks to Jen Chau, Swirl, Inc., and the Swirl reading group—especially Rebecca, Anna, Marilyn, Martha, Loren, Lisa, and Jen—for reading and discussing a prepublication draft; and to Laurie Zimmerman, the fabulous folk of Jewish Queer Think Tank and those who engaged the JQTT in public fora over the years.

Thanks to Miryam Kabakov and those who continue to organize various panels and programs on the topics of this work at the Jewish Community Center in Manhattan; Eve Landau, Barbara Dobkin and the women of Ma'ayan, particularly Tamara Cohen, for their tireless work and for drawing me into the circle of the 2005 study; Bertell Ollman and the great participants in The Marxist Theory Symposium at New York University; Sue Cobble, Beth Hutchinson, Marlene Importico and the wonderful group in The Rutgers University Institute for Research on Women and the 2003–2004 Femininities, Masculinities, and the Politics of Sexual Difference(s) Seminar participants; those who attended the Political Philosophy Symposium at Union College in 2002; the unique sessions at the Feminist Political Theory Conference and the Western Political Science Association meetings (and particularly to Mary Hawkesworth for organizing the 2002 Theorizing Difference session); Martha Ackelsberg, the related sessions at the American Political Science Association, and the 2001 day-long Special Session on Women and Politics and to Jane Bayes for organizing it; the marriage and monogamy session at the 2003 National Association of Women's Studies meeting; the Queer Seminar at the University of Massachusetts at Amherst and to Felice Yeskel for inviting me to present my work; and the International Association of Women Philosophers Conference, Barcelona, Spain 2002.

I would not be on the journey I am today without the fiery women of Bnot Esh. For additional opportunities to live out moments of *olam ha'ba*, the world to come, I am grateful to the members of the National Havurah Institutes, the Jewish Multiracial community, Kol Zimrah, and Congregation Bet Simchat Torah. Jews For Racial and Economic Justice continues to be a tough and beloved testing ground for theorizing in the way I do.

I stand in awe within the divine web of politics and biology, difficult routes and moments of excruciating individual agency. There are not enough words to express the gratitude I feel: for all the neighbors, friends, family, babysitters, child care workers, clergy, counselors, and teachers— including the doctors and lawyers—who have cared for, nurtured, and helped grow our kids; to Suzie Lowenger and Lanie Resnick for helping to keep me alive in the many senses of that word; to Mary Bonauto from GLAD for clearing the path; to those at MAPS, to Beth for answering the phone, and Gayle Merlin Knee *all* for making our family possible.

Sweet thanks to Walter and Emma Rous for sharing their nest in the magic forest, and to Joanne Jacobson for encouragement and good cheer.

It was a gift that my maternal grandmother was still alive and in my life when I began the work on this book. I have been lucky enough to continue to have the love and care of my parents, Sol and Phyllis, and my incredible sisters, Nina and Beth. I do not, in any way, pretend to speak on behalf of any one in my family. For good or ill, I realize that this one is all mine. Still, I thank Dawn Rose for walking with me along this unchartered path. I am grateful for all the forces in the universe that make Paris, Paris and Toni, Toni; their lives most certainly are a blessing.

Portions of this book are adapted with permission from pieces previously published:

Journal of American Jewish History 88, no. 1 (March 2000): 156–159. John Hopkins University Press.
Bridges: A Journal for Jewish Feminists and Our Friends 8, nos. 1 and 2 (Spring 2000): 124–127.

2002. "All Points Bulletin: Jewish Dykes Adopting Children." In *Queer Jews*, edited by David Shneer and Caryn Aviv, 238–257. New York: Routledge/Taylor & Francis Group, LLC.

Shofar 21, no. 2 (Winter 2003): 171–173. Purdue University Press.

"Judaism, Twentieth- and Twenty-First-Century." In *Sex from Plato to Paglia: A Philosophical Encyclopedia*, ed. Alan Soble, 533–42. Westport, CT: Greenwood Press, 2005.

The Good Society 14, nos. 1–2 (2004): 7–10.

V.
The Bronx
2006

Introduction

K-I-S-S-I-N-G

Beth and Stuart sitting in a tree, K-I-S-S-I-N-G;
first comes love,
then comes marriage,
then comes baby in the baby carriage.

We used to sing that song as kids. We would change the names depending on who was currently sweet on whom, or depending on whom we chose to torment that day. Beth is my older sister. Stuart Flurb was her first boyfriend; they met in Hebrew School. My middle sister Nina has a special knack for anointing people with nicknames, somehow revealing that specific aspect of their character you just couldn't put your finger on. Nina called him Fluart Sturb. It's hard to describe, but it was totally expressive. To this day, I still have to stop my brain in order to sort out which was the boy's given name and which was the one Nina dubbed him with.

I remember Beth bringing Stuart and some friends to the "den" in our home that served as her bedroom during her adolescence. I wanted to see what they were doing. I meant them no harm. But my banging on the closed door alerted my mother. All I remember after that is the scurry: kids hopping out the ground floor window from the room, mad dashes to stash stuff in the closet . . . and that I got my sister "in trouble." Beth never married Stuart; she's been in love but has not married nor has she born babies to put in baby carriages. She didn't even like to push my kids in their strollers. Why did we kids think that song made any sense? Why was its sharp edge double sided: meant to recognize and support

1

with one side, meant to estrange and harm with the other? Why was that ditty so powerful for us? What is it about desire and its supposed connection to the inevitability of family—as if enjoying the closeness that comes from sitting with a friend in a tree is linked, in the span of a sentence, a flash of thought, to the nuclear two-heterosexually parented family. The childlike fantasy can only go as far as the creation of babies. It cannot imagine staying single. It cannot envision queerdom, divorce, abuse, disruption, re-marriage, falling in love more than once. It cannot take in the long haul of child rearing and helping to develop strong independent beings on their way into the world. I never really hear people say: "I want to raise children," they say: "I want to have babies." Like the ditty, the circle ends with the most regressed aspect of the fantasy, being a baby.

My partner Dawn was a towheaded inquisitive child running barefoot through "cricks" and riding horses bareback. Her family were ranchers living in rural northern California. Not the rich kind, the earth is dust. I can barely breathe out there and can never stop thinking about Steinbeck. For money and to cope with the heat, in the summers the family ran a concession stand at a lake in the nearby mountains. Dawn played "garden" and considered one of the goats her best friend. They rose early in the mornings. While "mother" (in my New York Jewish home, a screeching "ma" would do) did her bible study and her own chores, she set the children down to practice piano for a full hour each before their chores and school. Dawn was raised a fundamentalist Baptist and her mom continued her early morning bible study until she died. Despite Dawn's—let's just call them "more ambivalent"—experiences as a member, from the outside her family embodied the ideal of "American family life" and could have been a poster family for the "Family Values" ideologues of today. Interestingly, Dawn found out at the age of forty-eight that her parents hadn't been legally married until the birth of their fourth child, Dawn's younger sister. That means her mom was a poor teenage white mother out of wedlock with three kids before she got herself "legitimate." Members of the right wing in this country have been working very hard to protect the "American Family." Crusaders charge ahead mobilizing the vast powers of the state to infantilize the family, to fashion Norman Rockwell paintings into living stories. This isn't an easy thing to do, even for those with actual access in the U.S. legal system. I mean my goodness, they even let Dawn's family slip through the cracks.

No one took Dawn's mom's kids away though. Being white and Christian, with a mother and a father, and passing well enough for a "legitimate" family, none of the kids were hauled off to foster homes or put up for adoption. Dawn had parents, and whether she liked it or not the ruling ideology—from church through the state to public opinion—

kept it that way. Now we live in a world where the law creates a category of children as parentless. (With the rather recent phenomenon of formal adoption, the law must create a child "parentless" before the child may be adopted.) This legal fiction goes beyond a PC acknowledgment that not everyone "has" a mommy and a daddy. The PCers mean not everyone is being raised by two married heterosexual parents; they still assume even abandoned children have progenitors commonly referred to as parents. In the biblical story, Solomon was presented with a child to whom two women made claims as mother. In the story the child has no voice, the women are hysterical, a great man must decide. He offers to split the child in two, knowing the "real" mother will back down at the threat of harm to the child. There cannot be two mothers. Child after child has been repeatedly told: "It may sound cruel dear, but King Solomon was very wise." In the United States, we have a similar problem recognizing multiple mothers. Leave it to those in the U.S. legal system to invent the concept of the parentless child.

I have two friends, a lesbian couple, who may "appear" conservative to some but can be rather frank about sex. They love to sing Starhawk's song about sex. (Did you know that Starhawk the witch, peace activist, and writer, is Jewish? Now why should that surprise you?) The lyrics begin:

> Sex, sex,
> we are all made from sex,
> put your fingers in each other.
> Yum yum yum.

I've seen them get up rousing renditions to delighted straight feminist and queer audiences. It seems they have found the primal life cycle commonality among us while playing with lesbian sexuality. This time we are at a Jewish feminist spiritual retreat that has been meeting for more than twenty-five years at a Catholic laywomen's social justice center. Any one of the women present might have been heterosexually married in a previous incarnation of her life and is now a famous lesbian, or formerly a famous lesbian agitator now happily heterosexually married with kids, or married to a man and raising a child while the lover to whom she refers is a woman, or a bisexual transgendered woman nonmonogamously married to a man and raising three kids with her husband. This time when the couple sing the song, someone objects. She has six children and the first four were not "made from sex." The woman is a lesbian. With the first four kids she was single and used insemination. These children know they do not have a daddy, they have a donor (in her case the sperm was actually a gift and not a purchase). The last two children she adopted while in a relationship with a gay man. These two younger children have two parents, a mommy and a daddy, adopted and each gay nevertheless. The youngest is around the same age as my kids. We have had wonderful times being away together at another Jewish retreat we love and the kids especially enjoy sharing living quarters so the girls can play and shower together. When the gay dad joins us at the retreat with the two youngest— the ones that call him daddy—I find myself making interventions lest my kids feel marginalized by what seems like their friends' "normative" family structure.

This is a world where for a few years my adopted daughters had legal documents attesting to their live births which recorded me as their mother. Although the men who served as sperm sources to their bio-mothers are known, their "live birth" certificates indicate no father. In these documents I am presented as the mother who birthed these children. I suppose if a child can be parentless altogether, there is no reason the miracle birth of a child with no human father cannot be recreated in U.S. law as well. It may be a Christian story, but like me, Mary was Jewish. For one of my kids, the line for father was simply left blank. If the law is going to make up these children's stories, why must the forms presuppose a father space needing to be filled in at all? For my other child the line for father read: "sole legal legitimate parent." An awkward name to be called out during a play on the basketball court. You would think in turn of the Christian millennium U.S. use of the word "legitimate" would be a mere anachronism applied to children—but no. And anyway, the father happens not to be the sole legal legitimate parent. This verbiage makes even less sense in that in the space for signature, there was none, but typed in were the words "sole legal parent & Marla Brettschneider." Suddenly, I am somehow two personages in the law, deserving an ampersand, not a qualifying comma. Years later, that ampersand will cause me trouble, inciting lawyers to question my legal parental rights.

I will discuss issues regarding the naming of my children later in this book, but for now I will let you know that on the certificates of live birth, the children have both my and Dawn's names. The documents are awash in contradictions they cannot synthesize. The requirement that a child can only have one mother at a time; with a new sensibility of "lesbian rights" the acknowledgment that she has two, me and Dawn. Why the impossibility of a third? The biological mother is legally disappeared. In the film *First Person Plural*, Deann Borshay Liem is a Korean woman adopted by white U.S. parents. She is emotionally scarred by her inability to imagine two mothers given the "trauma" of international adoption. Yet lesbians have been co-mothering children for years. It is actually a leap of faith in the development process to imagine mothering in a singular hue for many of these kids. A woman named Stefa gave testimony from her experience being a hidden child during the Holocaust: she notes that when she was reunited with her Jewish biological mother (after the mother was freed from Bergen-Belsen), and she was separated from her hidden adoptive mother, she cried so hard, for she "didn't understand why [she] couldn't have two mothers" (Kessel 2000, 61). Who ought to decide such things? The children, adult children, any of the mother claimants, the state, King Solomon, all together or some combination?

I live in a world in which I named my first adopted daughter after my maternal stepgrandfather, a man who raised no children to which he contributed biologically. Bloodlines be damned. With the naming of my daughter, the family feels he has been honored with a rightful heir. His wife, my maternal grandmother, escaped pogroms and came to the United States from Russia as a child with her mother. They arrived just as the United States began to close its doors to Eastern European immigrants in the 1920s. Back in Russia, my maternal great-grandfather was killed by Cossacks along the way of their escape, and his murder was avenged by the Red Army while they were still in transit. My grandmother's life was spared at the last minute by the murderers. The Cossacks came onto their train to take the valuables of the women and to kill all the males. Why then, you may ask, were they interested in my grandmother's life? Well, it seems my great-grandfather had wanted a boy so badly that they were raising my grandmother as one. Dressed as a boy, the Cossacks tried to pull my grandmother off the train too. A woman pleaded with them, "she's not really a boy." The Cossacks pulled down her pants and the matter was settled. No penis. Proof. My grandmother lives. It took my grand and great-grandmothers two years of traveling, but they eventually made it to a boat at port in Istanbul bound for "America." I don't know how, but with the help of some Christian peasants, changing birth dates to meet U.S. quotas, and a whole lot of love, luck, misery, and blessing, they made it onto Ellis Island and (more importantly) off to join the mass of immigrants early in the twentieth century.

While still a teenager, my unwed grandmother got pregnant. The man who became my mom's biological father was forced to marry my grandmother because even here in the new world things weren't quite new enough. There goes another unwed teen pregnancy. Eleven years later the couple had a son. The man beat and otherwise emotionally abused them all. My grandmother and the two kids escaped in the middle of the night aided by a Jewish social service agency. Before my mother's bio-father (my grandmother's first legal husband) was successful in getting my grandmother back, he had the decency to die. This made it possible for my grandmother to later marry the gentle man I always called Papa and until some time in preadolescence knew as my only maternal grandfather. He had escaped pogroms in Poland and despite his Orthodox kin (some of who made it here too), he chose secular Judaism once in the new world. He offered to adopt my grandmother's two grown children. My mother proclaimed she loved him as her father, but she was about to marry my dad. Legally adopting her wasn't necessary, she was about to have the stamp of law affirming her attachment to a husband instead. My Papa did adopt her younger brother. My mother's brother married and had two kids. Unfortunately, like his bio-father, he also went off the deep end, scarring his family in ways I probably couldn't begin to imagine. For many years now, the "family" I have kept in touch with has not been my bio-uncle, but my married-in aunt and my cousins.

My paternal grandfather made it to this country alone, also in the early 1900s. He was fifteen years old and fated for a terrible marriage to a U.S. born woman who hated him for being an immigrant. After birthing three children, she was bedridden from emotional distress and eventually died. My dad grew up separated from his siblings. His brother and sister were raised with their mother's extended family and my dad raised by his single father. Later in life my paternal grandfather remarried. I never knew either my dad's bio or stepmom. I always knew my uncle and aunt, and didn't come to know about their years separated from my father until I was older. My father's brother never married and lived a simple life. Unlike all of our other relatives, he never brought any friends around for holiday gatherings. In my young adulthood, friends and I often delight-fully speculated that he was gay; we joked that I would run into him at queer events around New York City. When he died, my sister Nina informed his only two friends of whom she knew. The next morning at his funeral, Riverside Memorial Chapel was literally overflowing with mourn-ers. (Just to be honest about those stereotypes, Riverside Memorial Chapel is the one on the Upper West Side of Manhattan that you see in all the funeral scenes during films about New York Jews: Woody Allen-type films, the opening scene of Tony Kushner's *Angels in America*, etc.) We had had no idea that my uncle lived within such an intense, and large, circle of relations (who were not very gay!). My father's sister married, had two girls, and then divorced. Her first daughter married an Israeli who was born to Hungarian Holocaust survivors while they were trying to enter a holding camp in Cyprus on their way to Palestine. My cousin had two kids, divorced, and later in life back in the United States remar-ried another divorcee with kids. We still consider her first husband and his family "family," including the woman *he* married later in life. My aunt's younger daughter married a Moroccan Israeli living in the United

States, a previously divorced man with two children; their kids play with the grandkids of their father. Despite anti-Arab racism I have witnessed occasionally in my family, I even heard his own bio-kids exhibit a similar racial bias when they were young.

Funny, I always thought of my family as unbearably normal according to the mythic ideal of the "American" family. I'm not sure my story is that unusual among Jews and many others in the United States. But on (U.S.) American standards as well, I guess with all this dislocation, transnational migration, abuse, divorce, single adults, dykes, multiple marriages and so on, we actually *are* quite normal, at least empirically. (The things you figure out when you grow up.)

This is a world where, as an adult, I run into the sister of an old friend of mine on the Upper West Side. We all met as teenagers going to work on kibbutzim in Israel. I haven't seen her in years, but now we have a new connection—we have kids around the same age. We're trying to figure out how to work the system and get our kids into non-failing public kindergartens in New York City (an herculean task if there ever were one). She is the unmarried heterosexual adopted daughter of my friend's father's third wife. She has had her daughter through insemination with sperm from (what in layperson's terms is called) "the genius sperm bank," she is currently letting her bio-brother stay with her while her adoptive brother (born biologically to the mother they share) lives in an apartment in the same complex owned it seems by their jointly shared grandfather. When we meet at the Central Park Zoo on a sunny autumn afternoon, she and her daughter and me, with my multiracial adoptive family with two moms, are the city's picture of families on an outing.

As a family we like to get out and about. My kids love to ride the subways and buses in New York. At two- and three-years-old, they were already swinging around the poles and hanging from the overhead bars like the teenagers that the undercover cops are always harassing. This is a world where I get on the subway with a Black man dressed in a black robe of an ultra-Orthodox Jewish sect, covered in a beautiful tallit (prayer shawl) over tzizit (religious undergarments), and sporting a necklace with a large flashy Jewish star. He's haranguing the travelers with fire and brimstone about racial degradation, sexual improprieties, proper gender hierarchy, the need for class warfare, and the love of Jesus. In the turmoil I have been forced to abandon my newspapers, the English language version of the Jewish *Forward*—an old Yiddish socialist publication that decided to publish an English version given the ever diminishing demographic pool of fluent Yiddish speakers. I've been reading about a guy who has come out with a new CD from the Jews in Uganda (I am confused because we bought one such CD from this guy a couple of years ago), about a non-Jewish Cuban musician who has integrated klezmer (an Eastern European style of music) into his new work, and about a public service campaign about Jews taking place in Sao Paulo. I've just read about the production of Woody Guthrie's Jewish music, the debut issue of a flashy Hollywood-style magazine conceived of by a gay Jewish immigrant from Iran, (I wonder how he fared in the post 9/11 INS roundup of Iranians in L.A.), and about the publisher who has all the English language publishing rights for Kafka's writings. I loved the piece on the then new Spanish-language Jewish newspaper (because, in contrast to the decline in Yiddish speakers, the Jewish "Hispanic"—as it is called—community in the United States has been growing). I know the Cuban rabbi who initiated it, Manny Vinnias, from Jewish multiracial circles. Since he's a beautiful soul and runs the most racially mixed class I could find in the Bronx, Manny would eventually become my kids' Hebrew school teacher for a spell. I miss my train stop because I am trying to figure out what the man in the tallit is getting at. With his heartfelt love for Jesus, does he consider himself some sort of Jew? I want to ask him a question. I'm trying to figure out how I can explain to my kids what's going on. I jump off the train when I realize I'm going to miss my appointment because I'm too far downtown now. I do not know what becomes of the man in the tallit.

In this book I hope to add to the ongoing conversation amongst feminists, queers and Jews, Jewish feminist queers of any number of races, and the variety of individuals and groups working on identity issues in politics as part of a larger project of justice politics. Here I interweave personal narrative, political analysis, philosophical critique, and plain old observations of interest. With a focus on the family, I look closely at an array of issues challenging us in our current struggles with justice politics. These issues are issues for families, critical theorists, Jews, feminists, queers, class warriors, and for antiracist activists. You may feel closer to certain aspects than to others, but I understand these as issues for anyone who cares about families and with an interest in what may still be challenging in identity politics, those: gendered any which way; sexual outlaw or proud member of the sexual mainstream; Jewish, not so Jewish, not sure if you're Jewish, once Jewish, your great-grandmother was half-Jewish, and definitely not Jewish at all (are you sure about that?).

I couldn't write a book about family without it fundamentally being about racial formation, queer lives and theory, feminist challenges and insights, class and economic politics, Jews and Jewish legacies. (Read on, you'll see why.) Some of the chapters tend more toward the theoretical and others concrete as the sidewalk outside my window. It's all here together because that's the way intellectual life is: a combination of ranting, musing, thoughtful reflection, down and dirty critique, psychedelic imagination, generous recognition, and obstinate argumentation. The way dinner conversation might be on any holiday celebrated with my family. Very New York Jewish. Usually loud and pushy. Another stereotype, you might ask? Yes, and also quite descriptive in this case. I hope that you like it.

This book is intended to advance the discourse regarding the mutual constitution of our multiple identity signifiers by incorporating the much under-theorized contribution of Jewish life and experiences. Oy, that's a big sentence. Let me say that another way: This book draws on and advances the theory that not only are identities multiple, and multiply situated with respect to power, but that each politically salient aspect of our identity is mutually constituted through the development of the others. This means that one is not simply a man, or a Jew, or working class, or bisexual: one is all of these and each aspect actually co-creates the others. In this view, the gender of Jewish men and Jewish women, for example, is explicitly "Jewed." This work brings together and develops principally feminist, queer, class-based, and critical race theories by informing the discourse with Jewishly grounded theorizing as well as bringing the variety of these critical theories to bear on an analysis of aspects of Jewish history and thought. Here I look at family matters to both apply and develop this orientation of mutual construction theory.

Thus, the concrete work in this book takes on issues commonly associated with "family." My aim is to examine the family in a way that is at once recognizable and close, and simultaneously held at a lovingly critical distance. The basic question is: how can we unfamiliarize ourselves with a construct, an institution, an experience as familiar as "the family?" How can we talk politically about a body presumed to be a creature of affect? How can critical theory be the language to discuss the supposedly private mode of love and generations? At this historical juncture we must wake-up, shake ourselves out of the sleep into which we have been lulled with childhood bedtime stories of hetero-romantic love, marriage, and forever. The institution of marriage and family, the multibillion dollar business of marriage and family, are at the heart of systemic modes of injustice which propel our social worlds into the future. Locally, nationally, internationally, the commodification of affect which squeezes us into the constraints of the nuclear family are grounded in and make possible the political capacity for hierarchy, degradation, and annihilation of the spirit and psyche as kin to the annihilation of the peoples and cultures wiped off the map as global capitalism runs rampant as wild fires in southern California. We the people, as opposed to multinational corporations and the U.S. military-industrial complex, need to do some shaking up. We need to make that which is cozy a bit more uncomfortable. Without doing so we will not be able to clear out enough space for insight, critical understanding, and relation with which we can re-engage in our worlds, in our desires, needs, passion in any way that is not simply reinscribing indignity and alienation.

Throughout this text on family business (we did have one, low-end textiles of course), I address issues within theories on identity itself grounded in the imbricating frameworks of Jewish, feminist, class-based, race, and queer critical theories. Here I also apply these co-constructed theories to a number of inherently related concerns significant in contemporary Jewish communities and families such as: racial transformations, adoption, various modes of family construction, marriage and monogamy, (trans) sexual and gender identity, and political activism. I address the fine balance that these newer contributions in the academy and on the streets may offer to Jewish life with traditional Jewish interests in continuity and communal self-definition.

With all the ruckus caused by feisty Jewish queers and activity on diversity more broadly in the Jewish community, I am often invited to speak or write for gatherings and collections with titles such as "The Changing Face of the Jewish Family" or "The Changing Face of Judaism." These titles are meant to open the audience to hearing from and about Jews with (in the words of the organizers) "black, brown, yellow, olive, and red" faces in addition to the U.S. stereotyped pink of northern European Jews. The symposia are designed to bring out into communal public spaces the experiences and contributions of queers, gays, lesbians, multi/bisexuals, transgendered Jews, feminists, divorced and single adult Jews, poor and typed-middle-class yet financially struggling Jews. People are wanting to address the needs and learn from the insights of elder Jews, young Jews, coastal Jews and those in the heartland, those who are Jews through conversion or living in interfaith families. Progressive Jews continue to mine radical Jewish history for inspiration and guidance; feminists, queers, and non-Euro Jews simultaneously blast the mines open to interrupt the unacknowledged hetero-patriarchal Euro-centeredness of the all too common reiterations of the mining. At these panels, many of the presenters feel compelled to use the first portion of our coveted speaking time challenging the premise of the gatherings themselves. (Such a Jewish practice.) The Jewish community has always been diverse; since ancient times and biblical stories, Israel has always been peopled by those of many nations. Jewish communities have always been in a state of flux.

The concern with continuity in the Jewish community mapped onto debates about the family might more properly be reconfigured as an interest in change. Jews around the globe have made it through history by change: through the dynamism of lives lived as Jews, through the dynamism of lives lived in community, of communities living with and against each other. Complex theories of identity, multiplicity, and change are crucial for understanding and caring for "continuity." When people say identity politics is dead, they are generally thinking of identities claimed as static, isolated components of a life. But identity politics remains very much alive, kept alive in part by those who condemn and deconstruct it. Struggling with identities—their multilayered, shifting, contextually contingent, and historically constructed politics—is alive and well. In consideration of the family, of complicated (and thus quite empirically traditional) kin networks, of the power of assimilation, the force of capitalism, the depravation of poverty, the indignity of prejudice, nuanced theories of identities are still called for in the messiness of our individual lives and our communal struggles for justice.

I know that I am not alone in these struggles. I have a great many comrades, both academics and street activists, producing works of beauty and critique on so many of the troubling political issues of our day. We are hard at work, serious at play, awestruck in prayer trying to untangle the jumble and meanings of our singular and collective lives in a new Christian millennium: in novels, poetry, and treatises; in film, dance, and all the arts; in experimental curating at museums willing to dare; in large and small demonstrations, marches, graffiti-ins; using the best of new technologies and the tried and true methods from knocking on doors to leafleting at neighborhood stores. In government, organizations, classrooms, yoga centers, comedy clubs, theatres, and places of worship, folks are creating new and bringing together the cutting edge political insights of Jewish, feminist, class, race, and queer theories and practices. Yet, we yearn for more. There is still so much to figure out and to change. We need more.

Feminist works are fundamentally transforming Jewish studies, exploding traditional assumptions and methods while reinvigorating Jewish life and scholarship. Queer studies also now has developed to such an extent that it is able to take on core aspects of Jewish life and tradition. A few Jewish scholars and activists are integrating contemporary work on class and economic justice while others are bringing antiracist concerns into Jewishly based analysis. There is, thus, currently a high demand for new approaches in this millennia-long tradition of Jewish scholarly debate. I consider myself part of these conversations, responding to this historic call by using my training in critical theory to bring multiple modes of identity-based critical analysis together in a Jewish frame. Among the few academics trained as political or critical theorists who have turned their attention to Jewish concerns, there are still too few drawing on the growing wealth of feminist, class-based, critical race, and queer scholarship and theory (let alone their mutually constitutive character).

What do you hear when you get quiet enough to listen?
I hear pounding.

I hear pounding all day every day as I write these words. I hear the pounding of children's fists as they cry out in frustration, the pounding of gavels in the courtrooms of our (supposed) justice system, the pounding of people marching in the streets, the pounding of radical activists at their computer keyboards trying desperately to get the word out, the pounding of hearts at the INS in a post-9/11 New York City detaining and deporting people with no due process. I hear pounding because for the past few months workers have been breaking through bedrock next door to build a new apartment building in what had been a rare patch of woods in the Bronx. Local activists tried to block the builders' securing a licence. Most of the local buildings are co-ops, the tenants in many of the nearby buildings are still the organizing type. We live in what we have nicknamed "amalgamated land." The neighborhood was built up early in the twentieth century by radical Jewish activists and union organizers: all co-ops, credit unions, and community services. I vote at Vladeck Hall, (I hope Vladeck was a Jewish anarchist!) because we still have old-fashioned community function rooms. A testament to the minority ethnic messianic vision within the labor movement. A little bit of heaven—that took a lot of muscle and perseverance to make—in the not so *goldene medina* (golden land) promised in the myth of "America." Those Jews worked so hard to get a local public school in the neighborhood to educate the poor and immigrant populations. The fate of P.S. 95 is the logical outcome of attacks on education and the dismantling of a democratic dream of universal education. Now our local public school is undersubscribed, a bussed school, meaning that the Board of Education uses it for the overflow of students in other Bronx schools, bussed in to fill-up the empty seats because too few local parents will accept the fate of sending their kids to what is now on the Chancellor's list of Schools in Need of Improvement. (SINI is the new euphemism for what the press calls "failing" schools.) Yet, the school is by now overcrowded. Go figure.

There are a good many of the founding generation still around in the Amalgamated co-ops and other buildings, and also many of their kids come back to live in this neat outpost in our beleaguered borough. Many also moved away, making room for an influx of every other ethnic and racial sort of New Yorker. In this book you will learn about the raced, classed, gendered, and sexed political forces that moved some of those Eastern European Jewish families up and out of the lower, urban mass. You will find out about the queer, and mixed race, and non-Euro Jews and non-Jews who moved into my community (to which community am I referring, you ask? All of them I answer) and those who have always been here and perhaps now are more visible. It's a great place to raise kids, where the families are a mix of the familiar and the unfamiliar. It's a great place to encounter the world. Mine is a queer encounter of the Jewish kind, where the "kind" is both familiar and unfamiliar.

I hear the pounding again. While the world pressed on, I had a few minutes of quiet. The workers must have returned from their lunch break. The building company won out at the district level and got their permit. One day we came home and all the trees had been cut down, wood shavings scattered everywhere by the wind and machinery. Can city kids still realistically sing about sitting in trees, k-i-s-s-i-n-g, when there are fewer and fewer growing among them? The Amalgamated folks said they wanted to preserve the "character" of the neighborhood. In white Christian and wealthy areas, that usually means something nasty (such as restrictive codes). This is a mixed neighborhood, economically, racially, and culturally. So what did these folks mean? Will the new residents care about the character of the neighborhood as seen by Amalgamated folks anyway? Will they become part of this changing amalgam on the south side of VanCortland Park? How will the new residents change? How will they change the area? I hear the pounding: families carrying mattresses or directing moving trucks, identities in formation, identities morphing, politics pulsing. Pounding.

Come with me on my encounter. It is an effort to acquaint us with the strange, and to estrange us from that to which we may be too close. It is a queer encounter, a queer encounter of the Jewish kind—where the strangeness of queers and Jews is both highlighted and undone, the familiar sometimes made bizarre, the bizarre occasionally made plain. I want to ask about when we encounter estrangement, though do not presume we are better off without it in any simple way. This book has four chapters, moving along in the mode of queer theory, of stories, of empirical research. I begin this exploration of family heirlooms by jumping right into the murky waters of mutual construction identity theory in a political discussion of raced identity formation of U.S. Jews. I rant about adoption practices, trouble family more philosophically, and then take on those mainstays of "American family life": marriage and monogamy. It's my life and my family's path. It's all feminist. It's all queer. It's all about Queers . . . and Jews, and race, and gender, and sexuality, and class, and politics, and love, and disappointment, and joy, and what's crude and what's subtle, what's a scam and what just might be the stuff with which we can make meaning in our lives.

The book flows from applied philosophical inquiry, the telling of our adoption story, and then back out to the theoretical and applied analysis. In the next chapter I use personal narrative of my family of choice in order to introduce a new mode of analysis and of understanding the contemporary Jewish community particularly in the United States, its multiple identities and intense politics. At different historical moments, certain groups "get whitened" while the "color" of others takes on deeper hues. How do these modes of racial transitioning work? How does bringing queer theory to bear on examinations of the diversity within communities challenge dominant tropes of racialization? Looking at my own family allows me to situate Jews within a grounded critical race theory in which I can take up gender, sexuality, and class as necessarily mutually constitutive aspects of the shifting racial assignment of Jews as individuals and as a group. Given my family constellation I am called to reexamine the idea and processes of "whitening and white privilege" of the U.S. Jewish community as I simultaneously decenter European Jews within the tale of American Jewish racialization. With the growing ranks of hundreds of thousands of non-Euro (i.e., African, Latina/o, Asian, Arab, and Native American heritage) Jews, it is time for a new telling of that tale. Including the work of political activists and of those Jews risking the treacherous waters of assimilation via their political commitments, in the chapter I am able to bring an array of identity-based critical theories into a complex articulation of a politically situated, changing, and multifaceted Jewish identity.

After theoretically grounding this discussion, I take on a concrete set of institutions, policies, and practices. Here the book sits firmly on the ground of our lived lives. In chapter two I undertake a detailed description of discriminatory practices in the complex world of adoption (our chosen method of family formation) in the United States. To do so I address some aspects for each of the three "parties" in adoption: (1) prospective adoptive parents, (2) children, and (3) biological parents (biological mothers in particular). I subtitle the chapter "A Guide to the Perplexed," riffing off the twelfth-century Sephardi Jewish philosopher Miamonides' great esoteric work by that name. The political issues involved are dizzying. I'm no Maimonides, but I can help readers sort some things out. In telling our adoption story, I utilize an analysis of identities as mutually constitutive to address the biases related to class (and various measures of socioeconomic status), race and/or ethnicity, gender, sexuality, religion, health, and age. Applying the method of mutual identity construction, I draw on my own experiences and research as a queer Jew in the adoption world to clarify and analyze the multiple layers of human hierarchy at work in this growing method of family formation.

Having offered the story of chapter two, in chapter three I then take an analysis of adoption to a more theoretical level. Still grounded in the narrative of my family life, I utilize a comparison between assumptions and policies concerning adoptive and biologically formed families not just to help end concrete discrimination against adoptive families such as ours, but to help us break free of essentialist elements regarding bio-families as well. Here we explore "going natural" to proclaim: The Family Has No Clothes! For the Emporer—and all the queens, riot grrls, faygeles, and families out there—theory can help us expose the political dynamics which enable presumptions, for ordinary folk trudging along in popular culture, that nature trumps style in the fight with the playground bullies of our lives. With a grounding in a Jewish history of continuity and dislocation, I feel compelled to take on the normative "American" (i.e., Christian) family. To do so I situate the analysis within feminist, class-based, queer, and critical race discourses deconstructing and challenging presumptions of what is "natural." Jews need to beware of complacency and the eugenics of family planning in the United States. Jews are out there in droves at fertility clinics, sperm banks, in vitro centers, and adoption agencies. Queers need to wake-up too. Jews will find queers at all the same places, many of whom will be queer Jews. Hell, everyone needs to deal with these issues because—whether you're currently situated within any sort of family context or not—they effect all of us. Ultimately I argue that we must come to see that the "natural" family is as much constructed as is the "constructed" adoptive family. I show that, under scrutiny, the framework "adoptive families are to culture as bio-families are to nature" does not hold.

As I seek to defamiliarize the familiar, within the family and without, the fourth chapter takes a critical look at the ideologies, practices, and institutions of monogamy and marriage. These days I get invited to more same sex "marriage/commitment/etc." ceremonies by Jewish friends than I do het ceremonies. In a time when the only feminist/queer analysis of these issues recognized in the mainstream media and the important work by many Jewish and large feminist/GLBT rights organizations focuses on demands to "marry," it is important to revisit radical critiques of the joint phenomena of monogamy and marriage. I recall discussions early in my relationship with my partner about monogamy in order to place the conversation. Then, grounded in Jewish historical experiences and the work of an array of Jewish political activists, thinkers, and their friends I use a feminist inspired queer theoretical approach. The argument breaks down monogamy into three modes: the practical, the political, and the philosophical; and breaks down marriage into its definition, component parts, strengths and appealing aspects, and a questioning of these together. Linking a discussion of the promises and ideological functions of the two, monogamy and marriage, I end with a critique of the failures inherent within them in terms of alienation.

A lovely note to end on, I know. That's the point. I refuse to stay there though. What about you? Whew. I'm glad I wrote an epilogue.

Chapter One

Whitens Whites, Keeps Colors Bright

Jewish Families Queering the Race Project

Part I

Identity and the Library of Congress

My daughter Paris is two-years-old. She stands in front of the hallway mirror gazing at herself, finding herself, questioning, exploring, discovering. My daughter Paris is two years old and she stands in front of the hallway mirror repeating a new phrase she has learned: "Jewish girl." "Paris is a Jewish girl." What does she see this time when she gazes and says "Jewish girl" that she may not have seen on a previous occasion? What image of herself is being created with these new words to accompany her constantly changing reflection? What could she possibly be thinking the phrase "Jewish girl" means? What does it mean for/to/about her?

I am her mother. I say, "Paris is Jewish." She repeats: "Paris Jewish." She asks about other members of our family, "Toni Jewish?" Toni is her younger sister, then about eight-months-old. I say "Yes, Toni is Jewish." She asks further, "Imma Jewish?" I answer "Yes, Imma is Jewish." She asks, "Ché Jewish?" I answer, "Ché is Jewish."

Ché is our nine pound, short-haired dachshund. We hope that Ché Guevara is honored, not appalled. Paris knows that Ché is different from the other members of her family. She knows that Ché is a dog. But what are boundaries and groups? When is some one or thing in or out, with or not with? When Paris asks, "Ché Jewish?", I figure it can't hurt to say yes. What have I done? Does all of this not yet have meaning for her anyway so it doesn't really matter what I'm saying? Am I being inclusive? Can a dog be Jewish? Have I avoided a more difficult issue by not including the possibility of a different repetition of the new phrase she is learning with the word Jewish in it? What are the implications of an alternative answer on my part?: "No, Ché is not Jewish." Would that be any more meaningful, any more true, any more descriptive than leaving Paris with her current pattern of repetition? "Paris Jewish." "Toni Jewish." "Momma Jewish." "Ché Jewish."

With regard to the humans, Paris hasn't asked about anyone who isn't Jewish, so I have not yet said to her, "No, . . . is not Jewish." We take as a given, from the social constructionist point of view, that the creation of any identity is made possible by the processes of separating phenomena, people, body parts, land masses, etc. and with it the exclusion and marking as "other" of some to make the subject identity. If this is a given from social and political philosophy, how does it work in the raising of children? In my example, how does the suggestion of an identity that does not yet have a "not" work in the creation of identity?

I look forward to a time when my children will ask if "so and so" is Jewish, and we will explain that she is not. I am not afraid of claiming identity and acknowledging boundaries. In contrast to a common insight which people seem to suppose is a criticism, to have a group likely *does* suggest that there are limits. What the critique does not take into account is that identifying (an even somewhat bounded group) also suggests expansiveness, because it means that there are other groups. I'm *glad* "my group" isn't the only group out there. (Oy, if it were . . .) To identify does not only mean you negate others, it also means you recognize others. It does not only mean you recognize them in order to place them as your nonexistent negations (where you are the single referent), it means that you can also be recognizing that others exist and that we are different.[1] This is also an affirmation. Perhaps it is common for majority or dominant groups to identify through the creation of an other which is marked as inferior. But it may also be common for minority and nondominant groups to identify as part of a process of recognizing difference where hegemonic modes often homogenize. Further, perhaps we can see—against the grain of the common critique which negates the power differential between dominant and nondominant groups and thus their potential philosophical and political differences—that to identify can entail (1) acknowledging differences, and (2) do so with multivariant systems of valuation. In the case of many minority groups, this suggests that noting difference does not have to come to meaning in either a bi-polar subject/object ontological frame, nor an hierarchical one in which difference exists because some characteristics are esteemed and others are abject. It is common in the United States today to interpret a Jewish (or others' at times) insistence on identity as insular or xenophobic. For many of us, however, Jewish historical modes of identity provide helpful guideposts in a contemporary politics in which diversity, multiple and shifting identities, and difference offer new avenues in the creation of social relations based on dignity, respect, and fairness.[2]

Tell me about your image of my daughter Paris looking in the mirror, a Jewish girl.
Tell me about this nice Jewish girl who thinks of her family first.

Excuse me. Let me interrupt. (So Jewish of me.)
What is/who is a Jewish girl?

According to the Library of Congress, my daughter does not exist. Or, in a more recent political move, she was provisionally invented.

I say to my daughter, "African-American." She tries to sound it out. It proves more difficult for her to repeat than the word Jewish. Is "African-American" harder to say than "Jewish?" I am not-African American. As I've mentioned, I am Eastern European (though the "color" of Paris' skin is quite similar to that of various members of my family. For example, my bio-mother is often taken for Black, Arab, Greek, or any number of other racial/national/ethnic groupings. Ah . . . race). Is there something coming from me that makes "Jewish" easier to say? "African-American Jewish girl." She hasn't quite got the hang of it all yet. Am I looking into a crystal ball, telling us about the issues we will face in our future?[3] Her word play and its limitations are already certainly reflective of a current incapacity to understand identity as not only multiple but mutually constitutive, Paris' two-year-old meaning-making not withstanding. I have not only taught her to say the word Jewish in reference to her two-year-old self, I have taught her to say Jewish girl. I am doing my best to teach her to say African-American Jewish girl. Will I always feel that I can teach about being a Jewish girl, but still qualify my teachings for African-American Jewish girlhood with the phrase: "the best I can?" Again, to what degree or in what ways are our present politics and our future struggles already encoded in early childhood language acquisition? In what ways do our languages frame, make openings and make closings, individual empowerment and liberatory identity politics from our earliest days in life? As a political philosopher and activist, I presume to talk knowledgeably about mutually constitutive identity signifiers; as a mother I'm winging it and hoping for the best at each moment. Paris learned the words for girl, Jewish, and African-American from her momma and her imma all at the same time and by the age of two. This does not mean she will not go on to learn and also to cultivate continuously new knowledges, practices, and relationships about all of this identity business. But still, how could anyone look at Paris and write a theory of separative and bounded identities? I suppose that has been the point . . . those who have been able to do so have not been the Paris' of the world. Theorizing a seamless cloak of unmarked identities is the privilege/constitutive of elites, not of African-American Jewish girls with two mothers.

The very possibility of Black Jews is erased in the U.S. racial cre-ation/coding of Jews and other groups in numerous subtle and insidious ways.[4] For example, a subject search in my university library's catalogue with the title "Black Jews" yields nothing despite the fact that the library carries two books by women who are both Black and Jewish (Azoulay and Walker) and they use the words "Black" and "Jewish" in their titles.[5] This is because there is no Library of Congress subject heading for "Black Jews." Many Black Jews' origins in the early colonial West Indies fed the development of such groups later in the United States.[6] When I search for Black Jews, the computer system "helpfully" tells me to use the cat-egory "Black Hebrews," which actually refers to a specific web of African and African-American communities, some also called Israelites (living mainly in sub-Saharan Africa, the United States, and in the modern state of Israel) who use this self-identifier and to which Azoulay and Walker, Toni, and Paris do not happen to be members.[7] The search for Black Hebrews at the University of New Hampshire library yields one volume.[8] We also carry one volume on Jewish communities in Africa, a significant aspect of history for all of us and particularly the African-Americans who call themselves Black Hebrews, and yet the book is not included under the subject heading Black Jews.[9]

A subject search for "African-American Jews" also yields nothing, (again despite the fact that we actually carry the Walker, Azoulay, and Chireau volumes.)[10] In a post-1960s political challenge to library catego-rizations, activist librarians succeeded in shifting numerous cataloging methods. As heir to this legacy, the term "African-American Jews" did eventually become introduced as a Library of Congress subject heading though it is rarely and unevenly utilized. Because many databases will not have revised their categorizations, a random search of library databases around the country yields similar ellipses as in the University of New Hampshire system. Further, under the category search for African-

American Jews the University of New Hampshire system suggests for you the subject category "African-American Jewish Relations"[11] to which it directs the searcher to its more "proper" category: "African-Americans Relations with Jews."

Racial thinking in the United States so essentializes and separates groups that it cannot imagine African-American Jews. The closest it can come is to think of the changing historical *relationships between* an essentialized community now referred to as African-Americans and an essentialized community now referred to as Jews. The contradiction here is made further apparent because the listing of books the library carries under this subject heading even includes Azoulay and Chireau, though (for some reason I cannot fathom,) neither the Walker, nor the Parfitt volume. The voluminous writings on "Black-Jewish Relations" in the United States is often the result of caring and/or leftist activist intellectuals supposedly contributing to a more complex understanding of racial politics in this country.[12] What we also must take note of is the way that this whole genre of literature reinscribes essentialized notions of who Jews and Blacks are that also forecloses the possibility of imaging Black Jews.[13] The University of New Hampshire library also carries a number of books which tell the stories of African-American Jews within them, but erases this fact by identifying multiracial or transracial on a Black-white grid, where the Blacks are not assumed to be Jewish and often the "whites" referred to are Jews.[14]

Part II

On Lines and Lines that Aren't Lines

> The problem of the twentieth century is the problem of the color line,— the relation of the darker to the lighter races of men in Asia and Africa, in America and the islands of the sea.

> —W. E. B. Du Bois, The Souls of Black Folk

As I note in the preface to this volume, Paris has come to be my daughter through adoption. We are a multiracial Jewish family.[15] "Yes, Imma is Jewish," I say. Imma is also her mother. "Paris has two mommies," as the saying goes,[16] but more, she has a momma, and an Imma (Imma is the Hebrew word for mother). I was born into and raised by a Jewish family. There are about six million Jews in the United States today. I am among the approximately four to five million Ashkenazi (European) Jews living in the United States. When asked my *racial* identity, if given the chance,

I say Ashkenazi Euro-Jewish: a descriptive term I hope, yet specifically chosen to be responsible in identifying European/white privilege, simultaneously staking my claim in identifying my Jewish/nonwhite self. Dawn, my partner and Paris' Imma, has come to Jewish community through conversion. Dawn is one of approximately one hundred seventy thousand Jews by Choice living in the United States today. Dawn has cast her lot with the fate of Jews; when asked *her* racial identity she says "white." Growing up Baptist in rural northern California, she knows whiteness in her own way and knows what access to whiteness means in a way that I do not. Paris has an African-American Jewish sister, Toni, who has also become family with us through adoption. Paris and Toni are two among approximately four hundred thousand Jews of Color (or nonwhite and non-European Jews) in the United States today.[17] Right now we name their identities. Over the various courses of their lives, they will undoubtedly come to be identified by many others and hopefully to find ways to identify themselves.

Over one hundred years ago W. E. B. Du Bois wrote: "The problem of the twentieth century is the problem of the color line." He was correct. And there was also more to it. Today we are called upon to "Theorize the Intersections of Race, Class, Gender, and Sexuality in the 21st Century" (the name of a panel for which I was once invited to deliver a paper). We were called upon to do so in the twentieth century too. We have done much work, but a history of hard work does not offer us neat accomplishments. We have learned much in order to begin to understand what Du Bois could have meant. In many ways we have barely begun our project. Du Bois was right not because there are truths and finally some white folks heard one spoken by a Black man. Du Bois was right because he helped us make some sense of our world, fight injustice, create alternatives. At the same time, we know from the vantage point of the twenty-first century that the color line does not really work out as easily as a line.[18] Some folks go here, others there; don't step over the line/out of place. Where would Jews in the United States fall in reference to the line? Perhaps "the problem" was the problem of the political challenges engendered in the ways that the line(s) kept shifting throughout the last century, and now in our new one. The one drop rule for those here of African descent was and remains unevenly applied.[19] The U.S. Census Bureau kept changing the boxes you could fill out, meaning the racial options one could fit into (or not) actually changed. Sometimes Latina/os and Native Americans are white, sometimes black, sometimes in a mid range classified as people of color. Sometimes what mattered to certain people was the extent to which they were whiteable/white-able, able to become white.

What does the color line mean in these contexts? Where are Jews? Where am I, Euro-Ashkenazi Jew: white/not-white? Where is Dawn, convert, following Askenazi Jewish practices, white? Where are Paris and Toni: adopted African-American Jews being raised in the Ashkenazi tradition by Euro-Jews? Technically three out of the four of us are converts. What does that mean for the line? We are all four Jews, though contrary to contemporary popular expectation, only one of us identifies as straight-forwardly white. We are all four Ashkenazi because the religiously related practices of this ethnic group will most likely guide much of our creation of a Jewish home: yet only one of us has an Eastern European Jewish biological family heritage. How does the fact that our daughters are girls (for now, by our identification) position them with respect to power, privilege, access, alternatives . . . position them with respect to a nonlinear line? How does the fact that they (currently and until further notice) are being raised in a family with two mommies, and specifically a momma and an imma, constrain and enable their life paths, most likely not to be very linear paths? While Dawn and I have both self-identified as "mothers," already in the course of their short lives, Paris and Toni have had parents who have shifted widely around the gender continuum—a common term referring to the multiplicity of genders within a sociopolitical architecture that is anything but a continuum between two opposite reference points. How does this fact fit in: their mothers come from different class backgrounds, but are now both members of an intellectual elite, holding relatively prestigious jobs, but can barely scrape together enough funds to pay the landlord each month?[20] How does class position one with respect to the line that really isn't?[21] Both their mothers are serious students of Marx's, but class issues remain ever befuddling. We must look to geography and history.

For those of you newer to throwing Jews into the mix of complex theorizing about identity, here is a quick history/geography lesson. A vast number of Jews in the world are non-European/not of European ancestry. They are Indian and from other parts of Asia, Arab or Persian from all over the Middle East and North Africa, African from other areas south of what is referred to as North Africa, Latin American from all around Mexico, and Central and South America.[22] But these racial/geographic categories made up in Western modernity do not necessarily offer the most useful explanation for racialized Jewishness. One of the central ethnic differences significant to (not all, though still a large percentage of) Jews (perhaps as opposed to European Christians) for the past half millennium or so, for example, is between groups labeled Ashkenazi and Sephardi. Ashkenazi Jews have become associated with "European" peoples, including all the contradictions that being part of Europe's excluded entails in identifying as European.[23] Sephardi Jews are associated often with the darkness of the rest of the continents, and yet Sepharad is the Hebrew word for Spain.[24] Sephardi Jews are of European ancestry as well (in the ways that ancestries are complex only semicontiguous routes),[25] meaning they are ethnically or in terms of their communal norms or religious practices related to the Jews of Spain prior to the Catholic Inquisition.[26] But the racial/ethnic differences significant for even Western Jews have not necessarily worked the same ways as they have for modern Western Christians. Spain might be part of Europe, but Sephardi cultures are considered racially/ethnically/religiously different from other technically also European Jewish cultures that may or may not come under the rubric Ashkenazi. With the Inquisition, some Jews made it into more northern areas of Europe, many went back south into Africa and on to areas now called the Middle East. There are significant differences between Mizrachi (Eastern, Middle Eastern, and/or Asian) Jews which have developed over time. It would not only be a mistake to consider Mizrachi Jews a homogeneous group, but also reinforcing Western hegemony not to point out that Eastern Jews are only eastern at all through the creation of the West as west. With these points we must ask: to the degree that many North African, Middle Eastern, and other Eastern Jewish communities may have roots in/have been created en route from Spain, does it make sense to lump them into the category of European? Perhaps for certain purposes, but not necessarily in the current usage of the term as used in U.S. race discourse. For that matter, since the terms European and white largely presuppose Christian Europe and/or Christian white, identifying Ashkenazi Jews as European is also quite complicated.[27]

Despite their demographically circumscribed status among world Jewry, the majority of the Jews now living in the United States are Ashkenazi.[28] This means that at the start, U.S. racial categories which cast those of European heritage as "white," and therefore many who now associate Jews with whiteness, are already skewed by the ignorance which accompanies (makes possible/is made possible by) U.S. dominance. The rest of Jews in the world associated, in currently popular U.S. racial/geographical terms, as nonwhite are erased by the narrowness of the historically construed "problem of the color line" in the United States. This erasure is effected by both majority and minority groups.[29] It appears, at least in contemporary multicultural politics, that many minority groups have mostly inherited the knowledges produced by dominant discourses on race which derace/erase the majority of Jews.[30] The majority of Jews are forgotten, or perhaps never known, by most folks of goodwill working in antiracist politics in the United States. The majority of Jews become deraced when presumed to be the U.S.-created vision of Jews as Ashkenazi. In this move too, then, their re-racination serves to erase.

The first Jews to come to the Americas, and the territories which would eventually become the United States, came as crypto-Jews. The first Jews recognized as Jews publically came in a group of twenty-three Sephardi men, women, and children in 1654 fleeing persecution, traveling north from Brazilian territory under Portugese rule. Upon their arrival, the Dutch governor in New Amsterdam, Peter Stuyvesant, attempted to expel them. That the majority of this group were women, Karla Goldman (2004) writes: "we must pay careful attention to the stories about these beginnings and the three hundred fifty years that have followed. Unless we take full measure of the ways that Jewish women have shaped both Jewish community and American society at large," we will be left, she cautions, "with impoverished notions of whom we have been and whom we might become.[31] She makes no comment on the shift from U.S. Jewish Sephardi origins to Ashkenazi dominance. Jews participate in many ways in our own racial erasures. There are records of Black Jews in the U.S. colonies dating back to 1668 (an African-heritage man by the name of Sollomon is recorded as perhaps the first Jew to live in New England), and to 1683 (Berger 1978, 10–11). By the mid-1700s more Jews lived openly in the New World's West Indies: some Ashkenazi, mostly Sephardi, and including communities comprised of those of African descent. By the late-1700s, Berger (1978, 12–13) reports that census figures from Surinam note "834 Sephardim from Southern Europe and North Africa, 477 Ashkenazim from Northern and Eastern Europe and 100 Mulattos." There were likely also ties between the Portugese-Jewish community in early New York of the mid-1850s and Jews of African heritage who might have occasionally come to the Sephardi Portugese synagogue (the first synagogue in New York) and those still living in the Carribean/West Indies (Berger 1978, 30).

Sephardi dominance of the U.S. Jewish community would not last into the twentieth century. So, what of the current majority of U.S. Jews who come from non-Sephardi Europe? Where are they on the color line? European stereotypes of Jews are not related to any actual history of the Jews of sub-Saharan African descent (a history basically unknown in Europe of the period).[32] In Europe, "European" (or those who might be now coded as white) Jews were cast as other, as dark, as Black, as non-European/ Semitic. When whiteness was invented, Jews were not included in the category. Jews were not considered ethnically of the European nations in which they resided. When the nation-state was created, Jews (not being of the nations) were not included as subjects/rights bearing citizens. The legacy of European Christian anti-Semitism intertwined with the legacy of struggles to end the exclusion and oppression of Jews in Europe are the legacies gifted to U.S. racial politics. Still, when European Ashkenazi Jews began to come to the United States in large numbers they were cast as nonwhite. Yet in much of today's racial categorizations Jews are presumed to fit into the box called white/European. They crossed the line? Did they? Did some? The line can be crossed? What could make that possible? Who might be able, under what historical conditions, at what costs? An historical perspective on Du Bois allows us to see that the problem of the twentieth (and thus far this) century was the challenge of the politics involved in the shifting definitions of both the color and the line. An historical perspective on Du Bois allows us to see that whatever "the color" and whatever "the line" mean, they also only exist as creations mutually constituted with other aspects of what has come to be politically salient in human experience such as sex/gender, sexuality, class, ability, and a host of other matters that matter.

Part III

Paying for Whiteness

> The price the white American paid for his ticket was to become white—: and in the main, nothing more than that, or, as he was to insist, nothing less. This incredibly limited not to say dimwitted ambition has choked many a human being to death here . . .
>
> —James Baldwin *The Price of the Ticket*

Race and Class: James Baldwin teaches us about race as a social construction in the United States with particular cultural and political consequences. He also shows us that there have been some differences for racial politics between those who have been identified as "immigrants" and the varied groups of people who came to these shores on slave ships, as indentured servants along with those whose ancestries have long been associated with the territories which the United States governs (such as: Puerto Ricans, Alaskans, Hawaiians, southwestern natives formerly living under Mexican rule, and an array of other indigenous peoples typically comprising the tribes referred to as Native American or those living on the Pacific Islands which are not official states but are within U.S. jurisdiction).

In order to both appreciate and trouble it, let us look at Baldwin's insight a little more closely. For example: not all indentured servants were from Asia, as is commonly thought. Since before the founding of the American Republic, the United States imported "white"/European servants, debtors, and criminals for servitude and hard labor as they did African slaves and later Chinese, then Japanese, then Filipino (mostly men). Even many of those we might call "immigrants," collected in Baldwin's reference to those who paid the price of a ticket to come here, often got their ticket by promises of indentured servitude to those who actually paid the money. Many men and women paid in work: whether in Europe to get the ticket, on board, or once on shore—many women's work price was/is sexual. Many stowed away. In Jewish communities already organized in the United States, self-help organizations and free loan associations made it possible to purchase tickets for relatives or other known persons from Europe without any one individual or family having enough funds to pay the monetary price themselves. Further, getting on the boat was one thing. Surviving the trip and passing U.S. economic, trade, health, and other quotas in order to get off Ellis Island and stay legally in the country also proved challenging. One reason this was such a challenge was the U.S. government's fear of the high numbers of Jewish radicals: politics makes immigration policy on many levels.

But let us listen to Baldwin for those who did get to stay here as immigrants, regardless of the myths that cover over the variety of circumstances of any individual's arrival. If you made it here, whatever costs you had incurred thus far were only the beginning. Coming to the United States held the promise of life, liberty, the pursuit of happiness, and the possibility of moving beyond abject poverty and extreme forms of organized anti-Jewish state violence. But these promises, once you got off the boat, also came at significant cost in other terms of racialized politics and cultural practice and memory. When the masses of poverty-stricken Jews came to the United States in the twentieth century in an effort to outrun anti-Semitism, they arrived into a racialized world which prelabeled them in the nondominant category "nonwhite." Yet at this point in U.S. politics, Jews are usually associated with the race/economic/power category white. How specifically did this shift occur and what specifically were the costs to which Baldwin refers?

We are looking at the erased/deraced Jew in the United States in the twenty-first century. "The Jew" is now (although most folks who perform this elision do not have the words for it) the Euro-"Ashkenazi Jew": a person presumed to be whiter than a stereotyped African-American, of immigrant stock from Europe.[33] In the race section of an average application these days in the United States, there is no box to check off for "Jew." It is now usually expected that a Jew will check off "White." Okay, there are hundreds of thousands of Jews in the United States who could also check off (the categories change, depending on who has drawn up the form): "Black, not Hispanic; Hispanic; Asian and Pacific Islander; Native American, Alaskan Native." Now the U.S. Census Bureau allows individuals to check off more than one "race" box in order to "count" mixed heritage people. This new addition to the Census was the result of years of long hard struggle and political compromise. The new option has its possibilities and its problems.[34] But, still, I doubt anyone expects people to use that category to name their Jewishness: Paris and Toni are African-American Ashkenazi Jewish, I am "white/nonwhite" Ashkenazi Jewish, Dawn is white Ashkenazi Jewish. The "other" or "check all that apply" type options were not intended for us. Yes, there are those who, like Dawn, may easily check off white; but let's face it—those of us who were raised rural poor Baptists are not really in the minds of the people who now claim Jews to be white folk. Of course, there are the stereotypical Euro-Ashkenazis like myself who find it necessary to confuse the statisticians and check off "other." So who are those white Jews? And how did such a category come into being if Jews as a group in the United States started off as nonwhite, and many remain so?

At mid-century, the United States was in the midst of an intense ideological struggle. In a postwar environment, the world reeled from news of racial and cultural genocide in Europe, women were being asked again to redefine their identities as men returned home and needed the jobs they had recently been asked to perform, and economic opportunity became available to some in a partial financial boom. In the mid-1950s, news of Christine Jorgensen's "sex re-assignment surgery" was splattered across the popular U.S. press as well as the medical literature. This was an historical moment when aspects of one's identity presumed to be as immutable as one's "sex" were suddenly open to change, shifts, switches. Across lines of race, class, "sex," gender roles and sexuality, religion/ ethnicity and culture, identities long held to be "facts" were morphing, and the facticity of such facts called into question. Simultaneously, there was a move to shore up such identities, to fix them in more permanent ways. Much of the new openings in identity crossings in this era were made possible only through complex processes of reessentializing identity categories, and the communities created in and moving across lines previously held to be impermeable.[35] The changing status of Jews in the United States, perceived as a community, at this historical moment was both product and producer of such intense ideological transformations and contradictions. What we need to see is in what ways the Jewish community both crossed a race line at this delicate moment, and in what ways it did not. What made this perceived collective crossing possible and what was required to effect it? Who were among the many individual and subgroups of Jews either unable or unwilling to meet those requirements and why? The basic politics of the U.S. Jewish community today continues to be constructed and constrained by these mid-century dynamics: those conceived as part of the collectivity, and those marginalized, what opportunities for Jews as political agents are opened up and which narrowed?

In *How Jews Became White Folks and What that Says About Race in America*, Karen Brodkin offers some excellent insight on these questions. Her book makes an important contribution to the study of (U.S.) American Jewish history and beyond. Brodkin offers a highly developed analysis of how the category of Jews came to be equated with the category of "white" in the United States since World War II. To do so she also explains how racial categorization worked prior to that time so that previously Jews were not considered properly within the boundaries of whiteness and its privileges. As the subtitle suggests, Brodkin engages in this examination not only by drawing on the U.S.-based literature of critical race theory more broadly but also so that she can say something about racial formation and racialization in the United States beyond the case study of Jews.

Brodkin's work is situated within a discourse and political movement which understands that not only do we all have multiple identities, but that these multiple identities are mutually constitutive of one another. As Brodkin discusses, the ethnoracial construction of Jewishness is gendered, it is sexed, and it is classed.[36] For example, according to Brodkin, Jews fell into/helped to create an economically stratified shifting racial system. Changing racial classifications for these new "Americans" depended in large part on the taxonomy of trades, and the political forces that went into classifying certain trades as skilled and others not, certain groups of people as "intelligent" and others not. As new immigrants, the Irish, Jews, and other eastern Europeans as well as southern Europeans were originally lumped together with peoples already living in the United States who were considered, for the most part, nonwhite.[37] Each ethnic immigrant group was generally steered toward certain geographical locations and trades. Although most of the trades pursued by these new immigrants required a variety of skills, they were often classified as "unskilled" laborers which was a major contributor to their off-white racial categorization. Labor unions and other institutions helped to create classifications of trades and jobs that were ethnically segregated and then stratified, creating the imbricating economies of class and race. Though Brodkin notes that all of these classifications were gendered as well, she is best at showing the mutual constitution of class and race.[38]

Brodkin critically examines the interplay between what she terms ethno-racial assignment and ethno-racial identity as it transformed over time and in relation to larger political phenomena in the United States. The story she tells of this interplay provides valuable insight into the changing nature of U.S. Jewish identity in its ever mutating raced/ gendered/classed formulations. Simultaneously, the story she tells provides valuable insight into the changing nature of the ethno-racial construction of off-whites (those not quite white and not African) in U.S.

history and how that re-created the very (and continually binary) categories of white and Black in this country over time.[39] For U.S. Jews, a major
shift occurred at mid-century with postwar governmental programs geared
toward already designated white men and men of certain immigrant backgrounds. These affirmative action programs included the GI Bill, opening
up educational opportunities to some groups previously excluded, as well
as new housing subsidies which made possible the phenomenon we commonly refer to today as suburbia.[40] Given certain peculiarities of Eastern
European Jews (many of which were effects of those earlier processes of
racialization, that is, literacy rates, urban culture, a system of self-help
organizations translated from their home countries and political traditions,
and skills associated with the trades they had been steered into), relatively
large sections of the U.S. Jewish community were able to access these new
governmental programs as ladders to economic advantage and more prestigious work options which were made possible by a certain honorary crossing of the color line.[41] This was so not only in contrast to indigenous
populations and African-Americans, who were either expressly or de facto
excluded from many of these programs, but also in contrast to numerous
other European immigrant groups (whether from Ireland, Eastern or southern European countries) whose racial placement in the labor market over
time left them with fewer opportunities to access such programs.

However, in the move Brodkin makes from the Jewish particular to
the ethno-racial universal, she does at times conflate the two and reinscribe
certain problematic aspects of U.S. racialization.[42] Some of the limits of
what Brodkin is able to accomplish in this generally very carefully argued
text are themselves interesting for analysis. In many ways the limitations
exhibited by Brodkin's analysis demonstrate the challenges many face right
now in thinking about these issues. For example, Brodkin has a tendency
to generalize in such a way that has significant consequences for the study
of Jews within the context of critical race theory. Some illustrative examples may be found in her own inability to complicate the common
U.S. *postwar* equation of Jewish as white. Brodkin does not challenge the
characterization of the postwar U.S. as middle class, nor, concomitantly
the postwar equation of U.S. Jews as middle class. She accepts a highly
controversial historical account of a lack of anti-Semitism in the late
nineteenth-century United States and replays a tendency to portray
Yiddishkeit as a common, unitary culture. As one final example, Brodkin
herself employs an uncritical use of the category Black as the mark of
race. The author simply did not need to make the overstatements and
create such exclusionary or unitary categories.[43]

Race, Class, and Gender: Indebted to Brodkin, and therefore able to
build on her work, Debra Schultz offers us *Going South: Jewish Women in*

the Civil Rights Movement. Schultz's work is able to more centrally place Jewish women in a race critical study of Jews in the United States. This book on the civil rights activism of women who are Jewish is an important contribution to the literature on Jews, feminism, race and the civil rights era, class struggle, and the legacy of Jewish political activism. Utilizing Schultz's work will thus enable us to further complicate the co-constructed aspects of U.S. Jewish racial identity shifts.

Schultz draws on oral histories of fifteen Jewish women to develop her analysis. There is some writing on Jews in antiracist movements, but those studies tend to focus on Jewish men. There are also some studies on women in the civil rights movement, though if Jewish women are mentioned their Jewishness is erased and they are thrown together with a cluster of white Christian women. The oral histories help Schultz to develop a very thoughtful understanding of the complexities of the era and complications Jewish women faced working to be a part of it. The book utilizes the oral histories in conjunction with extensive research in the literature and history of Jewish communities in the U.S. South, Jewish feminism, Jewish political activism and identity, the role of Jews in an emerging multicultural politics in the United States, the civil rights era up to the beginning of Black Power, and the origins of mass-based mid-century antiracist activism and coalition building. Despite the sub-title, this book is specifically about Northern Jewish women who went South in the early days of the civil rights movement. Through this lens we learn about struggles in the new movement and the emergence of a new kind of political imperative for African-Americans. Through her particular study, we also learn about the precarious status of Southern Jews.[44]

Schultz's work is a terrific counterpart to Brodkin's in that it also takes on the pivotal period in U.S. history when portions of the Jewish community entered into the middle class and the community's concomitant "whitening." Schultz's study of the northern Jewish women who went South expands the historical analysis by showing the alternate routes taken by many Jews at that time and since. Especially given the invisibility of non-Euro Jews in the United States, Jews as a community must struggle with the wager on whiteness and power that developed in the postwar period. Regardless of any erasures effected in the creation of the truth and non-truth of the Jew-White equation, and because of them, we must critically engage this fraught communal wager even as distinct portions of the community maintained their relationship to progressive and radical politics, their deep thinking about social justice and the costs of assimilation, and their high levels of involvement in concrete movement activism.

Although studying basically the same historical moment as did Brodkin, Schultz's analysis clarifies that not all Jews went the route of middle class into whiteness. Many Jews did not then, nor have now, entered the middle class (the move Brodkin demonstrates which was key to the whitening of the community as a whole) with significant portions classified in U.S. terms as low income and below the poverty line.[45] Many Jews who did make use of new access to education and developing skills often associated with the white middle class (regarding areas such as the law, health, writing, organizational management, public speaking, or working the media which Brodkin analyzes and relates to becoming middle class) rejected or chose an alternative path than the yellow brick road to accumulating wealth for personal gain. Many Jews, whether consciously or not at the time, forfeited "earning" the potential privileges of whiteness because their politics made them traitors to "the race"—in this case traitors to the so called white race. These gendered and classed historical analyses show that some Jews were coming to be granted honorary membership as whites if they also towed the political line of "mainstream" U.S. values. To remain committed to progressive and or radical politics generally, to remain committed to racial justice in racist (U.S.)America, to eschew the myths of capitalism and consumerism make one a traitor to whiteness—each and all serve as a barrier to those who might otherwise want to hitch a ride on the backs of others across the tracks to white (U.S.)America.[46] If Brodkin shows us that *class* climbing made possible some Jewish crossings of the *color* line at mid-century, Shultz's work on Jewish women civil rights workers further shows us that toeing a certain *political* line is also required in order to cross the *color* line.

Shultz discusses the women as daughters and as (later for most of them) mothers. She is able to explore multiple ways of being Jewish that do not underestimate the power of secular Judaism and the spirituality of political Jewishness. Schultz does not shy away from the difficult issues of the limits of whiteness, of privilege and class struggle, of Jewish identity forged in the wake of the Holocaust in Europe and the scourging of Communism and radicalism in the United States. Schultz gives us real insight into the class, racial, sexual, familial, educational, and other life factors of the women she studied which does not end with the women themselves. Her portrayal of these women's lives is both steeped in good historical insight as it offers us new perceptions on the social construction of identities and communities, on the importance of carrying on a legacy steeped in *tikkun olam*/social justice, and on a fiery Jewish sensibility.

In a post-McCarthy world in which mass and directly class-based activism was no longer a political option, the civil rights movement became one of the most viable avenues for historic Jewish work in radical politics.[47] Jewish women were among the earliest northerners to go south at the beginning of the civil rights movement. Moreover, Jewish women were often the only women at many of the sites, and were usually the only non-Black civil rights workers at the start of the movement. Schultz offers us a contrast to the common postwar view that equates Jews as a whole with wealth, and therefore with whiteness and power. In the tradition of contemporary activist Jewish feminists, who have contributed much to Jewish and general challenges to capitalism,[48] Schultz recovers an historical legacy of a different *Jewish* understanding of the relationship between wealth and power: if you've managed to get any of it, use it . . . for justice. In this Schultz is among those such as Kentrowitz who turn the equation of how to use wealth, access, skills, and power on its head: from one that is automatically in the service of oppression to one that seeks to end oppression. From this Jewish feminist historical study of gender, Schultz shows us that those who have followed this Jewish practice were left out of the new classification of Jews as white folk described by Brodkin.

Race, Class, Sex/Sexuality, and Jews with Queer Genders: There have also been many important works published addressing the intersection of Jewish identity and sex/gender and sexuality.[49] This frame of analysis is central to the work of theorizing the shifting processes of racing, deracing, and erasing in the United States. The sex/gender/sexuality triad is constitutive of race as are other politically salient aspects of identity. Becoming white has required conforming to certain sex/gender/sexuality norms which are troubled by the changing historical status and practices of Jews in the West. White gender norms are bourgeois Western and Christian constructions and these have been anything but static. They have also generally differed from Western Jewish constructions of gender, if even in response to transformations in normative expectations. Recall that in the early 1900s my maternal grandmother was being raised as a boy in Russia. She was not the only Jew to have a cross-gendered experience.[50] Examining the situation at another level of abstraction, we can see that due to their "different" gender assignments more broadly, Jews historically have been seen as queer in the Christian West.[51]

As class is also part of the racial construct, we must remember that the gender norms of whiteness are also often expectations of elite Christians in the West and cross with class-based constructions of gender among Western Jews.[52] The general wisdom of Jewish history acknowledges the importance of any Jews who may have become wealthy in the political functioning of a local community. But class as a form of status, prestige, privilege, and enfranchisement in decision making in Jewish communities was also largely a matter of learnedness. The learned were also often quite poor. So even Jewish class categorizations have had a different history than common Marxist or other economically based versions in the West. Further, the elite aspiration was generally defined in terms of the ability to study (Jewish texts). Surely many poor Jews dreamed of riches, but the hegemonic paradigm of status was being able to study in a religious house of learning (*yeshiva*). This was also out of reach for the majority of Jews not only because most were workers, but also because most could not reach the levels of learnedness required (or required to find fiscal and/or political sponsors). As Western Christian notions of manhood came to include physical prowess and chivalry, Jewish self-identity further reinforced its commitment to manhood through study, in part to differentiate itself from the surrounding nations.[53]

Though most Christian women in the West were also poor and engaged in physical labor, the elite association of white womanhood with fairness and a quiet etiquette excluded Jewish women from not only the category of woman, but then also as being of the Gentile race. It is no coincidence that the word Gentile, meaning racially/nationally non-Jewish, came to be related etymologically to the word for Gentility—as in of the upper class. Though it is too easy to paint an homogenous portrait of "Jewish womanhood," it can be said that an elite Jewish expectation which corresponded to men as scholars was that of their wives as the businesspeople who would financially support the household.[54] Again, most families needed numerous workers as most people were extremely poor. Further, within religious settings women were expected to be quiet and without a voice in the arena of men. However, Jewish businesswomen were a far more common occurrence than Gentile independent business-women and Jewish ones were generally respected within the community as one way of conforming to *Jewish* gender norms. Also, although ex-cluded from formal settings of religious study, Jewish women still tended to have higher literacy rates than the women in their surrounding areas. Noting examples of physically weak, "effeminate," studious men, and strong savvy women as independent agents in the economic sphere and interact-ing with Christian neighboring communities helped to cast Jews as a whole as queer (in sexed/gendered terms) and also served to preclude them from consideration for membership in the sexed/gendered con-structs of the European nations (later equated with whiteness).

Part of what made Jews eligible for honorary status as whites in the mid-twentieth-century U.S. was select groups of Jews' entry into the economic middle class. Part of the "cost" of that whiteness was the classed expectations of assimilation to certain sets of norms related to sex/gender/sexuality. New ideas of the Jewish man as businessman, or man of the professions, emerge as a stereotype. With the development of the State of Israel, Jewish men claim a stake in military capacities, physical strength, and physique as markers of manhood.[55] Nice Jewish girls are then ex-pected to be quiet, not feisty. New Jewish women are then supposed to be "kept," not working outside the home with an independent income base and bearer of strong opinions. A race critical analysis of Jews in the United States from the perspective of queer theory allows us to see that crossing the color line required a "straightening up" like the pretense of the mythic line itself.[56]

Without explicitly devoting analysis to this phenomenon, the work of both Brodkin and Schultz helps us to get a clearer picture of mutually constitutive constructs of heterosexuality, gender/sex, class, and race as they have come to work for Jews in the postwar United States. Brodkin shows clearly how one of the costs of whiteness that was required of these Euro-heritage Jews as some moved into the middle class was the quieting of women: unbending the Jewish style of queered gender-bending in the West that accompanies whiteness. Relying on Jewish daughters to marry up heterosexually was also important in the generations of social climbing that made it possible for some Jews to be granted honorary status as whites. Thus, complying with Western, Christian, middle-class norms of heterosexuality was necessary for the "whitening" of Euro-Jews as a group in the postwar era. But Schultz shows us that the large numbers of Jewish women activists threatened these new sexualized gender roles which some Jewish parents were coming to demand of their daughters. Some of the Jewish women activists married up, in the sense of marrying men in the professions only newly available to Jewish men; they also tended not to simply class climb with this newfound access but to use it in the service of radical and progressive political movements. Other Jewish women partnered with and/or married nonwhite men and founded a new genera-tion of not-so-white Jews in ways that some of their class climbing par-ents hadn't exactly expected either.[57] Also, many of these women coupled with other women and became activists as lesbians, bisexuals, and transgendered Jews,[58] fundamentally challenging their potential status as part of the U.S. American mainstream. My sisters and I have long joked: my parents got the *naches* (joy, pride, delight) of having a "son-in-law" doctor and a rabbi; okay she's the academic sort of doctor, a woman, and there's nothing legal about it. . . . Along my path in adulthood I also ran into some old friends of theirs who didn't turn out as expected either.[59]

Finally, drawing on a queer understanding of Jewish gender roles, we can use Schultz to help us locate these trends for Jewish civil rights workers within Jewish tradition. In elite circles, Eastern European Jews were used to women acting in the secular public sphere with non-Jews. Outside of elite customs, Schultz also links the kinds of work the women in the early civil rights movement were doing with a basic ethic found among working-class Jewish women that *their* traditional gender role was to "just do the work that needed to be done." Schultz brings us up historically to Jewish experiences in the United States, demonstrating that the more open sexual mores in the 1960s, of which Jews made ample use, actually made possible—as they were made possible by—the very involvement of these Jewish women in the early civil rights movement. As Jewish women made use of these openings in traditional U.S. hetero-sexual mores, they were able to take more risks in the kind of political work they could do, which continued to classify them beyond mainstream Western, Christian, gendered, and heterosexual norms of whiteness con-tributing even today to the ways that Jews are still often considered "queerly gendered."

Jewish men's work in the civil rights movement also continued to cast them as not-quite-white even as many might have taken the oppor-tunities to get advanced educational degrees and enter into more white-collar professions. To the degree that many Jewish men then and now might use their newfound privilege in the service of critical race and other justice politics, we find that they remain beyond traditionally (white) raced ideals of manhood.[60] Further, as we will see in the next chapter on adoption and new reproductive technologies, despite their elite academic credentials, most well-educated Jewish men and men in the professions—their individual places made possible by a *communal* shifting in U.S. racial designations—still don't meet the narrow standards of U.S. white mascu-line citizenship.[61]

Part IV

Bringing It Home . . . and Out Again

As an interesting point for reflection, I would like to look at one contri-bution to current identity politics that is not specifically a "Jewish" work, but a multicultural work that includes Jews. This piece, honoring its roots in feminist praxis, is significant in that its method itself makes use of and demonstrates the knowledges with which many are working regarding intersectionality theory. It also, therefore, helps clarify the limitations in the contemporary mode.

In 1998, World Trust released a video called *The Way Home*. Women from distinct ethnic groups were formed into "councils" which met sepa-rately over a period of eight months to engage in dialogue within their own communities. The main subject of the encounters was race as it intersects with gender, class, and sex/sexual orientation. The ethnic com-munities represented in the process were (as named in the video): African-American, Arab, Asian, European-American, Indigenous, Jewish, Latina, and Multi-Racial. Sixty-four women participated in these ongoing council meetings. The individual women were chosen from a cross section of age, class, education, profession, religious/spiritual beliefs, sexual orientation, political leanings and involvement, different histories of engaging in such groups and in individual self-exploration.

At an advanced point in the dialogue process, video cameras are brought in to tape the conversations within each of the councils. In the film, we as viewers are introduced to each of the councils, a first layer of important diversity issues within each group is exposed, and some major themes of concern to the different groups are brought up. The mode then switches to collages of clips from the different councils according to specific topics. In this portion, thirteen specific areas are addressed such as land issues, internalized oppressions, finding identity, becoming "American," standards of beauty, individual and cultural realities, power-silence-privilege, and so forth. By looking at each of these areas directly, the video takes on more difficult content-based discussion, deeper layers of diversity within each council are revealed, and viewers have an opportunity to see a bit more of the dynamics among some of the members within the councils.

The video has many strengths. Not only is the diversity of ethnic communities represented in the councils refreshing, but also many issues of diversity within each community are brought out. Too often, teaching tools and diversity programs rely on only one or two voices from different communities. Although usually intended as an effort to include diversity, these individuals will usually end up as mere tokens, expected to symbolize a whole community. Such an approach too frequently loses the important historical dimensions of community life as well as the dynamism rooted in the multiplicity within communities.

This dimension of the film brings up significant issues for Jewish feminists engaged in multicultural work. That some aspects of Jewish diversity were acknowledged and addressed was indeed welcome (i.e., not all participants were Euro-Ashkenazi and this situation was discussed among the women). The tendency to have a single "Jewish" spokesperson on a diversity panel or program similarly tends to essentialize "Jews" as a monolithic group and generally as an ahistorical community. Part of the reason that the presentation of this diverse group of Jewish women seems so extraordinary is that "multicultural" programs usually fail to address any Jewish issues at all, let alone a complexity of Jewish peoples and issues.

Still today, many conferences and texts whose purpose is to educate on multicultural issues lack any overt Jewish presence. We often find Jews participating, but they are subsumed under the European section. As discussed above, this occurs due to the historically recent categorization of Jews as white in the U.S. experience based on the false assumption that all Jews in the United States are of European/Ashkenazi descent. As opposed to the narrowness of the new U.S. Census, on the rare occasions that a non-Ashkenazi or nonwhite/Euro Jewish woman appears on a diversity program, she is often placed as multiracial. By placing African-American, Latina, Indian, Ethiopian, or other more traditional Mizrachi or Sephardi Jews as multiracial and not doing so for white and/or Euro, Ashkenazi Jews is one way in which U.S. politics both draws on and reinforces white/Euro and Ashkenazi hegemony within the U.S. Jewish minority. I will therefore focus most of the following analysis on the Jewish, European, and Multi-Racial councils as portrayed in the video and some of the issues for discussion such portrayals stimulate.

The Way Home makes clear that for Jews of European Ashkenazi heritage or lighter skin, concerns regarding racial privilege are a primary experience. However, as argued above, the usual subsuming of Jews under the banner "European" and therefore white does not make much sense in either historical context or current reality. Such a designation actually contributes to white privilege in that, in the U.S. example in particular and the Western example more broadly, white has meant white-Christian. In not addressing the Christian privilege that helps to construct white skin privilege we leave both Christian and white privilege intact as we obscure the ways in which Jews have both understood themselves and also been understood historically in the United States and the West more broadly.

Central to this problem is, again, the fact that so many Jews are not light skinned or of European and Ashkenazi background; a representation of us as such excludes the majority of the community (and the way that the very interpretation of "light skinned" shifts according to geographical and other contexts even currently). Even if the majority of Jews residing in the United States are of Ashkenazi European descent, then critically challenging processes of "Americanization," assimilation, internalized oppression, and access to cultural or skin privilege for the community as a whole or individual European Jews will be off balance by not situating the U.S. example as a particular Jewish experience and not the universal Jewish experience.

Also central to this problem is that the precarious position of the Jewish community in the United States (and therefore of many individual Jews) relies inherently on mutually constitutive hierarchical constructions of class, sex, sexuality, and gender. The ways that whiteness becomes a socially constructed category not only have been made possible by assumptions of a Christian norm, but of certain classist, sexist, and heterosexist systems of oppression that shift over time. As the discussion above following Baldwin's insight suggests, the Jewish community has achieved whatever levels of status and access it has relative to other groups in large part as segments have climbed the socioeconomic ladder and visibly acquiesced to too many gender and heterosexist processes in U.S. politics, culture, and society. To give voice to the very presence—and then also the contributions and struggles—of women, the working class and poor, and the range of sexual minorities within the Jewish community in *The Way Home* is to disrupt power dynamics in the United States at large and to build Jewish communal power democratically rather than through further oppression.

Similarly, the inclusion of a distinct European-American council and a Multi-Racial council in the film also help to disrupt all too commonly made assumptions about power in the U.S. context of specific interest for Jews. Although its presumably shared Christian identity was not addressed, the European-American council had within it its own diversity. The area of "white studies" is a newer avenue for examining power and oppression, and gives European-Americans a place from which to engage in the complexities.[62] That those on the European-American council did not address their own identity issues, but only began to deal with privilege with respect to others, reflects a stage common in anti-oppression justice work. It is not only minorities who must engage in multicultural work, but also majorities as well. It is not only the marginalized who must acknowledge their own situated stance in cultural and political work. Until those in power can recognize their own specificity and how their power is rooted in their own experiences, activists from marginalized communities will be stymied in their work for justice.

When the film was made, including a Multi-Racial council unto itself represented cutting edge work. Many of the most contentious aspects of diversity politics in recent U.S. debates have been played out over the turf designated by those calling attention to multiple racial and other identities.[63] Attempts to include a multiracial category in the 2000 U.S. census generated an unexpected backlash exposing the deep-seated investment those in power have in the current racial hierarchy. Questioning a monoracial presumption challenges the Black to white hierarchical divisions of the populace. But most U.S. citizens are themselves the products of multiracial reproductive unions (whether legal, illegal, chosen, or forced) over time, with the trend on the rise.[64] Although minority critics of a census multiracial box (as opposed to a "check all that apply" option) point out that its use only further inscribes racial reasoning, giving a sampling of self-identified multiracial women an opportunity to gather together in council to begin to examine power and identity issues—and that their process may spark further dialogue through the use of the video—is an important step in unlocking additional aspects of the seemingly iron grid of identity-based systems of oppressions.

Having said all this, it cannot go unmentioned that none of the Asian, Indigenous, Latina, Arab, and African-American women identified as Jewish, nor did the European or Multi-Racial women. Although the film expressed many current issues in diversity politics, the very makeup of the councils betrays the (il)logic of distinctive racial categorizations.[65] That Jews had their own council and were not subsumed under European, Multi-Racial or other councils seemed an "advance" from the ways Jews tend to get silenced in diversity settings; the choice, however, to have the only Jews present only in the Jewish council further exposes the limitations of such an approach.

Part V

"You Don't Have to be Jewish to Love Levy's"

—From an ad campaign for Levy's Rye Bread

In the late 1960s, Levy's Rye Bread did an ad campaign that reflected progressive identity politics of the day.[66] The campaign ran a series of photos of individuals from different racial and ethnic backgrounds eating a slice of rye bread. Yes, the point of the ad campaign was to sell products. It is also revealing of a certain set of political possibilities and ideas about race during the period. Many people found this a forward looking, urban-style addition to the new attention diverse ethnic/racial groups were receiving in the decade. It seemed to challenge the notion of ethnicity as a thickly walled, natural category. The Levy's ad suggested that non-Jews can participate in and enjoy some of the more worthwhile contributions of Jewish culture in the United States (Yum . . . a seeded rye bread.) This meant that non-Jews were being invited into a Jewish world. It also meant that Jewish things can be part of life beyond the Jewish community (occurring at the historical moment of the shifting racial assignment Brodkin and Schultz examine).

The Levy's campaign illustrates both the lingering limitations found in more contemporary work on identity, such as in *The Way Home*, as it also shows us how thinking has changed. Unlike the Jewish Council in the film, the ad campaign relies on a Euro/Ashkenazi presumption of Jewish identity. Rye bread may be seen as "a Jewish bread" found commonly in Jewish homes, but those homes are historically likely to be

Ashkenazi European Jewish homes. Jews from the Middle East and North Africa generally are more likely to associate with pita bread, a bread specialty of Yemenite Jews is called "malawach" (a finely layered round and flat bread), and Ethiopian Jews with a large fluffy flat bread, and so forth. In *The Way Home*, the film makers purposely intended to disrupt such an equation of U.S. Jew with Euro/Ashkenazi. But who were the non-Jews figured in the ads that suggested one doesn't have to be Jewish to love Levy's? There were head shots of smiling people from various cultural backgrounds. Before researching the campaign, I most clearly remembered at least one image of a Native American and one African-American boy.[67] At the same time that the ad campaign appeared, a tribute to the newly celebrated diversity and ethnic boundary crossing characteristic of the 1960–70s, it simultaneously reinforced essentialist and static notions of those very same identities (also characteristic of identity politics at that time). The Native American man sported "traditional" garb, and all of the figures presupposed a multiplicity of *individually fixed* ethnic/racial groups. The ad campaign worked because it was assumed consumers would see the face of an African-American-looking boy and presume that he was not himself Jewish.[68] In *The Way Home*, the film makers made certain to upset such boundaried and separative understandings of identity. At the same time, the critique above suggests that, still—in its use of councils as they were constructed conceptually with the lack of Jews in all of the other councils and the un-remarked Christian presumption of the European and non-Jewish presumption of all the other councils—the problem of Levy's remained a problem for *The Way Home*.

After I wrote the first draft of this section on Levy's, I was all hyped up and so I talked about it to Dawn. This Levy's ad campaign loomed so large in my memory, I assumed *everyone* knew the cultural reference. Dawn had no idea what I was talking about. One week later a former student of mine from the University of New Hampshire (basically, my only self-identified Jewish student up until then in my many years teaching there) gave me a copy of the first edition of the then new Jewish magazine: *Heeb, the New Jew Review*. Its tone and style is young, hip, urban, boundary crossing.[69] On the front cover is a photo of a round hand-made matzah meant to look like a record album on a turntable. (Matzah is the bread of affliction, symbolizing the Jewish flight from slavery in Egypt, which is eaten on the holiday of Passover.) These particular kinds of matzahs are usually associated with certain groups of ultra-Orthodox Jews who make them in this way. They are called "shmura" matzahs, the rules and traditions for making matzah especially guarded. This traditional image is juxtaposed with the modern technology of the turntable. (Interesting that the turntable in youth culture today is considered both an outmoded form of nontechnology for personal use, but is central for hip-hop innovations.) There is a pair of hands, the left one adorned with funky gold rings, placing the matzah/record on the turntable. The pair of hands are very dark-skinned. Inside the covers, amongst an array of serious and quirky artifacts and analyses of turn of the Christian millennium U.S. Jewishkeit, is a five page spread on JEWFROS, Jewish Afros in all their wild curly kinky Jewish glory. The final page in the spread includes homage to the queen, a hair cholesterol product long used by African-Americans to soften their kinks. Perhaps Jewish—African-American segregation is coming to an end in a new generation?[70] But wait, there is also page three. On page three of the debut issue of *Heeb* is a full page ad for subscriptions. There is an African-American-looking older man. (Hair clipped short under a cap. No Afro. Interesting.) He is holding open before him a copy of this first issue of *Heeb*. The tag line runs on top: "You don't have to be Jewish." And on bottom: "To love Heeb." It seems that I'm not the only one that remembers Levy's. What did the funky founders of *Heeb* think about the essentialized and exclusionary identity constructions of the Levy's ads? An apparently unreconstructed Levy's is revived in the same magazine which dares to take on JEWFROS. And anyway, does the very naming of "Jewfros" presume a necessary distinction between "Jewish" fros and "Af"ros (African-American Afros)? Do I have to ask the question: are we dreading my daughters' Afros or Jewfros or what? Even *Heeb* does not help me here. How am I supposed to make sense of this? Does the world have anything new to offer my Library of Congress logically impossible yet very real African-American Jewish daughters?

Having presented this critique, it is also important to note that the range of possible interpretations of any of these representations is unknowable. In the *Bridges* special issue on *Writing and Art by Jewish Women of Color* there is an interview which Reena Bernards (2001) did with Toni Eisendorf. Reena Bernards is a Euro-Jewish adoptive mom of two biracial Jewish children, an activist and early framer of an organization called the Jewish Multi-Racial Network. Eisendorf is an African-American woman. (She was born, and spent her early years, in Italy.) She was not raised Jewish, but explains that she had long had an attraction to Jewish culture and sought out Jewish environments and learning from an early age. She had already moved to the United States as a child when the Levy's ad campaign ran. Although the logic of the ad campaign suggests that the people represented in the headshots were not Jewish (otherwise the tag line would make no sense: "You don't have to be Jewish . . ."), the then young Eisendorf interpreted the ads in an entirely different fashion. To her, the ads meant "that you don't have to be White to be Jewish" (2001, 22).[71] Eisendorf was a young Black girl with a yearning to be Jewish in a

New York cultural context that had by then largely come to associate Jewishness with whiteness. To *her*, in contradiction to what *I* have presented as the racial logic of the ad, the ad gave her hope and possibility for new identity constellations and personal fulfillment. She writes that it made her feel "good" and "relieved."

What potential does Toni Eisendorf's experience with the "logic" of Levy's hold for my daughter Toni? What does Eisendorf on Levy teach us about the "logic" of race, identity, boundaries and boundary crossings, disciplining borders, historical moments, personal experience, power, institutions, systems, ideology, hegemonic constructs? I can not say, and that is part of the point . . . at least for now. So we are required to say what we can say . . . to say what will help us best make sense of our lives and our worlds where we stand now. To raise our children and teach our youth to the best of our capacities at the moment. To see through Library of Congress categorizations and find those books on African-American Jews, to see through popular ideology and create multiracial Jewish communities. The call for justice requires this of us, to speak and to act although next year we may be shown to have missed the point. To deconstruct the "logic" of an illogical racist system. To note the twists, and tangles, and breaks in what presents itself to us as the color line. To twist, and tangle, to clarify, to break, and to reconnect the line . . . or not, given what we will know/feel/think/suppose about justice and its requirements at the time we are ready to do the work. Jews have been raced, deraced, erased, and are continually being re-raced. There has been much work done regarding this phenomenon, in writing and on the streets. Yet, again, hard work hardly suggests that the work itself is complete. In the next chapter, then, I take on a more concrete issue area where these mutually constitutive aspects of identity are explicitly negotiated, traded, priced, bought, and sold. I enter the fray of the debate on adoption as a queer Jew whose identity and family constellation has been and is being forged in the crucible of an ongoing politics of identities in the United States.

Chapter Two

Jew Dykes Adopting Children

A Guide to the Perplexed

Introduction

We're Jews living in Maine. We are also dykes but we were living in New Hampshire. We had to move. Until recently, New Hampshire would not let people adopt children if there was a person thought to be gay living in their household. You could be as straight as an arrow, but if you had taken in your Great Aunt Tilly, a raging bisexual in the 1930s, someone could cause trouble and the state could deny you that kid. We didn't have a Great Aunt Tilly. We were out and rather public, politically active queers. It would be difficult for a rabbi and a professor in a small New England town to be in the closet even if they wanted to (which we didn't and which we weren't), so adopting children was simply not an option as long as we lived in New Hampshire. We picked up and moved a mile, over the border into Maine. That's how we made it possible to have Paris (Peretz is her Hebrew name) in our lives. Once Paris joined our family, we turned right around and did it again. That's how we are also blessed with Toni (Tali is her Hebrew name) in our family.

In 1997, New Hampshire finally passed a law including sexual orientation in its civil rights code. Around the same time Maine passed a similar law, but the Christian Right organized like mad and succeeded in overturning it. The difference between the Maine and New Hampshire cases is that although Maine repealed its gay civil rights law, it never had a specific ban on homosexuals adopting children. Despite New Hampshire's

45

newly passed "gay" civil rights code, the ban on queers adopting was not originally overturned. Basically, we had to give up our newly won general civil rights in order to have the specific right to adopt kids. Admittedly, it is a complicated story. A Jewish lesbian couple that wants to raise children will usually have a complicated story. We're a Euro-Ashkenazi Jewish lesbian couple that chose interracial adoption while living in rural northern New England. Needless to say, over the past decade or so, I learned a lot about adoption.

Actions taken to dismantle formal discrimination based on identity-related categories of gender, race and ethnicity, religion, sexual orientation, and ability have been somewhat successful over the years. Transforming the less formal mechanisms of discrimination has been much more difficult. One arena in U.S. life in which discrimination, both formally and informally, remains *rampant* is the adoption world. The intensely intimate intricacies of the parent-child bond, familial ties, and inheritance interweave in the area of adoption in ways that tap deeply into sexism, racism, and other biased modes of human relation.

In this chapter, I tell our adoption story and thus undertake an analysis of discriminatory practices in the complex world of adoption in the United States. To do so I address some aspects for each of the three "parties" in adoption: (1) prospective adoptive parents, (2) children, and (3) biological parents (biological mothers in particular).[1] The main issues at stake are class (and various measures of socioeconomic status), race and/or ethnicity/nationality, sex/gender, sexuality, religion, health, and age. These issues are operative for each group's own situation as well as the cross between them.

My Story: Starting the Process

I am a professor at the University of New Hampshire, an activist, and writer. My partner was at the time, among other things, the rabbi in the university town. We were Euro-Am Jewish dykes living in rural Maine with two adopted African-heritage children. I had often been asked to write about my experience in the adoption world. For many years, however, I had only been able to think in response: where could I possibly begin? Folks often assume we faced "interesting" challenges being lesbians. What most do not seem to realize is that we faced as much resistance to our adoption plans because we are Jewish. Most people in the United States simply don't want their biological kids to be raised by Jews.[2] Because adoption is a big business, agencies in many states are therefore not going to waste their time taking on Jewish clients.[3]

Queers generally seem to know that they might face obstacles creating families through adoption. I've tried to understand why most Jews don't know the situation for other Jews. After all, Jews are doing a somewhat disproportionate amount of the adopting in the United States relative to our small percentage of the population.[4] My research suggests that the reason has to do with the fact that most Jews who want to adopt children either utilize the services of Jewish agencies and/or live in cities or other places with large Jewish populations. The agencies they use generally know that Jews can't adopt in most places, and the adoption workers therefore know to focus on the organizations that *will* work with Jews. Prospective parents are rarely informed of all the details involved in creating an adoption placement. Jewish prospective parents must also, therefore, not know the politics of anti-Semitism that frames their opportunities negotiated at the agency level.[5]

With our "highly normative" profile (that's supposed to be a joke . . .) as Jewish queers in a state with very few Jews, we were largely left to our own devices. I had to do the research to find the services and the available children out there, tasks that many Jews in cities can delegate to their adoption agencies. With a lot of research I found a number of agencies and brokers happy to work with queers, Jews, older people, those without tons of money, folks who had been arrested protesting at the Pentagon in the 1960s and were thus shut out of most of the adoption world for having a criminal record, individuals with some aspect of their health histories that sparked irrational biases of many state-paid social workers. Occasionally I found the kindness of a stranger along the way. These random moments of kindness significantly helped me to stay on course. I needed those moments badly because most of what I found in my foray into the adoption world was ugly.

In late November 1998, we moved over the state border into Maine, a state where a gay person can legally adopt children. I called the Department of Human Services adoption office right away to get the process rolling. I wanted to be up-front from the start that we were gay to help avoid homophobic surprises later. A senior state employee then told me all the reasons that, although Maine does not discriminate, they would likely have trouble placing children with us. Every sentence she uttered began with the phrase, and I quote: "Although the State of Maine does not discriminate on the basis of sexual orientation," and then proceeded with examples of why we would not be considered as fit parents for hypothetical little Janie, Dexter, Matilda, and Lewis.

I got concerned. I knew I needed to come out about being a Jew too. Same response. "Although the State of Maine does not discriminate on the basis of religion," we would not be considered fit parents for Mary,

Chris, John, and Kathy. The woman further explained that it was her job to determine what was in the best interest of the child.[6] Because there are no children in the Maine state system born to Jewish parents,[7] her office would be left to determine what was a good fit. Because every child in the state system would have been, more or less, raised Christian, it was up to her to evaluate just how important Christianity had become to the child. Although (U.S.)Americans pride themselves on, in Thomas Jefferson's words, "putting a wall of separation between 'church' [need I say more] and state," U.S. institutions are de facto Christian institutions. Regardless of the religious background of the birth parents, any child in the state's care will most likely have attended state-sponsored Christmas parties, been sent an Easter basket, been blessed by a Christian clergy member, been brought to church on Sundays, or received any manner of Christian instruction and influence. This meant that she could potentially claim we were "unfit" parents for any child in the system.

Our chances looked bleak. I began to do some research. In 1988, the Child Welfare League of America issued a policy statement saying, "Gay/lesbian adoptive applicants should be assessed the same as any other adoptive applicants. It should be recognized that sexual orientation and the capacity to nurture a child are separate issues." Despite this, innumerable instances of discrimination occur against queers trying to adopt. I learned that queers sometimes waited for years to have children placed with them. In states where it is not expressly illegal for homosexuals to adopt children, there are likely to exist numerous homophobic practices foreclosing placement options for queer clients. Individual social workers and/or local adoption bureaus might accept funds and applications to do home studies from queers wanting to adopt children, but be either unwilling or unable to negotiate placements on their behalf. Although not expressly or legally prohibited in most places anymore, many states *practice* discrimination and will reject applications from those whose home studies state or suggest that they are queer. The politics of anti-Semitism may work similarly, though often operates within a specific field of prejudices and practices.

Queers find it difficult to adopt children due to a set of intermingling homophobic assumptions about who queers are, what we believe, and most especially how we live. Queers are still too often thought to be, for example, unstable, anti-"family," predators of children, poor role models for the young, without morals or religion. On this score, contemporary stereotypes about Jews can often come together in a pro-"family" cluster. Some of the stereotypes of Jews in the United States are that we have strong families and "good" family values. We are presumed to be smart, education-minded, emotionally stable, economically successful, drug and abuse free, tradition and family oriented.[8] This particular set of positively valenced stereotypes of Jews aren't necessarily any more reflective of Jewish lives than are the clearly skewed queer ones.[9] Even so, when it comes down to it, however, many Christians still would not want Christian children sucked into one of those "good" Jewish families. It's like the straight people who give a lot of money to the AIDS walk but freak out if their kid comes home with a rainbow sticker on their car. Not for my daughter. Not for our children.

There certainly are examples of children who used the foster system and developed bonds, grew in self-esteem, and generally thrived. Yes, there are also hundreds of thousands of children drowning in foster care.[10] There are tens of thousands of children yearning to belong to new families.[11] Yes, the state works very hard to find adults willing to adopt the overload of kids in their dockets. We, like many Jews and queers, were happy to take kids in all sorts of the categories the state deems "hard to place" and "special needs." Unfortunately, we found through our efforts and the delays we experienced that we probably would not have had any kids placed with us. (Some workers in the system told us this outright, I tell some of what we learned by "experience" below). Given the data on discrimination that my research was yielding, over time I realized we would have to find a private agency and pay sizable sums.[12] So much for my desire to be a good citizen, to work with the state and also receive the medical benefits and other support offered to children placed in adoptive families by state agencies. I suppose that I shouldn't have found it surprising: minorities too often wind up with extra financial, and other resource-draining, burdens. Due to discrimination we would not be working through the state and thus we would be required to employ numerous levels of intermediaries and brokers, and to hire costly lawyers specially trained in discrimination and adoption law instead of using our resources on our hoped-for child. By using a private agency when we had a child, we would be ineligible for an array of free or subsidized health care, special needs, and child care programs, financial allowances, and free placement follow-up services made available through state agencies.

I make my living writing about and working against injustice including especially racism, sexism, homophobia, anti-Semitism, and classism. But if anyone had tried to explain to me in advance the depths of the hierarchies of human worth at work in the adoption world, I admit even I might have found it difficult to believe. Some of the ugliest aspects of U.S. versions of discrimination and dehumanization are crystalized in the trading in human beings that all too frequently occur in the adoption world. There are clear hierarchies of human worth in this country and the adoption world has done the market research, assessed the situation, organized a filing system and very neatly attached price tags to services and humans according to their appropriate rank. I was constantly surprised by the intensity of the biases in play, shocked by the unabashed and "matter of fact" manner in which agencies marketed the biases. What follows are some examples from research and my personal experience.

Prospective Adoptive Parents

We, as the prospective adoptive parents, faced forms of privilege and discrimination in complex ways. As Jews and queers we were effectively disqualified from consideration in large portions of the country. We also very much benefited from a stratified and hierarchical social system in other ways. We are both highly educated, with eight advanced academic degrees between the two of us. (Shocking, but true. Dawn tips the balance with five of the eight.) Despite being Jewish, we are also both Euro-heritage, often enough enabling us to engage in the great "American" past-time of passing. "White" in the United States means "white-Christian." My partner and I are both "white-enough-looking" so that average (U.S.) Americans can sometimes forget the fact of our Jewishness which they find so inexplicably disturbing. We appeared somewhat healthy and young enough. Finally and significantly, we were able to pretend we had a sufficient amount of money to support ourselves and the bundles of joy we hoped to raise.[13] Discrimination operates in multiple imbricating ways. We faced negative bias just as we also tapped into aspects of privilege that are denied other likely "perfectly fit" and loving people who want to adopt children.

Our being a presumably monogamous couple also contributed to our "privilege." "Family" in U.S. ideology largely means a *set* of parents, so that even if we are queer and Jewish there are at least still two of us. This plays out in specific ways for Jewish queers. Often queers seeking to adopt children as singles, not as part of long-term couples, may "benefit" by presenting themselves as "just" single, leaving heterosexuality presumed and therefore avoiding being targeted as queer. This is usually of more assistance for women, as women are assumed to "naturally" want/need to be mothers. Surely, women's single status may call into question their ability to provide a proper (read: with a male) home. Even so, they can still rely on social institutions and ideas which seek to fulfill the natural destiny of women: to be mothers.[14] Single women are at times even favored as it is assumed that they will have more of a capacity to focus on the well-being of their children, and not be harried by the divided loyalties heterosexually married women are assumed to have between their demanding children and their demanding husbands. For a number of years, for instance, single women were looked upon favorably for these reasons in adopting children, particularly girls, from China.[15] With all this, however, single women are still stigmatized for being so in family building, particularly where the state plays as large a role as in adoption. Men face a different set of biases. Single men are presumed to be potentially dangerous to children. They are seen as a threat to the physical safety of children as single men are presumed to be gay—and therefore child molesters. Single people generally may also be seen as a potential threat to the moral development of children, because it is assumed that they will expose their children to "inappropriate" sexual behaviors otherwise safely hidden within the legal arrangement of single partner marriage.[16]

There is a further consideration regarding the benefits for and biases against singles adopting. The multiple factors of discrimination make it difficult for many people to fit the mold sufficiently on their own. Single people who want to adopt children, therefore, may have fewer chances than couples do to arrange the details of their life stories to make the grade. As a couple, my partner and I could pool our resources of privilege, and work to deflect our individual "deficiencies" as categorized in society by highlighting the other's socially constructed "proficiencies."

For example, despite my partner's many publications, high profile and prestigious positions, and despite the fact that she has always economically supported her needs just fine, she was concerned about her financial credibility. This is a situation common to many women, especially those working as professional Jewish feminist dykes. Women rabbis generally earn less money than their male counterparts for the same work, when they can get it. Despite the large institutional apparatus of U.S. Jewry, full time or adequately paid positions with any benefits are a rarity for Jewish women professionals, are more so for out lesbian and bisexual women, and are extremely difficult for gender outlaws of all stripes.[17] As a full-time tenured professor, I'm the one with the more normative financial profile and I happen to have a health history that looks "nicer" on paper. I'm the one within the requisite age spread agencies deem acceptable between adoptive children and parents. (Though the fact that Dawn "looks" younger than she "is" explicitly helped us when our agency showed our photographs to birth parents.) Is it any wonder: I'm the one the home study consistently names as "parent-to-be;" my partner was given the shifting labels: "other adult who resides in abode," "partner," or " legal guardian." Once we entered into the maze of adoption laws and markets, "family planning" in its conservative manifestations—designed through instances of state structures, ideologies, and practices—forced society's power hierarchies further into our home and relationships than they had been before.

Regarding the racialization of Jews, as discussed in the previous chapter, in our case my partner has the dubious advantage of having been raised Christian. This means that anti-Semitic Christians can sometimes excuse her self-identification as a Jew, because they can classify her as not "racially" Jewish. They think of her Jewishness as "a religious thing." In fact, to many Christians she's just an interesting *kind* of Christian. As she was not born a Jew (here race retains it biological base), they don't project all of those "problematic" Jewish racial characteristics onto her. Those they reserve for me. Christians presume that she can "understand" them more than other Jews can; they may feel "more comfortable" with her when they find out she is a convert to Judaism. Further, they do not necessarily interpret her strength and intelligence as superior, overbearing, rude, devious, and untrustworthy. They do not necessarily equate the financial stability they demand with trickery, usery, or miserliness. There are likely many contributing factors to this aspect of her acceptance, though that she avoids biologically based racial stereotypes of Jews figures largely. Also, my partner is a member of the clergy/a rabbi, and (although people don't always know what to make of women religious leaders) this scores points. But that Jew thing often still gets in the way. For example, many people in "America" don't know what a rabbi is, so she often misses out on the clergy perk.

Race is a factor for prospective adoptive parents also in other ways rarely discussed. As will be examined in the next section, the common wisdom in the adoption world is that there is a scarcity of children to meet white clients' demands. This is explained as follows: white adults want to adopt white children and there are not enough white children available domestically to fulfill the requests. There are, however, an "overabundance" of Black children available within the United States. What this means in adoption-speak is that there are more Black children available than meets the white demand for them. The "crisis" of "overabundance" is in myriad ways a creation of the adoption market, ideology, and government policy. Here I will focus on the aspect of the "crisis" related to prospective parents.

The "overabundance" of Black children up for adoption is part of a deeper system of racism than the mere racial preferences of white prospective adopters. As for many in our situation, there are plenty of non-Black prospective parents happy to adopt transracially, but due to mutually constituted factors of discrimination (in our case, for example, being queer and Jewish) adoption as a mode of family formation is closed to whole classes of prospective adopters. Another dirty secret rarely discussed is the racism faced by Black prospective adoptive parents.[18]

In the novel *Edgar Allen* (Neufeld 1968) about a white family living in a white town who adopts a Black child, and the tragic fate as a consequence, the eldest daughter has a conversation with her friends. Neither M.N. nor her friends want the child because he is Black. Her friend says, "What I don't understand, though . . . is why a Negro couple couldn't have taken him in? Why do you have to?" To which the equally horrified M.N. replies: "Well . . . there just aren't enough Negro families, I guess, who can afford another child" (33). Despite the obvious economic discrimination directed at African-Americans, this view that the community cannot support its own is simultaneously belied by the rather widespread historical phenomenon of informal adoption through (often multigenerational) kin networks.[19] Basically, however, what is presented in adoption-speak as not only the "scarcity" of white available children, but in fact also a "glut" of Black available children (what might have been separate phenomena always paired in adoption world logic) is presumed to have to do with lower demand by Black prospective parents. This long-standing assumption must be problematized.

The comparison between the success of agencies who target same race placements and those that do not specialize in such reveals a hole in the logic that there simply are not enough Black families to adopt the Black waiting children. Agencies that consider finding Black parents to adopt children in their dockets as fully part of their mission have high levels of success. Those that just occasionally have Black children to place tend not to find Black prospective parents as easily. As the adoption market in this country was designed to provide white parents with white children, the system has not sufficiently developed to work with Black clients. Most social workers are white and know too little about Black communities. It has been argued that agencies do not adequately recruit in Black communities, either as locales or sufficiently using community resources. Moreover, African-American groups have pointed out that the criteria for eligibility—such as marital and socioeconomic status, characteristics of neighborhood of domicile, and high fee scales—discriminate against Black adults trying to adopt. Black GLBTQ folks face imbricating discrimination regarding sexuality and gender status.[20] These are not necessarily standards African-Americans would consider crucial to identifying "fit" parents, and the white standards de facto exclude large portions of Black people. In addition, working-class Blacks are more likely than white adults to be encouraged to become foster, rather than adoptive, parents. Further, given the history of welfare agencies' discrimination against Blacks, many either tend to stay away from voluntary engagement or presume they would not be found worthy if they did approach a service worker.

With all of this, it has been the case that Blacks have adopted children who are coded Black at approximately the same rate at which whites adopt children coded white. Further, regarding adoption more generally, there is evidence that "Black heterosexuals tend to adopt at a higher rate than do White heterosexuals, [and that] Black LGBT people appear to adopt at higher rates than do Black heterosexual people."[21] As more research is done, the notion that there are not enough Black prospective adoptive families seems less likely to be a cause of the phenomenon that there are more Black children than there is demand for them.

We must continue to evaluate the morphings of racism in the adoption world. As birth families become somewhat more empowered in the process and have more to say about the families with whom their bio-offspring will be placed, racism may come in new ways. For example, I have heard from an African-American couple trying to adopt that they were told some African-American birth families were *choosing* white placements over Black ones, given the idea that the children would fare better in white homes. In another vein, a new move has been reported that some agencies have begun placing U.S. Black children in international adoptions with Canadian white families. In the report, the agency head was asked directly if he had tried to place the children with U.S. Black families first. He answered no.[22] Thus, much more research needs to be done on the experiences of adults of color, and specifically African-American adults, as prospective adoptive parents before we continue to recite the ideological mantra that there is not enough of a demand for Black children, especially by Black adults.[23]

The Children

The standards by which adults are measured, however, barely compare to the intensity of the racism, in its many forms, which charts the life course of children and prospective children in the adoption world. After all, if no one picks them, prospective parents still have their homes, lives, and autonomy. If this is their issue, there are services to help cope with disappointment and depressive responses to "childlessness." I have met individuals who spent some or much time in foster care growing up and consider their lives a blessing. Too many children are probably placed in foster care who may not have needed this service in the first place, or get lost in the system once there (Roberts 2002). For all too many children slated for adoption, however, kids who don't get chosen are likely destined to a living hell. These are children who end up being bounced around foster homes and state institutions.[24] What makes certain children "undesirables?" Children who are considered "special needs." This designation may be limited to children with health "issues" or physical "deformities." The classification of children as "special needs," or (especially given the discrimination waged against so many groups of potential adopters discussed above) "hard to place" also usually includes young people older than infant age,[25] who are not "white,"[26] who are to be placed with their biological siblings, or for older kids who are queer. [27]

Children are considered "undesirable" if the system labels their birth parents "riff-raff." As will be discussed further, this means that children may be deemed "undesirable" if their birth mothers were the victims of violence and poverty. These designations apply but are not only related to battery and sexual assault, drug use, IQ, education level, job/welfare status, truancy, prison record, mental and physical health, as well as the racial makeup, legal status, and "coherence" of the biological mother and her birth family. Occasionally such information is gathered and disclosed about biological or legal fathers.[28] Generally, the state and other adoption workers do not attend to the status of fathers the ways they do birth mothers.[29] Despite the challenges faced in Europe as a result of Jewish children hidden during the Holocaust, in the United States there are proportionately few children of Jewish heritage on the adoption market. Where this has been so, since the 1950s their ranks have tended to be swelled disproportionately among bi-racial and or disabled Jewish-heritage children (mirroring trends among non-Jewish heritage kids).[30]

In the state system there are thick books (usually three-ring binders so they can be updated easily) with page after page of information on individual waiting children. Each page has a photo of a child and some facts about race, gender, history, and health status. Each page is dated with the month and year the child officially entered the system and became a waiting child. Each state has a book and large cities often have thick binders separate from those of their state. The stats are like war records. Private little wars. Children scarred from abuse, neglect, violence, poverty. Children that suffered unending physical, psychic, emotional syndromes as a result. Intended also to "sell" a "product," the descriptions of the children are also often quintessentially gendered. Four-year-old Stanley has improved greatly since his placement in foster care three months ago. Stanley loves to play basketball. Ten year old Shanika likes to help with the housework. You will find pages of older Black kids, with comparably few war stories. They are still in the system often simply because being Black makes you a "special needs" child and "hard to place."[31] As I said, there is much that is ugly, and exposed, in the adoption world.

In the private adoption world, there are a number of agencies that specialize in African-American or Latina/o infants. This can be helpful for those who want to adopt children of color. It is also necessary because many more agencies will only trade in white kids, based on so-called market demand. Due to the supposed lack of domestic supply of white children compared to the demand, international adoption is a special favorite of, the majority of adopters, white folks.[32] These people may take incredible risks to adopt children from Bulgaria, Romania, and the former Soviet Union. They want a newborn but will compromise on a two-year-old. The information they are given is too frequently unreliable, the orphanages are often in terrible condition, and the adoptions are extremely expensive.[33] For some Euro/Ashkenazi Jews, adopting a child from these parts of Europe feels like a connection to their past. In a post-Holocaust world, some Jews have described their adoption of Eastern European children as a *tikkun*/repair in the face of murdered relatives and family bonds torn asunder in formerly Nazi occupied lands. In general, however, the prevailing logic in the United States is (inscribed within the economic bias regarding the distinct class positions of the parties in an adoption): who wouldn't pay up to fifty thousand dollars for a white kid? Many agencies play up the idea that the domestic pool is too small for the white demand. Why wait? Go to Eastern Europe. There are thousands of kids waiting to be adopted domestically, they just aren't white.

Certainly many people, including those coded as "white," who choose to adopt "Latina/o" children are doing so as a result of much self-conscious and race-critical research. I believe in adoption as both an (admittedly complicated) issue of social justice and as a fabulous mode of family formation. Many adults who adopt Latina/o children share similar beliefs. However, some white folks get involved in very questionable deals trying to adopt children from Central and South America. I have heard many people who identify as white say (either explicitly or implicitly): "Well, they look almost white and if they are raised by us they won't even have those accents." Some prospective parents specify "white looking" or "light skinned" when they agree to pursue adoption options from Central and South America. Critical race theorists may be busy analyzing the supposed Jewish-white power alliance in recent years, calling attention to the ways that many U.S. Jews seem to have "opted" for being white, and accepting whatever privilege comes with that designation. Given the vagaries of race, however, it may not be surprising that I have heard from many U.S. Jews that they chose to pursue adoption in Latin America, because they wanted their children to "look like" them. When it comes down to the sensitive issue of family and lineage, many U.S. Jews have decided that their "racial" features look more "Latino/a" than U.S. "white." On a related note, stealing children and trafficking in babies from the south is a terrible reality for many poor women from the southern western hemisphere.[34] I know many people who have adopted children from Latin America who have made certain that the birth families of the children offered to them actually did put these kids up for adoption. Many people, however, do not undertake such investigations or are confusingly thwarted in their efforts.

Another favorite for white folks is to get kids from Asia. Chinese girls, kids from Vietnam, Korea, and Cambodia are some current favorites. Many white adults in the United States who adopt children from Asia do so out of a sincere commitment to social justice and love that crosses constructed racial difference. I know lots of loving families, Jewish and non-Jewish, with white and/or Euro-heritage parents and Asian children. However, given the fact of so much racism, particularly in adoption, I was interested to learn about this option more broadly. The prevailing logic in the adoption world appears to be that, whether domestically or internationally, Asian kids come in only one rung lower on the ladder of racial worth than Latina/o children who can pass as white (or in the Jewish case, go unmarked as Jews).[35] U.S. racial classifications categorize "Asians" as a distinct group with presumed distinct phenotypes. Despite the assumption that racism is about excluding those with nonnormative (in the U.S. case, a cluster of characteristics grouped as relating to the peoples of Christian Europe) observable features, racist stereotypes operate on many levels. In this example, discrimination against Asian children for the fact that they will "stand out in white society" is occasionally offset by other stereotypes. The primary factor here is that (U.S.)Americans think Asians are smart. And "smartness" is certainly valuable currency among many U.S. Jews.[36]

Related to the partial desirability of those from Asian countries is the phenomenon that Native Americans are also somewhat desirable. Again, what I am about to say in no way means that every white adult adopting Native American children does so for problematic reasons. My concerns here are historical trends and political context. White-coded adults who have done their homework already well know about and probably consciously and courageously confront these dynamics on a daily basis. Thus, as to the critique: Prompting cultural genocidal policies for centuries, European/white people in the United States often think that Native Americans can be made to "look white." Children born to Native American parents are commodified as "almost white" in the adoption world by the ideological fiat that given the "proper" cultural upbringing, Native Americans can be just as white as the biological children of white parents.[37] Further, in current practices, propaganda as advertising is used to enhance the desirability of Native American children by suggesting that one can basically raise these children to be white, but retain certain commercially advantageous public claims to their Native American blood lines. These advertising strategies in the adoption world rely on and reinforce the growing tendency for U.S. whites to appropriate and commodify Native American history and customs.[38]

Sometimes racial classifications in the adoption world separate and categorize children into two groups: white and nonwhite. In these instances all children of color are put into a common set of files distinct from white children. Other times a different classification is utilized. Many agencies have three sets of dockets: white, colored, and Black.[39] Whether brought together officially with other nonwhite children or distinguished as a class unto themselves, African, African-American, and African-Carribean children have a problem. Their problem is the racism of others. Here as in the Latina/o example, shading makes a difference. The majority of white adults adopting Black children in the domestic market involves children who have one bio-parent that is self-identified as Black and one that is white (as will be discussed below, the paradigm in adoption-speak for "biracial"). Further, children identified as Black (with two self-identified Black bio-parents) and are lighter skinned or look "biracial" are placed with white adoptive parents at higher rates than those with more stereotyped "Black" characteristics.[40]

In the adoption world as in many other realms, Black often signifies race itself.[41] Many scholars and activists have discussed this notion.[42] Let two examples from the adoption world suffice here to demonstrate this tendency. First, when children are classified as "biracial" this does not generally mean that they are biracial in any way. In "adoption-speak," this term usually does not refer to a child who may be any combination of white, Latina/o, Indigenous, or Asian. The term is generally used to refer to a child who is any part African heritage. In these situations, it is not only significant that Black is the signifier of naming race as a matter of import, but the issues of power at stake. Naming a child biracial to call attention to Blackness alerts consumers in adoptions (ie: prospective parents) of the "quality" of the goods in a system of racial hierarchy. To be part *Black* means that one's adoption costs less than that of most other children.[43] To be *part* Black can also be cause for an agency to raise the price of the adoption above that for "all Black" children because non-Blackness is a desired commodity.[44]

Transracial adoptions domestically are another example wherein Blackness signifies race.[45] For sure, many white people adopt children of color.[46] However, when domestic transracial adoption is treated as something to be problematized, it is almost always regarding the adoption of Black children. As with the case of mixed race children, it is not only the Blackness that is significant but the power relations involved in a system of racist discrimination. Basically, what are referred to domestically as "transracial" adoptions involve white adults adopting nonwhite, and usually Black, children. The notion of a minority family being eligible for a white child is almost a joke among workers and service providers in the adoption world.[47]

All children of color are devalued in the U.S. adoption world. However, as Blackness still most likely defines race itself, children of African heritage, whether domestically or internationally, are treated as a special case. African-heritage children are treated as *extra* with regard to other children of color. Increasingly, notions of social equality as well as concrete law lean in the direction of treating African heritage and all children of color with due respect and not as a separate category of discount chattel. Even so, as differential treatment becomes more frowned upon publically, agencies still often likely practice, in less overt ways, discrimination. Agencies commonly charge less to adopt Black children, because they say "people will not pay as high rates for Black children as for other children."[48] Sometimes adoptive parents are actually paid to adopt Black children, this in a huge moneymaking industry. Most adults adopting children are white, comprising approximately 67 percent of the market.[49] If one controls for class status, Black adults adopt at higher rates than do white adults.[50] Additionally, Black women give their children up for adoption at the same or lower rates than women of other racial groups.[51] Due to a number of intricately woven racist practices, however, Black children are overwhelmingly disproportionately represented among those the state makes eligible for adoption, they will usually wait longer to be adopted, and are less likely to ever get adopted than children of other races.[52]

Birth Mothers

Race is a central matter of concern in adoption, though as I said above there are hierarch*ies* of human worth at work in the adoption world. For example, along with race in the private system, there are gradations of health risk. Health risks and other factors are determined largely with reference to health and status issues for the child's birth mother's, for example, drug, alcohol, and tobacco use during pregnancy. There are gradations related to class locations, the birth mother's amount of schooling and/or her "intelligence." Adoption workers also prepare bizarre calibrations presented as trade-offs: birth mother used alcohol at times during pregnancy but is college educated; birth mother is schizophrenic but is white and from a "good" (meaning middle-class) family. There are gradations and then there are price tags to fit.

Technically it is illegal to pay for a child. One can pay the expenses of a birth mother: her rent, medical expenses, maternity clothes, counseling, sundries. It does not take a Ph.D. in math to realize that the sums do not add up to the thousands of dollars prospective parents are often required to pay. When you hear of people paying twenty to fifty thousand dollars for an adoption, that money is mostly not going to the women who bear the children. For example, in cases I have seen, in a twenty thousand dollar adoption, approximately fifteen hundred may go to the birth mother or more accurately, toward her "expenses." The majority of the money billed to prospective parents in an adoption generally pays fees of agencies and lawyers. While supposedly working to enforce an ethic that humans cannot be bought and sold, the government ignores the large fees paid to agencies. In U.S. law and custom, the money paid to birth mothers is seen as buying humans. However, money paid to agencies is protected as free market capitalism. Most women give their children up for adoption due to poverty and an assessment that their class/ life circumstances will not improve. There are agencies who will find jobs and homes for women only once they sign over their legal parental rights. Though there is certainly nothing inherently wrong with not raising a child one has birthed, our culture does not sufficiently support women before they reach the point of considering or opting for adoption.

These birth mothers lack the resources to live their lives independently and to support the children they are trying to raise or are pregnant with. It is the agencies, however, that make the money. There are a very few organizations that *do* provide care, housing, counseling, and other services to pregnant women in need who might be thinking about surrendering their parental rights. These agencies work with women to help ensure that adoption is the best solution, while giving women concrete support to see if they can redirect their lives and possibly care for children they birth. These efforts are woefully understaffed, underfunded, and too infrequently available and advertised to the women in need. Sexism, racism, violence, poverty and classism, our cultural inadequacy to educate and deal with sexuality, gender power differentials, and reproductive choice all contribute to self-fulfilling doomsday predictions of unwanted pregnancies. Minority/and/poor women may respond to cult of motherhood propaganda as may any majority/and/elite women in this country. Some buy into complex, culturally created desires to have children only then to find that they cannot adequately support themselves and these children.[53] Racism, anti-abortion policies, and negative attitudes regarding and obstacles to safe and affordable contraception directly complicate women's capacities to make choices about conceiving, birthing, and raising their biological children.

Among other factors, race fundamentally effects the manner in which birth mothers are treated. In general, to be sure, women who choose to give their children up for adoption or whose children are forcibly removed from their care by the state face social stigmatization.[54] Society tends to view and treat all these women badly as they challenge the notion that women *are* mothers naturally and that mothers represent all that is good and wholesome. As class plays a large role in women's "choice" to put their children up for adoption and in the state's assessment of which women are "fit" to parent, poor women across race suffer with regard to adoption practices in particular ways. Poor and/or uneducated women across racial groupings will have less access to adequate medical and psychological care and material support than wealthier women in adoption bureaucracies. They are less likely to be treated with respect and have their rights and dignities honored. Having said this, race continues to make a significant difference among birth mothers in adoption bureaucracies regardless of class.[55] Women from racial minorities are generally likely to face the circumstances I mention of poor and/or uneducated women and more. Beyond stigma and racist assumptions about their status (as illicit sexually, irresponsible, etc.) minority women are likely to receive less medical attention and be treated worse by health care professionals. They tend to receive less attention from agency social workers, be given less information about their rights and any prospective adopting parents. Minority women as birth mothers are more likely to be treated in a paternalistic manner and their participation less solicited in choosing adoptive families and the circumstances of the adoptions. They are also likely to receive smaller portions of the funds paid by prospective parents than are white birth mothers.[56]

I Love Paris in the Springtime . . .

Back to Our Story

So what happened with us? In August we got a call: you are mothers. Our agency in Maine was contacted by a southern agency with two girls, sisters, available for adoption. Jews and queers cannot usually adopt children from the South. As the self-proclaimed Bible Belt, the U.S. south is generally written off as practicing conservative, ideologically based discrimination. But here we were being offered the chance to adopt children from the South. We were overjoyed. As siblings, as "older children," as creole/African-Americans, the girls were considered "too hard to place" and with these unusual circumstances we were contacted. We went into full swing to make this adoption happen, working with Scott, the head of the southern agency, who prepared us to talk with the birth mother. She knew we were a lesbian couple. She had had some concerns, but Scott had talked to her and smoothed things out. I asked if she knew we were Jewish. I had been briefed that in meetings with birth mothers you are usually expected to talk about your religious beliefs and how you plan to raise the children. "No," Scott replied, the birth mother did not know that we were Jews. We were surprised and inquired as to why. The head of her agency told us that he thought it would jeopardize the placement. This was a problem and also probably illegal as law requires disclosure of all relevant information to both birth parents and to prospective adoptive parents. Religious affiliation is a standard piece of information that disclosure laws require. If particular state laws are vague on the details, the general ethic in the industry is that religion is considered "relevant" information.[57] We reminded the agency director of this, but he said that he had put too much time into arranging this placement already, and he could not afford for it to fall through. He would stand to lose too much money and would have to start looking for another placement all over again. He found this particularly problematic as his family and that of his co-worker were about to go on vacation for a few days together and he did not want to disrupt their plans. He continued to refuse to tell the birth mother that we were Jewish because he "knew" that she would then refuse us. Despite his earlier hard sell approach, there were further complications. We lost the opportunity to adopt the girls.

The next fall we received a call from social services (the state agency which was so concerned about protecting the interests of "Christian" children). In Maine prospective adoptive parents have to register formally to be foster parents in order to adopt children. We were asked if we would take in a little boy who was coming into their custody. He would be placed originally as a foster child with the intent of adoption as a longer range plan. Nathaniel did not fit the profile we had signed up for at all. (Since we were forced to place ourselves into a variety of categories over time, we eventually were slotted for older, African-American, girl siblings.) We said yes anyway. They said they might bring him over that night or the next morning. We said, "great!" so they told us more about him. One of his birth parents was from a Native American tribe in our region. I inquired how they had worked through the process of offering him to non-Native prospective parents so quickly. According to Federal law, the state must protect "Indian" "children who are members of or are eligible for membership in an Indian [*sic*] tribe" by working to place them in Native tribes. The federal government passed this law in the direct interest of the children and the tribes. The law states clearly that "an alarmingly high percentage of Indian [sic] families are broken up by the removal, often unwarranted, of their children from them by nontribal public and private agencies and that an alarmingly high percentage of such children are placed in non-Indian [sic] foster and adoptive homes and institutions."[58] The worker on the other end of the phone said that they did not bother to try to place Nathaniel within his or any other tribe. She reminded me that it is within her purview to determine what was best for the child. It would take "too long" to try to find a Native American family to adopt him, in her estimation being bad for the child. The law notwithstanding, his lifetime interests and identity concerns notwithstanding, the rights of his kin and the tribe not withstanding, they were offering him to non-Native families. I said we would be happy to take him, assuming that if he was offered to us as foster parents, at least *we* could try to work something out, but how could they ignore this constellation of needs, let alone the law? Needless to say, the foster care worker placed Nathaniel with a different (nontribal) family.

We had a number of other possibilities which all fell through. Word got around in our region about the Jewish dykes in Maine trying to adopt kids. I received a call from GLAD, the Gay and Lesbian Advocates and Defenders, which had begun researching discrimination in adoption for people who faced multiple barriers in adoption. The GLAD lawyer explained that they wanted to be able to work on GLBTQ concerns where they also overlapped with other aspects of discrimination. Would I help? I told her that we still had not been able to adopt children and that I did not want to jeopardize our prospects. I had decided while still in New Hampshire that I would help fight discrimination in adoption, but not put our own process on trial as a test case. The GLAD lawyer told me that it was enough now to write up a report on being lesbian and Jewish for their records only. I told her I would do it. (And I did.)[59]

We got another call from our case worker. This time she had waited until further along in the process before she contacted us. The family knew we were queer. They knew we were Jewish. They had picked us. Increasingly, domestic private adoptions work by the birth parents choosing the adoptive parents, and then the prospective parents get to choose back. We chose back. On the last night of Hanukah 5760, Paris Mayan was born. She's beautiful and happy. As an infant, she came with me to the meetings of the UNH Presidential Task Force on GLTB Issues which I chaired at the time. She took naps during the meetings of the Jewish Queer Think Tank I coordinated. She would come with us to services at Dawn's shul (synagogue) where Dawn served as rabbi. Paris went to work with Dawn to the rabbinical seminary where she was on faculty. Paris traveled all over Israel with us her first summer where we went to give lectures for Bat Kol, a feminist *yeshiva* run by a lesbian couple who are both rabbis. Basically, Paris came and still comes with us everywhere . . . everywhere her out, loud, political Jewish lesbian moms go in the course of their wanderings. People can't help falling in love with her, even total strangers. She's great and we are truly blessed to have her in our lives. Paris was barely six months old when we began the paper work to try it all again . . . we thought Paris would love having a younger sister.

Toni came to us in her own surprising ways. You have the basic story: bias, courage, ugliness, beauty . . . a stubborn Jewish woman who makes a habit of fighting the system and a child who entered the world to see how she would become. I don't know if you'd call it destiny, accident, a particularity of a rather predictable political system steeped in inequality. In early spring we found Toni and Toni found us. Toni is a Passover baby. She emerges from narrow straits[60] and is hopefully destined to be part of great nations experimenting with freedom. She gets around with us plenty too, and along with Paris likes to take over at any gathering. I shlep the two of them around to demonstrations of all sorts, into class with me when I can't get child care . . . they're quite a hit.

In our cosmic search for Toni, we had numerous trials, fall throughs, and miraculous moments of connection as well. In an experience I find is common to many adoptive parents, we had to become "experts" in any number of medical and social issues usually literally overnight. Reams of health records and social histories get shuffled around in the flurry to place a child for adoption. With the help of my own internist in New York City, a pediatrician in New Hampshire who often accompanied prospective parents on their journeys to Asia to find children, friends, institutes, government agencies, progressive health clinics, etc. we would learn about issues, find contradictory research on pros and cons, and ultimately engage in something of a cross between rational choices and outrageous acts of faith. Over the course of our searches in response to a variety of prospective placements, we found that STDs (sexually transmitted diseases), Attention Deficit Disorder, attachment disorders, various developmental delays, marijuana use, secondhand smoke, intermittent prenatal care at public clinics, and any number of medical/social/political debates would require our attention.

Like Paris, Toni became our child through a complex circuitry of politics, perseverance, and luck. The luck thing sticks out for me in our finding Toni. I had never been to Las Vegas before, town that has ruined so many, and where lady luck has deigned to visit others. I was prepping to fly out there for jointly held Feminist Political Theory and Political Science conferences. I had never had any desire to go as a tourist. I may be a risk taker at times, but I am not much of a gambler. The night before

I was to go on this business trip, I found out about a child available for adoption. It wasn't through "our" agency, but another with which I had been in contact. The agency was fine with our being Jewish queers, but we hadn't succeeded with placement through them since so many of their birth families specified that they would only place their kids with Christian adoptive parents and/or they were not interested in us because we are dykes. In this case our being Jewish queers wasn't seeming to be a barrier. The child was due to be born within two days and they wanted to secure a placement for the child as a newborn. In the morning I received a more detailed presentation including a health history. The adoption agency wanted to be sure (disclosure of "relevant information") that I knew the birth mother had Hepatitis B. If this placement was to go through, I would be expected to be wherever in the country the child was being born. I was scheduled to be on a plane to Las Vegas that afternoon. We made a mutual decision with the agency that I should get on the plane to Las Vegas, and if the placement went through I would just go directly from there, possibly upon arrival, to where the child was to be born. (There are actually a couple of travel agencies that specialize in booking adoption travel, able to get special rates on last minute flights and so on.) Thus, even as I was traveling around the country, I had this one day to find out about Hepatitis B (about which I knew next to nothing . . . yes a factor of my own class, racial, geographical identity constellation), and its potential impact on children born to women with it. I was still somewhat new to the cell phone. I remember sitting on the floor in the airport in New Hampshire where I could plug in my cell to recharge it; I needed to simultaneously make calls to my doctor, my friend the radical nurse, the Center for Disease Control, and whom ever else. I was trying to find "information," enough to have us feel "informed" in our decision. If I recall correctly, we didn't end up thinking that the bio-mom's Hep B would cause us to turn down the option of adopting the child to be born.

I had to leave my cell phone on during the gathering of some thirty to forty feminist political theorists in case I got called that the child had been born. Later that day, I found out the child had already been placed with another family. The next day I was using a break between sessions to read a manuscript version of Mary Shanley's chapter on adoption for what would eventually become *Making Babies, Making Families* (2001; to be discussed in the next chapter). I was sitting on a real comfy, overstuffed couch in the lobby of our off-the-beaten path hotel in Vegas (not one of those extravaganza self-contained metropolises where the shows and gambling are), when my cell phone rang. I still had it on from my earlier potential emergency blast off. It was Dawn. She has just gotten off the phone with our social worker from our agency. They wanted to suggest a placement. The birth mother was living in the midwest and the child was due shortly. Again, like with Paris, they had waited before approaching us to hopefully avoid the kind of fall through we experienced with the sisters in the South. Specifically, no one in the agency believed they would be able to get a homestudy talking about lesbians accepted in that state. But it was accepted. It turned out I got lucky in Vegas. Who would have thunk? I finished out the next couple of days of my conference, returned to Maine, and flew again westward soon after for the birth of the child who was to become our younger daughter Toni.

Toni's name in English is Toni Louise. As their last name, both the girls have a combination of Dawn's and my last names with a slash in between. You'd be surprised that folks full of joy about our interracial, adoptive Jewish family with two moms have drawn the line and given us hell about their last names. For some it's the length . . . but hey, I grew up a Brettschneider and survived just fine. For some the real sticking point is the SLASH-too Mary Daly, not Melanie Kaye/Kantrowitz's story . . . basically too unorthodox. One of our kids' birth certificates uses a dash, the other from a different state uses a slash. I find the U.S. government a perfectly rational and predictable bureaucratic operation, don't you? It's true the Social Security Administration doesn't like the slash . . . but why invoke orthodoxy over a slanted line when so much of our family constellation is straight as . . . as . . . as W. E. B. Du Bois' color line?

Dawn and I went with the U.S. mainstream practice of a first and middle name, and the U.S. practice of a dual set of (U.S.) American-ish names and Hebrew names. As we are an interracial adoptive family, each child is named after someone important to us in our families and each child is named after a famous African-American woman important to us. Names are, after all, also about legacies. Paris Mayan is Peretz Mayan (Mayan already being a Hebrew name), after my maternal nonbiological grandfather (remember, the one from Poland) and after Maya Angelou. Raised an Ashkenazi Jew, my family's tradition is to name a child after a member of the family who has passed on. (Many Mizrachi Jews name children after living relatives.) My maternal grandmother's second husband died early in my grad school years. Toni Louise is Tali Lilit, after Dawn's mother and after Toni Morrison. Raised a Christian, Dawn's family does not have any particular tradition about naming after living or deceased relatives. At the time, Dawn's mother was alive and well and living in rural northern California. The Hebrew choice, Lilit, is for Lilith— according to Jewish tradition the first woman in the garden of Eden; she was exiled for being uppity. Here you have quite a Jewish mix of family traditions in all of their biological and adoptive diversity, roots and routes, feminist creativity, bunches of love, and some wonderful small human beings. Names say a lot.

Our Family

Part Luck, Part Hard Work ... and how much an unintentionally queer product of a raced political system

There are also whole realms about the construction of our family that I had little idea about at the time, and many I will probably never know. Psychoanalysis I'm sure has lots to say about stories such as ours. Do you want to try to retell our story through Jewish redemption mythology? What about Christian fundamentalist urges to usher in the messianic age? How about: "Lesbian seeks to re-capture lost childhood due to abuse and neglect." Sociologists and others have a lot to contribute regarding the ebb and flow of cults of motherhood. Are we simple products of a lesbian baby boom, itself just another mechanism to keep people in gendered boxes, and in this case expunge the fear of lesbian gender dysphoria by having all those dykes getting pregnant and exhausting them with through the night feedings and the entire business of raising children? There are many ways to tell a story.

There is a set of specific dynamics, however, that I have come to understand somewhat better since the adoption of our children which bears discussing at this time. It involves the war on minority communities in the United States and in particular how many African-heritage women have come to find themselves in the class of people called birth mothers.[61]

Our family is a transracial family formed through adoption. We began our adoption process in earnest in the mid to late 1990s. We encountered the extreme racism of the adoption system from the very start, sought hard to comprehend how it worked, how we played a part in it, and experimented with various strategies to confront it over time. In even preliminary inquiries regarding the possibility of adoption, we were always asked what race child we wanted. As mentioned above, the system of essentializing racial groupings, and then separating, tracking, and ranking them is at the core of the organizational mode in adoption. At first we thought we could just get around this framework by refusing to answer those questions. Then we tried saying that we were open to all races. In such a stratified racial system, staying outside categories does not really work. Agencies just interpreted this within their own racialized system of signs and placed us into dockets for children of color, or particularly Black children. The logic was: to not name "white" meant a specific nonwhite track.

In the past, two out lesbians would have had a nearly impossible time trying to adopt children. We had difficulty, but were ultimately able to bring children into our lives through adoption. Depending on the era, we as Jews would have been racially marked in a variety of ways. In the current era, as Euro Jews we were in some ways marked racially as "Jewish" and in other ways marked as "white." Depending on the era, Jews may have had an even harder time adopting children who were not born to provably Jewish birth mothers. In the current era, this is nearly the norm for U.S. Jews. Thus, actually almost all adoptions by Jewish parents are "transracial" adoptions of a sort. Depending on the era, folks who are not discernably Black would have had easier or more difficult times adopting children called Black by the system. By the time we found an agency and our search became formalized, we were told we would have a better chance than in the recent past of adopting transracially.

This bit of information was presented to us, in our otherwise homey and progressive agency, as a market plus for us as the potential parent consumers. I was vaguely told here and there about new legislation making adoption easier for prospective parents in general, about changes in foster to adoption precedents, and about legal developments easing the way for creating interracial families through adoption.[62] At the time I had not yet begun (nor had even thought) to research adoption as a scholarly endeavor . . . living it was plenty. Even so, with some of these vague references I knew enough to care for the fate of poor and minority women who are more likely to have their children removed from their homes by the state. Since it turned out that our children did not come to us through the state, we did not end up seeing through the full course of the array of political concerns and strategies to face and challenge these tendencies. Due to the bias we were facing working with the state, and the relative lack of experience we and our agency had in negotiating in the system for queer Jewish prospective parents, our agency asked us if we would consider children who came through other agencies or intermediaries (i.e., not necessarily through the state system).

Eventually we agreed to stay open. We were told that our chances at having our placement be transracial was improving, and that therefore we were more likely to be approved for adoption sooner than our process might have left us in the past. Since U.S. racial law does not code for Jews at all, at this point in the process of "transracial" adoption we were being coded as white middle-class adults "reaping the benefits" of a complex set of then brand new legislative measures. In 1996 the U.S. Congress passed three related sets of laws: one regarding immigrants, one regarding use of illegal drugs, and one supposedly changing the "nature of welfare as we know it."[63] In a post-9/11 world, readers might relate first to the new situation regarding immigrants. Let me explain how these laws constituted the legal context of the expansion of our particular adoption options.

Since 9/11/01 the forced registrations, arrests, and detention of immigrants targeting the very vulnerable populations of Muslims, Arabs, Middle Easterners, and South Asians in the United States are a moment in the evolving methodology of strengthening the military industrial complex more generally. Laws passed in the mid to late 1990s to limit the mobility and choices of immigrants were only sporadically enforced and resistance to them had nearly succeeded in getting them overturned when the events of 9/11/01 occurred. After that day not only were these laws not repealed, but they were both stepped up and more systematically implemented. The new effort appeared to be directed at men, and particularly younger men, from these communities but was also designed to disempower already rather disenfranshised groups of women. Snatching away the men fitting these profiles has continued to tear apart families and communities economically, socially, religiously, and otherwise. Not merely relegating women from these communities to the sidelines, the situation has left women with the multiple hardships of supporting the men in—and under threat of—detention, as well as holding families and communal structures somehow together in an historical context for which there has been little preparation and a national climate in which these same women face verbal and physical harassment and abuse everyday at every level.

The immigrant-based boost to the prison industrial complex has also been made possible by "complimentary" sets of antiwelfare and antidrug laws passed around the same time as the 1996 effort to crack down on immigrants from non-northwestern countries. The new welfare and drug laws of 1996 also targeted mostly young peoples of color though they brought women into the prison-industrial complex at faster rates than before.[64] Splitting up families and communities through the surveillance and incarceration of women helped more solidly bring to fruition the self-fulfilling white peoples' fantasy that women of color are producing generations of humans unfit for an "American way of life" and are thus a threat to the nation's well-being. Although immigrants of color were effected by these laws, communities of color long residing here have been devastated. The growth of the immigrant population now in detention came as a more recent extension of the boom in the criminalization of the public, resulting from the 1980s and 1990s domestic "wars" on drugs and welfare. These three pieces of legislation allowed the government wider access into the lives and autonomy of women of color, both immigrants and those with long histories in the United States. Stereotyping increased, this time particularly aimed at challenging minority women's status as proper women. The goal has been to delegitimate minority women as mothers, to create a question in the public mind of the soundness of minority women bearing and raising their own children.[65] The anti-immigrant and hyped up drug laws exist hand in hand with the welfare reform act to dehumanize women of color in this patriarchal society which casts women's humanity as expressed in the "right" to be mothers. The most important feature of these interlocking legislative moves for the current discussion is a little known provision in the welfare law which actually changes the legal tenor for transracial adoption.

As will be discussed in more detail in the following chapter, formal adoption is a recent development and began as a strictly race matching escapade (despite all the forging of documents this required!). As part of a new movement against racism in the United States, in the post 1960s-era, many white-coded progressive adults sought explicitly to adopt non-white children. This included a number of newly white-coded Jews. There were of course many different understandings of what these white adults were doing. Some understood themselves as "just" building their families, now simply without regard to race. Some sought to personalize their political commitments against minority poverty by raising minority children. Many sought to challenge efforts at creating monoracial families, long at the core of race-based genocide in this country, with the adoption apparatus mimicking this process.

In the 1970s, the new experiment of transracial adoption had mostly come to a halt. Many cite the public statement made by the National Association of Black Social Workers discouraging the practice, as they assessed the new trend in adoption as yet a new form of cultural genocide. For many progressives, the NABSW analysis was at the core of shifting attitudes favoring same-race adoption placements once again. I am guided by this analysis today. But let us face it, in racist (U.S.) America, policy and practice dominated by the elite is not first motivated by minority community's needs as expressed in their own voices. Politics is a complex business. The move away from transracial placements was sought by a number of prominent public figures in the Black community. It also clearly served to reinforce white supremacist concerns against racial mixing. Perhaps further suggesting the ambivalence in the racial assignment of U.S. Jews, in contrast to problems voiced by majority whites with transracial adoption, Jews were less likely to find TRA a problem for the adopting parents. At the *same* time, Jews as a community have been better able to understand the logic of the NABSW regarding cultural genocide than many majority whites as well.[66]

In the 1980s and early 1990s, transracial placements in adoption were either expressly discouraged or implicitly avoided in most states and by many individual agencies. The year 1996 was a historical moment in the aftermath of *Bakke* and numerous other efforts to undo policies and practices that had emerged which named racial difference for the purposes of ending racial discrimination. At that moment many white folk, claiming to speak for progressives generally, began to make public headway in the effort to yet again "ban the ban" on transracial adoption. I have no doubt that many who lead this fight sought justice as they understood it. It also must be said that such efforts helped pave the way for new versions of antiwomen of color legislation. Included in the 1996 personal responsibility act was a change in the law regarding transracial adoption. The trifrontal attack on women of color—through anti-immigrant policies, intensified drug criminalization, and welfare cut backs—included provisions making it easier for white adults to adopt the biological children of women of color.

Many have described this move as a renewal of the white savior strategy to end "the race problem" in the United States. This understanding of the race problem recognizes the incredible disparity between the lives of people according to race, and the tremendous disadvantages faced by those within minority communities. Long a staple of Christian/white identity construction, the more white/Christian, the better off one is. In this analysis of the race problem, however, the equation is not merely empirical. This is to say that wealth, health, status, agency, and other important differentials that fall into a racialized hierarchy are not simply matters one can quantify . . . and then leave room to critically untangle the web of racism that has brought us to this day. Instead, white/Christian identity is *essentially* understood to be associated with more dignified humanity. The twist has long been that various groups have vied for, and been sought out for, designation in this group. To be *white* then meant one *was* better off. After years of analyzing the failure of civil rights to effect equality in the United States, many have revived the essentialized notion that the problem is not discrimination against Blackness . . . but Blackness, or other minority status, itself. [67]

This movement drew on historic policies denying minority women's reproductive rights (in many ways differently than the denial of elite women's reproductive rights). In conjunction with the anti-immigrant and antidrug laws, the 1996 welfare reform sought to solve the race problem by whitening as many Black and other minority children as it could. Taking children of color away from their bio-families and making it easier to place them with white families was a strategy to solve the "race problem" by a new mode of cultural genocide. The thinking was: if raised by "good" white families, Black kids can *be* white, and thus avoid Daniel

Patrick Moynihan's (1965) notion of generational cycles of poverty and loosening of moral stature.[68] What is often missed in analyses of the tripartite set of laws targeting minorities through the hand of the INS, drug enforcement, and welfare workers is the ways these laws turned so many more minority women into the "birth mothers" of adopted children than previously in history.

This method was a favorite in the 1800s with respect to Native children; legal efforts at whitening Native Americans operated by forcibly removing their children and placing them in "good Christian" homes and Christian boarding schools. It was also quite effective in terms of devastating Native American communities, cultures, identities, and modes of survival. I cannot predict any linear outcome of the 1996+ legislation which made it easier to make transracial adoptive placements. In what ways is it good, or not, for the children? In what ways is it good, or not, for individual women of color and also for minority communities? In what ways is it good, or not, for non-peoples of color seeking to build their families through adoption? What potential avenues are opened for interrupting racism? What potential avenues are broadened for reinscribing racism, even if in new ways? How does the complex class and racial classification of Jews in their diversity effect these dynamics? How are Jews in their diversity navigating the tumultuous waters of racism and anti-Semitism, as the tides are ever changing and the currents ever crossing? How are queers factoring into these new racialized systems? How are homophobia and efforts to resist heterosexism both at work in the constantly morphing adoption world?

These questions are begging for further analysis. In the meantime, we in my family seek to live out our lives with dignity, love, community . . . and in the spirit of justice to the best of our capacities.

I have shared with you some of our story adopting Paris and Toni. Over the years of our involvement in the adoption world and engaging in research since, the laws, practices, and attitudes have continued to shift (though not always in clearly laudable ways).[69] With all the problematic aspects, there are also so many wonderful ones. I find many practices in the adoption world awful, but still think that adoption is a beautiful blessing. There are many caring and informed people seeking to challenge the hierarchies operating in adoption processes. Specifically with respect to Jewish, queer, and other minority communities and how they engage also with issues of race, class, and health bias, there are numerous efforts to change social norms.[70] These people, agencies, and organizations need to be supported. We are called to keep the debate open and to take on state policy. I hope that in some small way telling aspects of my experiences will help enable more work to challenge the system and provide better care for children, for birth mothers and families, and for prospective and adoptive families.

In part, toward that end, I also offer the analysis of the next chapter. There I seek to extend this discussion to the construction of families more broadly. As a queer Jew who chose to raise children, I felt the extreme force of "family culture" and expectations regarding family norms from the beginning of my interest in creating a family with children. Here I have discussed some of what I have learned along the way regarding adoption practices in particular as a method of family formation. But I encountered the intensity of bias and essentialism operating at the meta level of "family construction" as well. I know many Jews feel invested in geneology, though as a post-Holocaust Jew I respond viscerally when public opinion makers talk about bloodlines. I notice when people romanticize bio-family ties in their efforts at racial pride and nation building. Thus, in chapter three, based on my experiences and also thinking things through as a critical theorist, I deepen the examination of families, more explicitly seeking to unfamiliarize the familial by denaturalizing the "natural."

Chapter Three

Going Natural

The Family Has No Clothes

Introduction

This chapter builds on the previous chapter's critique of contemporary adoption practices and looks to ideas about "the family" writ large. The thesis here is that the so-called natural family is in fact a social construction. On one level most critical thinkers of course know this. It is not especially new to point out that the norm is anything but normative.[1] The biologically related, two heterosexual monogamously parented family is and has long been far from an empirical mainstay of actual social organization. Extending this further, in the United States it is often said that the average family unit includes 2.2 children—one, of course, a boy and one, of course, a girl[2]—a cat, a dog, and even a picket fence. Okay the picket fence might be a bit much at this point in history. Nevertheless, the portrait remains hegemonic. On the one hand this seems obvious, and many would argue further that not only is this picture not an empirical "truth," but as an institution it is also normatively undesirable. It's not that it is *necessarily* a problem if you individually happen to be a member of a biologically related, two heterosexual monogamously parented family, even with one boy child and one girl child, and even with a cat and a dog and a fancy house. If this has been your particular experience, and it has worked out nicely for you, then yeah! Society as a whole has much to learn from how your family created and maintains happiness and mutually supportive stability and freedom.

To say that the "normative" family is not normatively desirable is to say that as an ideological structure, the hegemonic norms and its attendant institutions, apparatus, ideologies, rights, privileges, benefits, as well as the policing, pressures, oppressions, and exclusions required are unattractive and repressive. Again, although most critical thinkers, and particularly many feminists, queers, anarchists and other radicals, and progressively minded folk know this, time and again ordinary people as well as activists and critical thinkers will still fall into step of the Disneyesque parade of presumptions, biases, hopes, dreams, value judgements, and analytic ellipses inherent in the ideology of this particular notion of the bio-family as natural. In this chapter, therefore, I return to what may seem to some a much rehearsed progressive truism—that the so called natural family is anything but natural. However, the force and persistence of the dominant view in society and policy at large, as well as within critical discourses, necessitates looking at the issue anew.

The specific method that I will utilize here is a comparison between assumptions and ideologies concerning adoptive and biologically formed families. The goal is not just to help end concrete discrimination against adoptive families, but to help us break free of essentialist elements (such as ideas and politics) regarding bio-families as well. In terms of policy, yes, this work is situated within feminist, queer, class-based, and critical race discourses deconstructing and challenging biases in adoption and foster care. As the last chapter shows, that was the impetus for my research when I started looking into the "family business." But I learned a few things along the way. Then I had to write this chapter. Thus, here theoretically the context is deeper than concern regarding bias in policy. This work is also situated within feminist, queer, critical race, and class-based discourses deconstructing and challenging presumptions of what is "natural."[3] The aim here is getting us to look more deeply and critically at those aspects we tend to take for granted, consider given, unchangeable, immutable, exposing them as historically specific and founded within particular ideological frameworks.

Adoption as a Representation of the Real: An Historical View

Adoption, as a formal and legal practice, is rather new in U.S. history.[4] Globally, as well as in many communities in the United States, disruptions in the family unit were and remain all too common. Jewish history, from biblical narrative or lived experience, is a history of communal life within the context of constant dislocation, family ties and breaks, and reformations. For Jews and most folks, the reasons range from a variety of forms of domestic violence and abuse, poverty, war, natural disasters, illness, bad luck, death, all also inflected and usually mutually constituted through systemic modes of sexism, heterosexism, racism, able-ism, classism, anti-Semitism, nationalism and other ethnically/religiously/geographically based discrimination, and anti-immigrant hysteria.

Before adoption became a commonly legal arrangement, and still to some extent today, any number of children were and are being raised by relatives, kin, friends, and the kindness of strangers. The phrase the kindness of strangers actually comes from the common practice in ancient Greece where poor or otherwise marginalized parents brought children for whom they were unable to care to the city's dung heap. The child either died by neglect and exposure to the elements, or was picked up— by the kindness of a stranger—and brought home . . . usually destined for a life of servitude to the city's citizen-elite.[5] Many still have such stories to tell of their abandonment and stranger care for good and bad. In the modern United States, a connection came to be made between white, usually Christian, wealthy families who could not biologically birth the children they hoped for, and the socially stigmatized class of designated white women who became pregnant (from heterosexual intercourse either chosen or forced) without being married to the child's father. There were many unmarried and pregnant women who brought their fetuses to term, either for ideological reasons, by lack of folk or medical knowledge regarding how to end such pregnancies, or something resembling "choice." For both unmarried white women, as well as for those who were married and poor, experiencing hard times or other tragedies, if they or someone known to them could not care for the child, these children were generally either abandoned, sold into servitude, or left at orphanages. The United States eventually did away with "orphanages" and instituted the foster care system which led to the increased market in adoption.[6]

Shifting familial constellations comprised of complex and often intergenerational kin, not necessarily having any bio ties, have not been uncommon outside elite circles. Formal adoption, however, for the most part grew out of the informal practices wherein Christian white-elite heterosexual married couples raised as their own children birthed by others usually either far less well-off, or from other elite families to whom the child would be perceived to bring shame. The more these children were brought up as if they were the couple's biological children, and not simply acquired into "service," the more over time the arrangements were formalized.[7] The process of formalization was mostly to protect the elite couple from claims or potential claims by the biological relations of the children. In some cases, especially where the women who birthed the children were themselves from elite families, formalization was also developed to protect the bio-relational elite family from what was perceived to be a threat and potential harm to them, their reputations, and property (including the marriage-ability status of the daughter/birthing woman). Formalization also grew in response to similar concerns within the dynamics of non-stranger adoption—meaning within kin structures—in an effort to protect (again usually the more well-off parties who were generally) the adopting adults. As the previous chapter demonstrates, to the degree nonelites have been allowed access to formal adoption, they are effected by the ways in which the system has been set up by, for, and of elites.

Inherent in these developments has not only been stigmatization of unmarried pregnant women, poverty, migration, war, and other common causes for the disruption of bio and other kin groupings. Central to this phenomenon was also not only the class/cultural and race-based access of the elite to other people's biological offspring. Essential to these developments has been the intense stigma attached to childlessness as it has played out among populations differently positioned with respect to power. The barren woman is a key trope in Jewish life and mythology, but (also depending on her status) her avenues of coping and her options for agency have historically been different from elite Christians in the modern West.[8] At the same time, many people do not want to raise children nor are they concerned with biological heirs to their fortunes. Regardless of this fact, social pressures are intense: on women to bear and raise their biological children, and on men to contribute biologically to the creation of offspring and have them as benefactors of their legacy and/or of their estates. Society still today sees as inadequate those who cannot have children biologically. Individuals internalize these ideological pressures and often feel as though they have failed in life.[9] For the wealthy, acquiring the children of others to make up for this "lack" was both possible and desirable as a secondbest solution.[10] To make the best of the situation, those involved in the arrangement worked hard, and developed practices and policies over time in order, to keep the adoption a secret. It was important, given the force of ideology and self-worth, to have one's family appear to be biologically related as this was the valued type of family formation. Thus, in various ways, a growing trend of formalized adoption took place within an attempt to create new families "as if" they were real, biologically related, or following nature.[11]

Some of the practices developed for these ends included state-sealed records of the legal arrangements. Before World War I it was more common for friends and relatives to adopt children and keep open arrangements with the bio-parents. The secrecy and stigma that for a while came to dominate in adoption practice increased after World War II as states passed new laws that both required sealed records and that new birth certificates would be issued for the adopted children. (For example, my kids now have at least three sets of "certificates of live birth.") This occurred in a postwar, McCarthy-esque historical moment of refurbished policing of sexual and gender variation, the renewed glorification of femininity and motherhood, and an emphasis on the nuclear family.[12] Those who birthed the children they were not to raise were not given information about the children once out of their custody. The children were often not told they were adopted and access to information about their routes into their adoptive families was denied to them. Those involved in helping to place children in adoptive situations tried to have the children appear, as much as possible, as if they were biologically related to the adoptive family. And thus, related systemic phenomena of racism, sexism, classism, anti-Semitism, and a host of other biases shifted and gained import in additional ways.

What shared characteristics might suggest that people are biologically related?[13] What sorts of characteristics does anyone have, or think they have, control over identifying or adapting to have them appear shared?[14] The answers to such questions are by no means straightforward. In fact, the history of these questions themselves and various approaches to finding their answers is the history of human hierarchies, hatreds, and biases of U.S. history itself. However successful some have been in creating adoptive families to meet the changing standards of what appear to be shared characteristics of these "as if" families, the ideology of privileging bio-relations remains intact. It is that ideology, casting adoptive families as sloppy seconds, that creates the desire and practices of attempting "as if" versions of family formation and continues to effect the bias against adoptive families.

The Contemporary Debate

In recent years, a small number of political thinkers and other scholars have begun to address the political and theoretical issues involved in adoption practices in the United States.[15] Slowly, over time, adoptees and families formed through adoption *are* facing less stigmatization than in the past. Jews, queers, and other marginalized minorities who in the past might have chosen formal adoption but were excluded from the practice have increasingly gained access to the institution. Scholarship by political scientists and particularly political and legal theorists has been helpful in these shifts. Scholarship has addressed underlying assumptions people tend to have about families formed through adoptions, and then assessed how those attitudes have found their way into adoption policies and programming.[16] One approach in this sort of work has been to deconstruct the presumption that families formed through adoption are a response to a lack, or failure.[17] As mentioned, the presumed norm, (historically if the adults were members of the elite, but justice politics watered down to a politics of inclusion has been bringing these normative ideals into application to the lives of many "others" as well) is that children should be conceived by, gestated within, born to, and raised by their biological mothers/parents. As this was the presumed norm, or seen as the most desired form of family building, those in the adoption world originally tried to best approximate the "natural family." As demonstrated in chapter two, people's individual ideas here were concretely manifest in the programs of adoption agencies, the counseling of social workers, as well as in legal frameworks.

In more recent years, much evidence has been put forward arguing that treating adoptive families "as if" they were "natural" families has been a misguided strategy, with problematic consequences for all parties involved in the process.[18] In my own process of family formation, I have appreciated this move. The goal here is to end bias against adoptive families. The reason for the bias was that biological families were considered the norm, or better. Thus, the first strategy for ending bias was to try to make adoptive families seem as much like the preferred form as possible. However, this strategy for confronting bias against those party to adoptions kept intact the normative position of biological families. Creating adoptive families "as if" they were biological did not call into question the structure of beliefs, and mutually constitutive juridical and bureaucratic structures, that attributed more worth to biological families, found them more whole, wholesome, good, and natural. Scholars, social workers, and activists have been helping us to see this dynamic and its limitations, suggesting instead that we broaden our conception of what a good, whole family is. They argue that we should stop thinking of adoptive families as unnatural and therefore suspect, as compared to the natural/biological family. This has been a helpful turn in the discussion regarding adoption. In my view, however, it does not go far enough.

My argument takes another step. I argue that it is not enough to challenge the "unnaturalness" of the adoptive family.[19] It is not enough to stop the dichotomous pairings which suggest that "adoptive families are constructed while biological families are natural" as a way to show that *adoptive* families are not unnatural. It is not enough, necessarily, to claim that adoption is a good in and of itself in the effort to end discrimination against adoptive families. I would suggest that it is not a solution to the problem of the centrality of the bio-family to say that some people desire adoptive families without any relation to other people's desire for bio-families. Nor is it most helpful for people who want to claim that adoptive families are "okay" to say that they are not condemning bio-families, they just want people to see that there are a lot of forms of "okay" families. The situation is that out here in the world all of these particularities exist simultaneously. I have heard well-meaning folk, including myself, argue any combination of the above. None on their own necessarily challenges the root of the problem for adoptive families: the hegemonic character of the bio-family itself.

Instead, I argue here that if we want to move beyond biased structures (in both thought and practice), we must see that the natural family is itself not natural. This is important for "normative" bio-families as well as for bio-families marked as "other." More, we must come to see that the "natural" family is as much constructed as is the "constructed" adoptive family. We will find that the situation is not as simple as: the biological family is given, while the adoptive family is made; the biological family is natural, while the adoptive family is constructed; or that the bio-family is real or original and the adoptive family a copy or mirror. In contrast, I will show that, under scrutiny, the framework "adoptive families are to culture as bio-families are to nature" does not hold.

For this I am indebted to Butler's work on drag as not a "fake" version of a "real" gender.[20] In her work, Butler does not claim that drag is in itself, or necessarily, subversive. As opposed to some others engaged in the family debates, I am not arguing that adoptive and other "alternative"[21] families are in and of themselves radical formations of social relationships. In fact, the inclusion model of justice politics has expanded the amount of people able to form families in some socially recognized ways that often uphold the hegemonic ideals of family culture. What I am interested in is utilizing an exploration of adoptive and other "alternative" families to expose what just *might* be radical about them, what possibilities might they open up beyond the confining norms of the All American Family. Butler writes: ". . . drag is subversive to the extent that it reflects on the imitative structure by which hegemonic gender is itself produced and disputes heterosexuality's claim on naturalness and originality" (1993, 125). As a strategy, we can look to the subversive potential of affirming adoption as legitimate in itself and not trying to erase its difference such as in the "as if" model. To do this we must look into how an affirmative (not assimilationist) approach to adoption calls into question the "imitative structure by which hegemonic" family formations are themselves produced and disputes the bio-family's "claim on naturalness and originality."

Adoption/Biology: The Discourses of the Real and the Mimic

The point here is to demonstrate that even the natural, or biological, family is itself a social construction, formed in the charged field of historically situated power dynamics. By utilizing the comparison of the adoptive family as constructed, we can actually denaturalize even the "natural" family. In this section, therefore, I look specifically at the language and discourses more generally relating to biologically formed and adoptive families. Below is a list of terms associated with these two specific forms of family building. As a whole, or at first glance, I realize that the lists may seem overly determined, though I hope the discussion will demonstrate the currency of such in everyday life from individuals, to media and law.

Table 3.1
Family Formations

List A: Adoptive Families	List B: Biological Families
Public	Private
Convention	Natural
Legal	Fact of Nature
Contractual	Blood
Procedural	Emotional
Negotiation	By Birth
Agreement	Normative/Normal
Created	Fundamental/Foundational
Constructed	Norm
Changeable	Stable
Artificial	Unending
Copy	Actual
Duplicate	Unique
Replica	Legitimate
Imitation	Base
Representation	Official
Variation	Enduring
Replacement	Unchangeable
Substitute	Primary
Simulate	True
Resemble	Real
Mimic	Authentic
Mirror	Original
Fiction (or as in: Legal Fiction)	Fact
Alternative	Presumed
Subjective	Objective
Choice	Given
Control	Inevitable
Volition	Need
Voluntaristic	Involuntary
Questionable	Indisputable
Unseemly	Proper
Disruption	Unity

I find that by looking at these lists together we can learn about, and unpack, much of the seemingly oppositional discourse of adoptive and biological family formations. By analyzing the trends of adoption discourse, and setting it up next to its supposed opposite, we can see in what ways the trope of biology is an ideological construction. I certainly hope to help those working to end discrimination against adoptive and other families referred to as alternative. But more to the point here, by reading the trope of adoption discourse *back onto* bio-families we can come to see more clearly how much *not* unlike each other the two modes work out in practice.

There are two ways we can look into this mind-boggling dance: (1) one is to see the construction of adoption discourse as a projection of the hegemonic bio-norm; (2) the second is to examine how what seems different about an adoptive discourse has been, and is becoming more so, actually a norm in within the bio trope itself.[22] Let us begin an examination of the first concept of projection by walking through the two lists above.

Table 3.1, List A: ADOPTIVE FAMILIES. The Logic: Adoption is considered a public act, a family founded by convention through legal, contractual procedures. In this realm, people reason their way to agreements through rational negotiations. Thus, the adoptive family is seen as purposely created a postori, after the fact. Because it has been consciously constructed at one point in time, it relies on a view of families as changeable. Poised as artifice, adoptive families are thus often cast as copies, duplicates, imitations, representations, replacements, substitutes, simulations, and/or replicas. Through the processes involved in mirroring, in mimic strategies designed to replicate bio-families, we can see that there are variations among family forms. As "alternative" families, they are fictions, legal or otherwise, and thus elements of subjectivity enter into the picture. People are seen to engage in these arrangements out of choice and therefore to have control over aspects of the creation of their families. These are voluntaristic formations flowing from the expression of human volition. Exposing hidden issues of trust in "man's" imperfections when he applies his will, there are underlying questions about adoptive relations. These questionable elements stem also from actions by fallen women who challenge "natural" patriarchal roles leading to the disruption in relations necessary to bring children into the public realm whose fate will be determined through social workers and other guardians of convention under law. As you may have recognized, this list then reflects a set mutually reinforcing aspects of ideology which re-creates itself and the conditions for its very existence.

Table 3.1, List B: BIOLOGICAL FAMILIES. The Logic: A similar self-reinforcing cycle may be seen in the logic of the discourse of biologically formed families. The bio-family has been designated as of the private realm. As natural, the ties are created a priori in blood and by birth. With this foundation as facts of nature, the ties are seen as ahistorical: their origins a given and thus of no interest to politics; the presumption of their existence as stable and immutable lending to the sense of the family as a unit, or a unitary form of family; their futures as inevitable and enduring. The bio-family is an outgrowth of need, as an act of nature it is involuntary. As following the proper designs of an apolitical nature, it belongs in the private realm left to bodily functions and emotional impulses. Again, the mutually reinforcing assumptions regarding families built through bio-relations create the need for them, and re-create aspects which become the preconditions for their very formation.

The focus on adoption as a second choice, after failed attempts to have "your own children," replays the hegemonic ideal that the bio-family is the real one and the adopted one is always the imitation of the real. Dawn and I, for example, had no reason to think that either of us would not be able to get pregnant and birth children. We even had a great and willing sperm donor. We explored this and other options of family formation and chose adoption. Yet, we continuously had to sit through the "coming to terms with infertility" type sections of an array of sessions and meetings along the way in our adoption journey. My heart goes out to those who did so want to conceive, gestate, birth, and raise children in a certain fashion and grieve that they were not able to. That so many people assume, however, that one's true desire is to have bio-families constructs adoptive families as false families or at best replicas of the true form. We find here that the bio-family, even in one's inability to make one, remains in the center, originary position. Even when we are talking about adoption, the bio-family becomes the cause of creating an adoptive family even if it is only then seen to mimic the real family. Adoption, that which is counter to the normative bio-family, becomes a symptom of a failed desire and capacity for the having/producing of the real thing. In this way even the counter-normative is turned back into a reaffirmation of the truth of the normative. As the alternative, adoption becomes engulfed within the practices of the bio-family it is not and that which it simultaneously re-creates.

Just How Natural Is the Natural Family?

Family By Numbers

Having marked adoptive families' apparent "difference" from bio ones (if even as an inverted projection of bio norms), we must now turn to an exploration of the question: how much is the bio family actually like its adoptive constructed form? To do so, let us see in what ways the above assertions stand up to actual practices over time. First I will look at some empirical information about actual families. Don't be surprised to not be surprised: the research shows that the norm is anything but normative. I realize that hard-core conservatives, speaking in the tradition of "natural law," may discount the empirical evidence demonstrating how far the concept of what is normative diverges from lived practice. Such a divergence may be interpreted as our lack, just showing our need to shore up normative principles. To this we must offer the reality check of lived practice anyway, when demonstrating that changes in these ideological norms culturally and historically expose them to be just as much a product of contemporary conditions as the empirical portrait itself. But more, I think that most folks whose thinking invokes normative models are not necessarily doing so out of explicitly studied precepts of a natural law tradition. Most people, trying to sort through the complexities of family formations, options, potential stigma, feeling that they are alone in the makeup of their (and aspirations for particular) kin constellations, yearn to know about the state of the family today. Thus, I will both offer some information regarding current family makeup in the United States, and I will then move to a discussion of the political dynamics and changes involved in biological family formation and norms.

The State of the Stats

I have heard the following statement reiterated in any number of critical inquiry sessions: "only two thirds of families look like the norm." Let us break down this generalized portrait. First there is a slippage between the normative conception of what a family looks like from the perspective of a child and an ideological claim regarding how people live in society. It is important to delineate the types of families in which children are raised and the constellation of relations and living arrangements for the population as a whole (meaning including adults). What the statistics show is not only that the normative ideological image of children's families is far from normative, but also the notion that "people live in families," as normatively construed, is a fiction. Demonstrating these two points as separate points further challenges the hegemony of family culture and policies (legal, corporate, organizational), suggesting that making a pitch—ideologically or in terms of policy—in a family-oriented mode may not be reaching the majority of the population.

For example, in attempting to get at a portrait of the universe of children's kin structures in the United States, we can note that nearly 70 percent of children live in families with two parents. However, not all the parents noted in that statistic are actually married to each other. This figure, 69 percent, also does not necessarily suggest that the relations within the family are biological as one or both of those parents may be a stepparent, or otherwise related through adoption. (I have not found reliable statistics on how many of the married parents claiming to be biological parents might not be.) Three to four percent of all male and female jointly headed households are unmarried partners.[23] What are referred to as "unmarried partner households" are twice as likely to be of different races than are "married partner households."[24] Thus, even this 69 percent figure is a bloated statistic not actually reflecting the percentage of "natural" or biologically related children living with two married (and therefore currently by definition opposite sex) parents. Further, the statistics do not reflect same sex couples who may or may not both be the legal parents of the children in a household. Also, it cannot be stressed enough that such emphasis on the normative family is structured on concepts of racial purity and reproducing the nation . . . which often turn out to be fictive concepts. For example, though in any given case a statistic may show two bio-parents living with their children, Jews intermarry at relatively high rates,[25] interrupting aspirations for racial purity (whether Jewish or Anglo-Saxon Christian).

Compared to the ideological expectations that we are a nation of families, and the supposed centrality of the normative family to individual citizens, relatively few adults live in normative family constellations. For example, of those adults in two, heterosexual parented families, a portion have been divorced and this a second or later marriage. For example, 43 percent of first marriages end in separation or divorce within the first fifteen years. One in three first marriages ends within ten years, and one in five ends within five years.[26]

It is important to note that not all adults marry at all.[27] Only 69 percent of men and 76 percent of women marry at all, yet 13 percent of men and women have married twice. At any given time, only about half the adult population (55 percent of men and 51 percent of women) are married, whether in their first or later marriages. Approximately 15 percent of households in the United States are comprised of women living alone, and about 11 percent of men living alone. What of the stats on the children produced in marriages?

Twenty percent of all marriages have children with at least one stepchild and 20 percent of children live in families with no siblings at all.[28] More than half (54 percent) of married couples have no children, 19 percent have two children, and 10 percent have three or more children. One quarter of the nation's children live with one parent.[29] For Black children, 62 percent live with their mothers only. Four percent of children live in households without any "parents."

And how reliable are these stats anyway?[30] The surveys miss a large percent of newborn children and their older siblings. Not surprisingly, poor and minority children are *over* represented among those *under*counted in government studies. For those trying to get a national estimate of same sex families, those willing to report end up yielding numbers that are too low to be considered statistically reliable.[31] These numbers hardly suggest that the two heterosexual parent family with two biological children living together is a normative model of households in this country. And what of the political dynamics involved in the creation of biologically related families?

The Political Dynamics (1–10 and Beyond)

As natural, it is assumed that the bio-family is either nonpolitical or pre-political. As an inevitable expression of need and emotion there are no negotiations, rational procedural steps. Bio-families just happen, like a rainstorm. Turn around and there are four bunnies, turn around again and there are six. "Last time I saw you, you were just a little girl, now look at you, married with your own children." The force of the natural tide flows mighty. "One minute I was playing jump rope, the next I was planning a wedding. Before I knew it I was a grown woman with children of my own." Is this really the way bio-families happen? Under our noses without our noticing? Do the generations generate merely in the course of events without the premade choices of politics, hierarchies, and power dynamics? Do emotion and need gush without their contours having been constructed, constrained, and produced through hegemonic ideologies and institutions which work with the force of tides though are anything but natural?[32] I would say: No.

For Jews grounded in the wisdom of text, biblical stories offer countless examples of the politics and negotiations in setting up marital unions, the birthrights of children, adoption, and bloodlines taking detours. For mass audiences there are unending examples of the intrigue of courts, Shakespearean plots of marriage, positioning, betrayal. Yet, simultaneously we have a norm of the natural flow from Beth and Stuart sitting in a tree to Beth (not) pushing that baby carriage. Dawn often comes home with Disney films loaned to us by her congregants. I try to be gracious about it all. The films are appalling but some actually make it onto our TV for viewing. In almost every children's movie I have seen in these last few years, from *Bambi* (which Toni could watch over and over again if we let her) to the *Lion King* (through which the girls continue to sit in absolute silence no matter how many times they have seen it), I note that mass culture instills in us from our youngest years an emotional truism regarding the "great circle/cycle" of life. (Have you noticed how often the main characters' biological mother—or sometimes father—needs to die for the story to proceed?)

Many Jews, historically and today, have lived (often by choice) in a world of arranged marriages. This is not, however, the contemporary Western/Christian ideal. The contemporary Christian ideal figures itself as natural despite the myriad forms historically and culturally. Let us break down the aspects of normative bio-relational family forms. Here is the contemporary modern Western concept: You meet, are attracted to, and fall in love with one person of the opposite sex to whom you become married for life, have and raise kids. There are at least nine moments in this one sentence summation of the "natural flow of life" that we should stop to think about. Let me put it out there again, and slow it down this time: (1) you meet, (2) are attracted to, and (3) fall in love with (4) one person (5) of the opposite sex (6) with whom you become married (7) for life, (8) have, and (9) raise kids. Slowly now, step by step.

(1) The People We Meet: What are the politics of "the people we meet?" Regarding explicit choice, most are likely to be familiar with popular dating language: SWF seeks. . . .[33] Some Jewish newspapers now have sections for "women meeting women" and "men meeting men" alongside their columns announcing the fantasies of SJFs (single Jewish females) looking for SJMs (single Jewish males). Apropos of the last chapter: note that "Jewish" stands in the "racial" space. On a long drive one spring, a gay Jewish friend told me of his escapades using an online dating service. Interestingly, it seems a great way to find long lost comrades and lovers. Not everyone makes it into the grand archives of Google. You might be better off looking for Benjamin or Yitz through one of these servers. My friend told me he ran into an old mutual friend there from our earlier activist days. "Smart, fun, well-built, politically aware, synagogue-affiliated Jewish man seeks same. I am forty-one. You are thirty to forty-five." Who knows who how many old friends you'll drag up. The history of "*fill in the blank*" (relational status-race-gender) mass-market dating services is one founded on matching a variety of "choices/preferences" made so explicit they are taken for granted to a degree that they are basically "naturalized."

The people we "just happen to meet" on a broader scale are every bit a factor of chance *and* more structural concerns such as geography, nation, class, caste, religion, race and ethnicity, etc. With grand "natural" disasters, globalization, war, and poverty, people move around at astonishing rates. Of course, nothing is simply "natural" about why some communities fare worse during "natural" disasters than others: it's usually about race, gender, and class. Still though, most people live in quite cloistered circumstances locally (even with occasional shifts of locale) and will obviously never meet almost everyone else on the planet. So we must ask: what are the political forces at work that have brought one into contact with those one "meets?"[34]

(2) Are Attracted To: Attraction is similarly constructed and constrained through any number of political dynamics of human hierarchy. I went on a Jewish queer retreat with my kids one winter. Mine were the only kids there (due to programmatic problems, not due to a lack of interest on the part of lots of other Jewish queers with kids). Toni was about three-years-old and developed a personal spiritual practice of taking people's business cards off the information table and giving them out to participants. She went about her project quite solemnly, not disturbing programs but walking up to individuals and quietly saying "here's your ticket." When she ran out of business cards she reached for slightly bigger adverts. One offered creating the "life of your dreams" by helping you to find your *basherte*. *Basherte* is a Yiddish concept for fate, or destiny. Irena Klepfisz's poem (1990) captures the aura of the fates in the word. *Basherte* is then also used in everyday speech to signify your "one true love." As the advert promises, connecting to your soul mate. The service offers "coaching" on the concrete skills to develop, and steps to take, to find your *basherte*. How will you know you succeeded? How can the coaches help you clarify when you have the right "chemistry"? Why you need to pay someone to assist your living out your destiny is a matter too complex to explain on the little cardstock flyer.

Why are some people considered attractive, and attractive specifically to us? There are large feminist, critical race, class conscious, Jewish, and increasingly queer literatures on body image and standards of beauty. Certainly, racial, class, gender, and other historically situated cultural norms create a framework. Many Jews are attracted to features stereotyped as "Jewish" in the Christian West. (How many times I have heard Jewish dyke friends tell: "I'm looking for my dark eyed, olive skinned, curly haired beauty.") Since before Phillip Roth, we have also seen the Jewish fetishization of the blond haired blue-eyed specimen. Large or small, shade and color, religious affiliation, expression, and fervency—or none, ability status and what aspects of health risk or disability are within the realm of one's attractions, history of sexual or substance abuse, abandonment and neglect in the family all often factor into what is considered desire, or the forces of attraction over which one supposedly has no control.[35]

(3) Fall in Love with: Love is a whole other matter which is new on the historical scene as are meeting, attraction, partnering for life, and bourgeois conceptions of romantic love.[36] People often construct "love" out of their prior desire to have bio-kids to begin with. My thirty- and fortysomething friends, gay or straight, proclaim they are ready to fall in love now, because they are finally ready to have children. Will you love your *basherte*, or is the point of finding your *basherte* that the love part takes care of itself and is never in question? The aspects of the idea that there will be (4) one person (5) of the opposite sex (6) whom you marry (7) for life are such ideological and historically situated characteristics, that I will devote the next chapter to examining them.

(8 and 9) Have and Raise Kids: Interestingly enough, it has been the recent history of legislative acts and Supreme Court cases associated with women's reproductive "freedom" and interruptions in racist heteropatriarchy which have helped make possible the growth of adoption markets and an expansion of adoption rights to those outside earlier hegemonic norms of those "deserving" children. Yet in court cases from *Loving v. Virginia* to *Griswold v. Connecticut*, and *Roe v. Wade* to *Lawrence v. Texas*, the courts and legislature relied on and deepened a presumption of privacy which tends to reify the pre-political nature of family making.[37] In 1967, the government struck down 109 U.S. 3 (1883) with *Loving v. Virginia* making interracial marriage permissible in U.S. law;[38] in *Griswold* the Court legalized the use of contraceptives by married couples; in *Roe* it created space in the law for a woman (in consultation with her doctor, presumed to be male) to choose abortion; the vote in *Lawrence* overturned the *Bowers v. Hardwick* 1986 decision which excluded homosexual sodomy from the privacy protections granted to heterosexuals performing the same acts. To the degree that any of these laws and the practices to which they refer are under attack, what critics focus on are aspects of "deviance" from a right wing agenda of morality. Although these cases have been hugely important to decentralizing racist-heterosexist norms of the natural, each actually achieves its victory by placing certain acts and relations within a realm beyond the purview of the law known as "the private." In Western legal traditions, reiterated in such decisions, the private is understood as a sacred, extra- (if not explicitly pre-) political arena traditionally valued as natural. Specific aspects involved in deciding whom to marry regardless of at least racial factors, with whom and how to engage in consensual sexual relations, if heterosexual intercourse ought to lead to conception in any given event, and whether fetuses ought to be brought to term have new life as "private" decisions supposedly not to be mediated and curtailed by law. However, not only do any number of aspects involved in these very decisions continue to be subject to legal sanction, but the very designation of those named "private" is itself a public, political act, protecting a supposedly "natural" arena within a charged nexus of constantly morphing power dynamics.

Assuming that the point of love, sexual activity, and unions are to have bio-kids is an aspect of the hegemonic ideology of marriage and monogamy that make the bio-family presumed to be natural in the first place.[39] Love and certainly most sexual activity—including heterosexual intercourse—are *not* generally connected in people's minds with getting pregnant, staying pregnant, birthing, and raising children. Even in a conservative read of traditional Jewish law, once sexuality is penned into a heterosexual marital union, there is a clear message that sexual activity serves an important function in the satisfaction of desire, experiencing pleasure, and developing intimacy between the couple. For a majority of people in the contemporary United States. I would venture to say that, most sexual activity, even heterosexual forms, happens in a manner divorced from the potential relationship to the formation of a fetus and the bringing forth of a new life for whom one directly cares. The very right to have children has long been actually more of a privilege of the elite. This is demonstrated poignantly in contemporary society with adoption itself. Why would so many women who get pregnant and bring their babies to term choose to have their relationship with these children be mediated through their adoption by others? I do not want to simply presume that getting pregnant and bringing a fetus to term necessarily implies the desire for parenting. Also, some children are raised by their nonbiological progenitors due to the untimely deaths of the adults (also often a factor of poverty and thus other historically changing, imbricating aspects of marginality). But let's face it: most of the people who do not parent the children they birth are in some socially named (and constructed) category of impoverished people who are told they do not have "enough to offer" children and that these kids are thus "best off" with people who can provide—based usually first on an economic rendering that easily shades into other aspects of human worth—for them.[40]

(10) And Beyond: I have not framed this discussion of family in terms of the U.S. legal standard of the best interests of the child or models of caretaking. That is because when the well-being of children and their care is surfaced in the hegemonic discourse, it remains largely instrumental to the prior ideological imperative to cluster society into certain kinds of kin/nation building arrangements. But not to avoid at least a comment regarding caretaking: even aspects of care, regarding what makes a "real" family in terms of the roles of bio-mothers and bio-fathers, are products of politics. Among the elite, historically being a biological parent didn't in any way suggest that it was the parent who would care for the daily needs of the children.[41] Today, the current version of the cult of motherhood eschews day care, though wealthy women might still employ nannies and maids, or involve their children in myriad "programs" (swimming, dancing, music, etc.) effectively filling up the day of caretaking that children in formal child care programs get as a matter of course. Breast feeding is another good example of changes in what is understood to be natural about the bio-family.[42] In the past, elite women hired wet nurses, considering breast feeding animal-like—which somehow translated into "unnatural behavior." Paps and various kinds of infant "formulas" have long been used even among the poor, especially when a woman's health was so compromised by poverty, war, or abuse that the pap was more nutritious for the baby. And yet today we live with pressure on (mostly those assigned as white and/or middle-class) women to nurse their biological offspring as if that is "what nature intended," even if it requires training, hormone injections, electric pumps, technologically advanced storage bottles, and freezers.

What is considered natural in terms of the size and makeup of even bio-families has also changed over time and according to culture.[43] Friends of mine in New York had a child utilizing some *new* reproductive technologies. We spent a summer in Jerusalem together before Toni was born, and so Paris and their daughter had lots of great bonding time. The couple then decided they wanted to have a second child. Again, using *new* reproductive technologies, this time they ended up with twins. Now they have three children instead of two, but they still live in Manhattan. It seems people often think they are freaks. Unlike large and poor families of color, however, they are not accused of "overcrowding," though people are relatively unsympathetic to their economic challenges. "If you can't pay for them, don't have them" functions as a middle class trueism. The middle-class child economy in Manhattan is generally geared toward families having one child and at the most two. Babysitting scales change after two kids, entrance rates to attractions shift, "family" seating almost exclusively allows room for up to two kids tops. (I recall such presumptions growing up in a family with three children—there were usually only spaces for four, not the five of my nuclear family.) This assumption that families will comprise two children is certainly culturally and historically specific. Aside from the tendency for TV families to include many children, to have more than two children (perhaps outside Manhattan three) now is somehow considered almost unseemly. It is even more improper, and in some cases nearly criminal, if one is poor or young or receiving public assistance. Living in a nuclear family would have seemed unnatural, uneconomical, and sad to many in the past and to many still today.[44] But calling this family form nuclear itself exposes the values of a culture which thinks it proper, and therefore natural, that the generations separate in such a way as to form particularly bounded units *then* re-defined as the nucleus of a family.

All ideologies have within them internal contradictions. It is often helpful to name these contradictions as part of deconstructing and showing that they are in fact ideologies . . . not natural. And so it is with the very discourse of nature. Think about it: how can you call something unnatural? Doing so is part of the creation and repetition of the discourse of nature itself. Designating phenomena as unnatural is part of defining the normative trope of what is marked, in any given cultural and historical context, as natural. Noting that within a culture dominated by ideologies of white supremacy, women of color are cast as somehow both closer to nature (more primitive and less civilized), *and* among those whose biology and mothering are an affront to nature is a prime example. (This follows a pattern in which, historically, Jewish women generally were cast as such in modernist Western discourses.) As discussed in the last chapter, minority women in contemporary U.S. discourse are seen as "messing up" nature.[45] Under the very pretense of the bio-nature equation, the state intervenes and interrupts many bio-connections, calling them irredeemably broken, in order to redirect nature back to its "proper" course. We live in an age where the natural needs a particular form of legal articulation, promotion, and policing. The next chapter will look at this dynamic in terms of monogamy and marriage: many folks in the United States seem to feel that we need to use the power of the state to "protect marriage" . . . as a natural institution. According to scholars such as Dorothy Roberts (1997 and 2002), there is a material aspect to this current incarnation of denaturalizing in order to shore up the natural. Given the intransigence of family ideology, elites still need kids, although for any number of reasons they can't seem to produce them biologically. What we see are moves to free up more kids for acquisition by the elite, meaning making it easier for elite whites to adopt children. In contemporary terms, we see this phenomenon expressed wherein a significant aspect of the popular debate over transracial adoption and reproductive technologies exposed many fears that white prospective parents' rights are being curtailed, hindering their access to children through adoption.[46] Some bio-connections must be deemed unnatural and in need of separation in order to enlarge the pool of children available for elites to fulfill their natural mission. To identify internal contradictions of the nature/bio/good ideological connection is to show that it is an ideology. That is to say, pointing out that (how and why) this ideological construct is mobilized differently over time and with respect to different populations is to say that it is a construction, and not what it claims to be: natural, or simply "human."

Adoption and the Stigma of Unnatural Choices

By this point in an argument challenging the naturalness of the natural family, we can bring adoption more specifically back into the discussion to push the analysis yet further. Utilizing the trope of adoption to denaturalize the biologically related family, we can see that the framework of comparison hinges on the complicated concept of choice. By this I mean that the adoptive family is consciously created as a choice while the bio-family is seen as natural and therefore somehow given. At the same time adoption is surely cast as a second best choice. The real choice is to have a bio-relation to one's children. But supposedly we have no control, no choice over that. And sometimes we are forced to choose adoption. Choice as a lack of "natural" processes involved in adopting children is turned against adoptive families in strange ways. People often assume that the ties in a family formed through adoption are not as strong or real because the relations are not blood relations. That a woman did not birth the children she is raising is used to delegitimate the family form. And yet, confusingly, there are moments when many adults with biologically related children seem to envy adopting parents, as if it is easier to create a family through adoption. There is a double flip in popular ideology: (1) valuing pregnancy, gestation, labor, and breast-feeding, (2) wherein the lack of such in adoption is envied even as, (3) this "lack" is the basis for judging the relations as less valuable.[47] The flips play out something like this: "I 'had' my kid. You didn't 'have' your kid, and therefore don't 'have' children in the same way as I do now. You didn't have to deal with pregnancy. You got to choose your kid. You had it easy." By this people usually mean: only I had difficulties or my process is worth more. "I had to deal with all the fear and vagaries of trying to get pregnant and complications and risk. That's what nature is—wild and unpredictable. In the sterilized legal process, you were dealing with a known product, and if there was a problem you could choose not to accept that child." Basically the idea "my process was natural" is translated into "I suffered more." This is then equated with "my situation is more real" whose ultimate significance is expressed as "mine is more important."[48]

With these norms, it appears that this notion of choice is what separates the two family forms. Yet, choice is often confused with politics. "Choosing" to give up one's child for adoption is created by and brings social stigma in certain ways. Getting to "choose" a child brings a different form of social stigma. Though used in everyday language, given the power dynamics, choice is not necessarily the most appropriate term here. Still, both forms of *stigma* operate because bio-families are presumed to be an inevitable and pre-political phenomena, countering the notion of "choice" in family formation. Yet, the politics of "choice" is everywhere in the creation of a biologically related family—from meeting a partner to raising the bio-offspring of a heterosexual union. So how is it that a process so infused with layers of choice (better put: or socially constructed possibilities and limitations instead of just "naturally" happening) becomes cast as opposite to "adoption as choice?" We must look into this question before pushing the choice/nature distinction. To do so we need to look at how society turns what now seem to be obvious modes of socially constructed moments in the process of bio-family formation into natural processes.

Textual Readings: Looking to the Pop and Scholarly Use of Family Tropes

Let us take a moment to examine some mechanisms whereby constructed relationships are not only passed off as "natural," but the processes of their construction become hidden within the process itself. In this section, I take up two forms of textual readings to demonstrate that what may seem overdetermined, when clustered as a list (as in the table above), are still alive and well in current discourse. In order to do so I specifically take up both pop and scholarly examples.[49] To help frame this portion of the analysis, it will be instructive to return to Butler's insights.[50] As Butler discusses with respect to heterosexual privilege, normative structures operate in multiple ways. Two manners in which they operate are (1) by naturalizing themselves, and (2) by rendering themselves "as the original and the norm." One way in which the bio-family naturalizes itself and then renders itself original is in the very publicity in pop culture of an anti-norm. Butler acknowledges (1993, 126) "that there are ways in which heterosexuality can concede its lack of originality and naturalness but still hold on to its power." She discusses the example of certain films in which "the anxiety over a possible homosexual consequence is both produced and deflected within the narrative trajectory." She writes that "such films are functional in providing a ritualistic release for a heterosexual economy that must constantly police its own boundaries against the invasion of queerness, and that this displaced production and resolution of homosexual panic actually fortifies the heterosexual regime in its self-perpetuating task." Can we apply this critique to families?

Any number of films might be cited as examples of this phenomenon in the context of bio-families producing themselves as originary and
normal. Think of the overused plot line wherein a wayward older man
meets up with a young challenger who both seem to be mavericks, defy-
ing a settled family life, and yet end up being "father and son," confirming
the "realness" of the "family man" behind the loner. We can find another
example—of a story that seems to defy family life as the norm only to
reinscribe it in the most (supposedly) appealing hue—in the use of the
dream sequence or angelic intervention such as used in the film, aptly
titled, *Family Man*.

In the film *Family Man*, "in real life" both the Nicholas Cage (Jack)
and Téa Leoni (Kate) characters eschew stable marital and familial relationships in pursuit of the glory and riches of their adversarial and capi-
talistic career ventures. They act counter to the hegemonic presumptions
of romantic involvement and family making, but within the equally hegemonic norm of capitalist aggression. At the outset these two norms are
presented as contradictory. Enter an angel ("Cash" played by Don
Cheadle). It is not incidental that the angel appears as an urban-blight
sort of Black man who is poor and robbing a small store. He functions
to present an antithesis to the great white suburban family myth, only to
be rendered not too challenging in that he makes it possible for that myth
to be replayed again and not defied by the wealthy heterosexual white
people themselves. Some may find the portrayal of an angel as a Black
man as subversive, and in many ways it is. At the same time this Black
angel functions to save the dominant way of life of rich white folks which
requires and produces young Black male gangsters. In returning the natural—marriage and family making—to its "natural" place, the angel's intervention is required to remind the upper class of emotions and kin. In the
angelic universe, the couple is actually a struggling middle-class one ensconced in relation with multigenerational family members and neighbors. Back in the "real" world, the characters, of course, end up forming
that Hollywood-esque marital bond. We are also led to assume that they
will produce an even richer version of the cozy domestic white Christian
heterosexual bio-family scene we witnessed in the angelic universe. This
use of a supposed challenge to the normalness of the normative family
that tends to reinforce its "reality" is so pervasive in U.S. society once we
stop long enough to look around. Let us look to two more examples that
seem to defy the mythic ideal of family only to reinscribe its "trueness."

One example is the classic soap opera,[51] multiplot tale of betrayal,
mistaken identities, and sexual infidelity, of long lost, marginalized, and
disowned family members. The families on soap operas are notoriously
messed up, plain and simple. Their appeal is in that they boggle the

imagination based on what we assume to be right families and human relations. Yet, notice how what provides the turning point is the claim of biological kinship and who really signed the marriage certificate. "Oh no, your lover is *really* your brother." "The troublemaker you just had killed is *really* your daughter." "He's not your *real* father." "They never *really* did get married." It is always the reference to the legally married or the bio-relationship that produces the climactic "resolution" or the final point of "understanding" the complications of the story. Soap opera intrigue appears to counter the normative notion of the family but instead constantly replays, reproduces, and relies upon it for the punch, making for its mass appeal.

A final example I will offer from within the realm of pop culture is another that seems to so outrage the defenders of the "good family" and yet also has tremendous mass appeal: the ordinary daytime talk show.[52] Common topics for these televised circuses are of the "are you the father of my baby," "your wife/husband is cheating on you," type or any number of scenes that seem to show the underbelly of (U.S.) American social behavior. In the first instance, the man protests he is not the father, that the woman sleeps around, that the child does not even look like him. The woman screams at the man, accompanied by a loudly jeering audience. They are brought back the next week when the talk show host will reveal the results of the DNA testing—the scientific "proof" of who is a "real" family. The talk show host opens the envelope in front of a live studio audience. The man is the "father" . . . the woman claims she hates him and at the same time that he take responsibility for the child. I'm sure she needs financial and other support. It is likely that she has been facing issues of loss, and the stigma of "illegitimacy." At the same time, why would the woman want this no-good-nick whom she hates in her child's life? Or, why she thinks this irresponsible person she despises will turn out to be the solution to her problems—and not just the cause of more— is somewhat of a mystery.

Occasionally the DNA results show the man is not the father. Then the woman is proven to be a hussy and is publically shamed. People cannot believe she is such an idiot. She can only be a Jezebel and there can only be so much power in this form of shaming if there is a norm of the good mother which she has so flagrantly countered. In either case, biology is the true marker of familial ties. The bio-truth provides the tensions and set up for the audience-pleasing mind-blowing finale. The pop culture, mass-based entertainment that shows the antithesis to the Cleaver family repeats, creates, and therefore more fully reinscribes the very norms and truths than the Cleaver versions did themselves. These families gone awry, similar to the adoptive "as if" family and those born out of failed bio-attempts to replicate the original desire, do not in Butler's words (with regard to instances of nonsubversive drag) "displace that norm; rather it becomes the means by which that dominant norm is most painfully reiterated as the very desire and the performance of those it subjects" (1993, 133).

I turn now to a brief discussion of one wonderful scholarly text. It may seem too easy to indict Hollywood, daytime talk shows, and soaps for their reinforcing the bio-truth-good triangle of ideas and values. Therefore, it will be instructive to examine a tougher example. Feminist political theorist Mary Lyndon Shanley published a book on a variety of family forms and numerous complications at present involved with them. In *Making Babies, Making Families*, Shanley takes on the bio-family, and the presumption of heterosexual normativity in creating repressive relational norms. And yet, *Making Babies* is a particularly illustrative text to examine here in that Shanley too at times seems to forget that the hetero-bio family is not natural.

Shanley is interested in moving beyond the Liberal-Communitarian divide on family issues. In examining current difficult issues in families and relationships, she seeks to move beyond a Western rights-based approach, a contractarian approach, an approach based on intention, an either-or nature/nurture approach, a functional paradigm, and even the legal tradition looking to what is called "the best interests of the child." In a refreshing turn, Shanley makes her alliances clear and is explicit about her principles and priorities. Wanting to strengthen the Liberal tradition, she enters the debates from a feminist perspective with the values of care and responsibility placed at the center. Ultimately, Shanley takes us through a maze of legal, philosophical, and emotional difficulties and disputes in contemporary adoption, gamete transfer, and surrogacy offering us her contribution which she calls "a child-centered approach." She has done this extremely well on so many accounts, that I find it instructive to also take note of some of the ways in which she simultaneously reifies the "natural" family.[53]

To begin, as I am mostly interested in the discourse of adoption, it will be helpful to note what it is about chapter one of the book (which explicitly addresses issues of adoption) that is so significant. Shanley's work is such an important contribution first because there is simply hardly anything written on the topic of adoption at all in the Political Science literature. There is basically nothing on the topic in the journals of the discipline.[54] It is actually quite astonishing. Her endnotes actually suggest this as well in that a good deal of her hard-core references, particularly in this chapter, are from Law reviews. This is not only because Shanley is adept at working with legal theory, but also because some of the most difficult issues requiring critical analysis have been taken up mainly in legal terms, not within the frameworks that political theorists may have to offer by way of broader political analysis. The brilliance of this chapter comes from the fact that she takes on and links the complex issues of open and transracial adoption in particular. In her analysis, the link hinges on her critiques of the concepts of the "as if" family (a nonbiologically related family created to "look" like the relations are biological), and the "parentless" child (where the law requires that the child's ties to parentage be fully broken, and in the past sealed off, creating a nothing space or history-less human before considering adoptive parents). Her intention is to care for the role of women and children in these practices and the debates about them in order to undermine a restrictive base in an ideologically construed vision of nature when we deal with issues of the family that tends to reinforce and re-create—if even in new ways—multiple modes of human hierarchies.

What also deserves notice for our purposes here is that Shanley does not always follow through on the implications of her intention not to dishonor genetic ties, but to denaturalize the family (in the ways that nature is socially constructed and in the field she is studying invoked too often for narrowing or discriminatory purposes). For example: Shanley gives some historical background on adoption so that it is clear that the practice has been around a long time. What is new are laws regarding formalized "stranger" adoption. Beyond this, however, she does not really historicize her discussion that in many ways what she and others call, for example,—from the title of the book—"reproductive technologies, surrogacy, adoption, and same-sex and unwed partners" have long been part of family life. Yes, there is much that is new. Though from a political standpoint, a lot of what is most interesting currently is not really the multiplicity of family formations itself (as opposed to a singular ideological norm) but that those in a capitalist yet conservative climate are again turning to/re-creating these as issues, as "problems" and "deviations" and therefore in need of government regulation and media propaganda campaigns.[55] Concomitantly, it only will make sense to care for the claims of individuals who experience custody challenges and other problems within this historicized and critical framework. A publisher's or other media's often glossy appeal to these as new, unusual, and alternative not only ignores the empirical and multicultured reality of family and kin formations, but itself also reinforces the notion that the two married parent heterosexual family that just pops out kids is what is natural, traditional, and the base from which we now deviate in order to need "new" ethics to guide family construction and change.[56]

To really push the implications of Shanley's work for its radical potential to disrupt what passes as natural, we can take note of the way that she frames a discussion of "alternative" families broadly conceived in terms of *deviations* needing to be *problematized*. She writes: "These families return us to the question of how far new family forms *should* [my emphasis] be allowed to depart from the model of the biologically related family?" (9). Shanley is perfectly clear elsewhere that the traditional biologically related family is neither an empirical norm nor normatively desirable. So what can this question mean then? Or, why would there be a decision to make about allowing the existence of nontraditional families, or not decisions about all families, or no one deciding . . . on anything, or who decides.

A similarly provocative point is why she asserts in another chapter on lesbian co-parenting that two heterosexually married people living together should be presumed to be the custodial parents of a child born by the woman in the couple (139)?[57] Any level of presumption in this case leaves so called "others" the burden of proof of difference and tacitly leaves in tact the constructed notion of heterosexually inflected nature as the ideological norm. Empirically, there are myriad reasons the cross-gendered pair may not have provided the bio or gestational routes to a child's existence. On the more normative level, this presumption allows us to avoid that challenge to nature and hierarchy with which Shanley herself is so concerned. I might add my own two cents here: there really is no reason every adult interested in having a recognized relationship to a child must not (1) name, (2) have accepted publically what that relationship is, and (3) declaratively agree on the consequences of that name, even if it changes over time.[58]

Another aspect of this point arises in chapter 5 (see especially 142–147) with the concept of *limited fathers*. Here Shanley takes up a suggestion for the creation of a legal category particularly for men who sell their sperm who may not choose anonymity or disconnection from the family formed as a result of purchasing such sperm. Shanley's work has much to offer here in the concern for the rights of offspring created through the use of sperm banks. She does not, however, take one particular step of clarification which warrants attention. Although Shanley points out that the concept of limited fathers may also be of use to others, including women, who stand outside traditional parental relations seeking to find alternative legal arrangements, she does not offer a preliminary assessment of the ways in which the frame of the conversation in general thus far keeps intact the notion of the father as natural—always there, always (at least potentially, if not in her rendering specifically) entitled. Like the birth certificates for my kids, given the context of patriarchy in this country—especially in a time of a right-wing crusade for marriage promotion and fathers' rights[59]—the wider discussion (if even at times unintended) presupposes a father-space and does not conceptualize a possible family constellation as full if of women or other beings who are not men/potential fathers.

In relation to Shanley's work, I actually have nothing in principle against offspring seeking access to their genetic ties, or if a man who has sold his sperm later becomes interested in the trajectory of his sale. Given custom in the United States, we will likely need new legal thinking to attend to such situations as the courts will certainly continue to be the prime arena in which the complications of such desires will be assessed. At the same time, however, in a family with the adults being a single woman, an unmarried woman, a woman in a relationship with one or more women, or any transgendered adults not recognized as men does not mean that in *their* universe there is a father-space that anyone could ever make a claim to. Just because there is not a man in the picture does not mean that there is a space open for one, nor that the law has any standing to even conceptualize filling in a father to a family constellation without a recognized man because it imagines that there exists a gap to be filled at all.[60]

Shanley's work is tremendously insightful. With Shanley, more of us need to continue to challenge the notion of "origin" and excavate its ideological function in identity creation. Along with Shanley, I want to honor this factor of social construction as having valence. The years that adoption has been assumed a dirty secret have harmed a great many people. The dynamics in families regarding shame, inadequacy, and fulfilment are pathologies in need of healing at the individual level through a larger social transformation. The state has co-conspired in these dynamics to the point it is now under intense attack not only to make adoptions open in the future, but also to open records sealed off in the past. Adoptees are demanding information on their bio-relations as part of undoing the damage. Many see this phenomenon as a bold new frontier in naming a harmed class of people, of rights claims, and of activist politics. The call to stop the secrecy and stigma is clear. The efforts to bridge gaps and rewrite histories are often heroic.

At the same time, there is an element in the discourse of adoptees' rights that itself falls into and reifies the bio-norm which creates adoption as the problem in the first place. The focus on adoptees' rights to "know their story of origin" prioritizes bio-links in ways that need to be unpacked. The explosion of rights claims gains force within a context of unreconstructed assumptions regarding the bio-truth-good triplet. Decrying adoptees' denial of their fundamental rights makes sense largely within a cultural affirmation of a mythic idea that there are "truths to be known in order to make us whole." Moreover, it is the bio-connection that makes for truth. The current discourse is predicated on an ideological presumption that people raised in bio-families "know" their truths at all, let alone know these so-called truths through knowing their bio-links.[61] Similarly, the language of "completion" and "wholeness" is used often among adoptees seeking information on their bio origins. Not only is such language ideologically loaded in modernity, but also such a framing leaves as implicit that biology can provide such fullness, and that those who think they know their bio-relations are complete and whole.[62]

I support and am a participant in open adoption. I want my kids to have access to their records, and am open to the kinds of needs they may have, even as they will change over time, with respect to their bio-routes. We as adoptive parents have committed to staying open to the needs of the bio-relations of our children. None of this prescribes in advance what those needs will look like or how anyone of us will move to meet them. At the same time I know that addressing issues which arise in adoption does not necessarily indicate bio-ties as the counterexample. Adoptive families are not "alternative" families, in the sense that they are not "alternatives to bio-families." They are families. Like other families and simultaneously specific forms of families as all families are specific forms of families. Aside from adoption, this challenge of interrogating the myth of origins and the "desire to know" is similar for children created with fancy technological assistance as opposed to some notion of "bio kids that just happen" as both an empirical norm and a mythic phenomenon not in need of critical analysis.

Is It a Choice or Not?

Stigma and the Lure of Consumerism

Having taken on some specific examples of textual readings to demonstrate that a long standing tendency to prioritize the bio-family remains very much intact, even when on the surface the presentations appear to contradict and even purposively challenge "traditional family values," we must now return to that nagging question regarding choice. It seems at first glance that the division between adoptive and bio-families grows out of this core concept regarding the "choice" involved in constructing adoptive families as opposed to the "found" quality assumed of bio-relations. Again, by reading the discourse that has grown regarding adoption *back onto* bio-families, we will further unpack the bio-nature-best triplet.

This focus on choice has grown hand in hand with the developing formalization of adoption discussed above and its concomitant commodification. As discussed in chapter two, if the form of adoption as a procedurally negotiated legal relation is new on the stage of history, it has been made possible by and grown within a complex market system within entrenched capitalist forms of understanding and relations. One avenue in which we see this is that changes in adoption practices regarding the concept of choice have developed as adoption has become targeted as a market. Relying on and reproducing the notion of the bio-family as better, many in the adoption industry have developed an investment in pushing for the "as if" family. As the previous chapter has helped us to see, one reason for this is that by preying on the fears of prospective adoptive parents, the industry can create demands, needs, and solutions which it can then price. As the majority of prospective adoptive parents are white, reification of the "as if" family helps to create a higher demand for babies who can be passed off as white than the supply currently offers. The industry gets to play up this created scarcity for economic benefit. Along the way, white women who birth children and decide to put these offspring up for adoption have become players in a market driven process. No longer are the women who birth the babies in the adoption triad only seen across the board as unfortunates, but now also as "having" a commodity that is very much in demand.[63] This means that especially able white women birthing children in the adoption world now get to have more "choices" than in the past, and are increasingly involved in "choosing" the adoptive families of their offspring.

As adoption becomes somewhat less stigmatized and also more formalized, the industry has responded by growing its target market of prospective adoptive parents through appeals industries commonly make to consumers: additional aspects of choice. Relying on the understanding of adoptive families as volitional and created, adoption agencies provide endless sets of choices to their clients who hope to adopt children.[64] Tapping into ideas that we can have the children we "want," the adoption industry creates this illusion that by answering endless numbers of questions, and firming up one's choices in advance, prospective parents can hand pick the qualities they most desire for the children they will raise. Of course any number of systemic hierarchies are mobilized for these purposes, including class inflected presumptions regarding intelligence, race, religion, health status, and ability. Blond haired, blue-eyed, educatable, athletic children become in demand, and people think that by answering questions on a form they can actually "have" their (very much socially constructed and sanctioned) "dream child."

This trend in the adoption world has found its way perhaps even more incipiently into the world of gamete transfers and surrogacy. Rapid growth in the adoption market, particularly the rise in those using rather unregulated methods such as lawyers and independent brokers, has occurred simultaneously with an explosion of other less regulated modes of family formation using reproductive technologies.[65] Sperm and egg banks can be even more blatant about breaking down the characteristics of donors to appeal to different market demands.[66] Since they are not talking about actual children just yet, the language tends to be even more crass. The creation of preferences and offering choices is becoming even more crude here than it has thus far been even in adoption. Facets of a donor's history that are likely to sell are brought out, making customers feel like they are making choices rather than being manipulated. For example, in a bank with a large Jewish clientele appeals to lost family from the Holocaust might be noted. Height, weight, race, skin color and tone, hair texture, athletic abilities, IQ and a plethora of other "relevant" features are written in brief bios of nameless donors.[67] Clients use the internet, sit in cozy offices, or are encouraged to take home books with the bios so that they can choose among them for their perfect "genetic compliment." The less regulated the market, the more "choice" is used as a selling point. This also means that higher degrees of "choice" are reserved for those who can pay more, and what they pay more for tends to fall more firmly within the realm of the history of eugenics than a simply random array of "choices."[68]

Bringing the commodification of such characteristics into the newer versions of technological assistance to family formation helps us move one step closer to rounding out the "circle." People consider using reproductive technologies and particularly gamete transfer and surrogacy as both on the one hand constructed like adoption and on the other hand more natural like bio-families. These forms of family building rely on science and markets and choice as much as, if not in various ways differently than, adoptions. But some genetic connection is common between the offspring and "parents," and thus people also often prefer these methods to adoption as they see them as somewhat more "real." The same may be said for the trend with single and queer folk (and often those who are both). Many singles and/or queers are producing children through a combination of biology and other technologies. For many queer couples, a family constellation that includes both adoption and some bio-ties is often seen as preferable to a no-bio-tie adoption. With surrogacy and gamete transfer providing a link between adoptive and traditional bio-families, we must now turn to a discussion of the growth of "choice" in bio-families themselves.

As readers may remember, the matter that matters in distinguishing adoptive from bio-relations, and the concomitant devaluation of the former to the later, was based on an ideological conception that bio-families are natural and given whereas adoptive families are voluntary and controllable. As the market built and built upon (U.S.) Americans' positive response to the notion of choice in adoption and then with reproductive technologies such as gamete transfer and the practice of surrogacy, the market also came to inflect these aspects of choice back into the language of more traditionally "natural" families. Through the development of genetic technology, for example, people are being told that they can choose the genetic traits passed on to their bio-children.[69] Some suggest genetic screening of fetuses to be able to "tell" parents about what kind of child they can have, and some people choose to abort certain fetuses if given the "wrong" answers.[70] Genetic screening and the promise of genetic engineering are big business, although at present only available to a small percent of the childbearing population. But beyond official genetic engineering, these aspects of choice are brought further into the process of conception, pregnancy, birth, and child care by other mechanisms.

This includes some extremely problematic policies discouraging undesirables (those who challenge aspects of the current incarnation of nature-bio-good equation) such as women who are unmarried, poor, addicts, convicts, and/or members of minority groups (both on their own and as they cross with these other categories) from birthing children. People have always shared knowledges and cultural ideas about how to have the "most worthy" children. People have long "paid" folk experts, witches, midwives, oracles, priests, and any number of others for their advice and interventions.[71] There is nothing new at the general level of societies placing value on the kinds of children adults want to bring forth and finding ways to encourage those births, and seeking to limit the births of the less desirable or those otherwise perceived as a threat to the elite.[72] A Pharaoh of ancient Egypt reportedly decided that the Hebrew slaves had grown too numerous and would overpower the non-slave Egyptian population. He ordered the killing of all their new babies. Women midwives exercised their own technological power and tried to birth as many of these babies as they could anyway. Today, women of color—particularly if they have criminal records, are unmarried, poor, and/or have histories of addiction—are encouraged to use sterilizing technologies to keep their birthrates down.[73] They are offered direct cash payments, plea bargain options if in the criminal "justice" system, forced without their knowledge or consent in hospitals, defunded in the welfare system, and any number of other methods. "Choice" for these women to temporarily or permanently accept sterilization is a cruel joke. "Choice" for elite populations is a different, yet powerful, form of manipulation. What may be said to be new is that we are seeing the differential uses of specific discourses of modern medicine, science, politics, and capitalist appeals to choice and control used as big business in a capitalist sense whether for poor or rich bio-families.

These newer techno-capitalist modes of encouraging/forcing desirables to bring forth and raise children, and discouraging/forcing undesirables not to bring forth or raise children in U.S. politics has emerged amidst a cluster of interweaving other phenomena opened up in U.S. culture that ought to be seen in relation to a supposed increase in "choice."[74] A somewhat lessened stigma associated with single parenting and multiracial families in addition to increased awareness, availability, and legality of some methods of birth control, abortion, divorce, protections of privacy, rape in marriage laws, and the counter-trope of love as opposed to formally arranged marriages are part of this phenomena as well. Each also is mobilized within larger movements to shore up our idealization of nature and promote the bio-nature-good discourse of the "deserving" while breaking those connections for those deemed "undeserving." The availability of information and services, as well as access to legal recourse, regarding birth control, abortion, divorce, privacy, rape laws, and love remain differentially applied and accepted among groups in the contemporary United States, depending on the interlocking aspects of their shifting enfranchisement, power, and/or marginality.

As argued above, bio-families and the paths toward their creation are never just "there," in a pre-political sense. They always reflect and co-create an intricate weave of who will meet, of socially designated categories, of constructed desires, of culturally coded family formations, lifestyles, and practices. The lines between the apparently counter discourses of adoptive families and bio-families are becoming now even more blurred. The creation of the "idea" of the adoptive family as the opposite of and lesser to the bio-family is turning back on itself. Cultural views of adoption have been created as different from, and less than, bio-families as part of the process of constructing what is considered natural about familial relations based on blood. But the once universally degraded caste has become a moneymaker. The very framework of choice that was once pitied has been created as desirable. Well-meaning doctors, nurses, social workers, community health policy makers, and activists all engage increasingly in adapting the trope of choice to bio-families. By this I do not mean to say that suddenly, *now* the naturalness of the bio-family is being interfered with. The influence of the market only *now* is tampering with the real and venerated family. But social fashion can, at all, work in this context because the bio-family never was simply natural. The natural family has always been, and is only being more so exposed currently as, an aspect of social power dynamics and political meanings. The natural family is not now, and it has not been, simply natural.

Chapter Four

Questing for Heart in a Heartless World

Jewish Feminist Ruminations on Monogamy and Marriage

Introduction

Many are familiar with Marx's famous line about religion being the opiate of the people. But that line, abstracted out of its context as it usually is, loses the deeper and more complex meaning of Marx's comment. In the introduction to the "Contribution to the Critique of Hegel's Philosophy of Right," Marx wrote: "Religion is the sigh of the oppressed creature, the sentiment of a heartless world, and the soul of soulless conditions. It is the *opium* of the people."[1] This final chapter takes its title from Marx's insight here, but it is not really about religion. In that text Marx refers to the bourgeois appropriation of institutions and ideologies extant prior to capitalism rendered instrumental no longer to the Ancien Regime of lords and noblemen, but now to a mercantilist system of businessmen. Marx wrote about religion as mirroring the alienated relations capitalism effects in politics through the state and in economics through labor and value. In Liberalism, religion is rendered private but suffers in terms of ideology and alienation nonetheless for its occupying also a supposedly more ephemeral sphere. Marx generally understood family in a similar fashion, but did not examine it as closely as he did things religious. By

107

drawing on their link via alienation, I hope to make use of Marx's insight regarding religion in an analysis of another "private" institution related to family formation. Thus here I propose to discuss the two primary institutions and ideologies expressing capitalist forms of relation between adults in families: monogamy and marriage.

Antonio Gramsci (1971), an Italian Marxist, demonstrates how what is generally thought of as "common sense" is actually the ideology of the ruling elite. We learn from Marx that a ruling economic class is always accompanied by a political system and webs of infrastructural institutions designed to serve its interests. Although capitalists are quite fond of outright force, blatant displays of violence, and deploying disciplinary power, in the mind of the masses these are masked through the power of ideology. To put it another way: how is it that the oppressive power relations inherent in capitalism receive such high popularity ratings? It is not that pollsters are out there asking questions such as: Do you think workers, immigrants, and other ordinary people should be kept poor and befuddled through trained attack dogs and automatic rifles? And yet, in every mainstream media outlet, and every best-selling introduction to American Government textbook, we are told time and again that "most Americans are nonideological" and yet at the same time that "the most important feature that binds us together is the democratic consensus, a fairly widespread agreement on fundamental principles of governance and the values that undergird them" (Burns et al. 2002, 87, and 69 respectively). In a Marxist sense, one of the central functions of ideology is to soothe the disconnect between people's varied and often contradictory experiences, and the "official story" of all that is good in the land of Liberal democracy. The estrangement of individuals from their work, from the products of their labors, from each other, nature, and their own and each others' humanity is both product and producer of capitalist forms of relation. Alienation, our objectification and our objectification of each other, is both required by and requires attending to in the not-so-seamless web of capitalism.

Beyond directly economic concerns, Marxists are more familiar with analyses of superstructural institutions of the state, ideology, and alienation in various forms including that of religion. These are seen as examples expressing the imbrication of ideology, institutions, practices, and capitalist propaganda. Despite Engel's full-length work on marriage and the family (1981), contemporary examination of other ideo-institutions such as monogamy and marriage have received much less critical attention. Long ago feminists critiqued patriarchal creations/distinctions of public and private spheres as mechanisms to make it at least difficult and usually impossible to undertake analysis and change of social phenomena in which marginalized groups experience particular forms of oppression.

Marxism is helpful, though traditional Marxists have generally shied away from this feminist challenge. I definitely think that this discussion is as relevant for Marxist analysis as Marxist analysis is necessary to look once again at these two institutions. At the same time, mine will also, of necessity then, be a feminist and queer critique.[2]

In the change to capitalism, religion is supposedly privatized. Marriage and monogamy are usually understood as relating to the private sphere as well. Yet marriage and monogamy are no less public, ideologically inflected, institutions co-creating, bolstering, and protecting the political apparatus of the bourgeois state and the economic base of labor and the means of production than are legally sanctioned religious activities and apparatus. With regard to monogamy and marriage, my basic argument here will be that under capitalism, society sets us up systemically, through our ideologies and institutions, to live out alienated forms of relation. A main mechanism through which it does so is by posing these two institutions as particularly fulfilling aspirations for mutual, expressive—basically non-alienating—relationships.[3] This is particularly weighty as the two are set up specifically as THE spheres in which human fulfilment and relation are possible given the antidemocratic hierarchies required within a Liberal political system and a capitalist economic system. They are *supposed* to provide counter spaces to the alienated forms of relation in politics and economics. Yet, as I will argue, they each carry through—albeit in their own modalities—the very same dynamics of alienation as found and noticed more commonly within the public spheres of politics and work.[4]

Personal Interlude

I'll begin with a story. A personal tale. It's from the days of old, when my current partner and I were still somewhat new to each other. Into our relationship about a year: some of the tale taking place when still less than a year entwined, much of it from more than a year bound up in each others lives. It's about a conversation. The actual conversation happened over many years, in varied locations. I remember one in particular—a bucolic scene, lying on the grass, smelling and hearing the rush of a nearby river. We were discussing monogamy. These were never really discussions only. They were always also negotiations, intellectual and emotional wrestling matches—playful romps, yet also struggles—a kind of sex themselves. At each match I was both wound into further "commitment" as I deftly wriggled out of "commitment" all together. (Note: I put "commitment" in quotes because below I will challenge its common sense paring with practicing monogamy in a love relationship.) My strategy was brilliant. It was never planned. I didn't even know I was doing it—didn't know *what* I was doing at all at the time, in fact. It was only later that we came to realize the strategy, the political framework I was inventing, or perhaps simply reinventing, in and through these dialogues and in the dynamism of living and being tested in relation. The conversations/negotiations were held at any number of beautiful lovers' hideouts, grassy knolls and river banks. You know, truth is we also probably took them up in various ugly locations—both physical and psychic. But who has time for reality, now—I'm telling you a story. Each time I was asked about, or to "commit" to, monogamy I invented new levels of it. When asked to "commit" to the next level I invented sublevels. We seemed to be living out that metaphysical quandary: if you approach an object by covering half the distance between you at each move, you will never actually reach the object. By inventing levels of monogamy, and then sublevels and aspects to the sublevels, I agreed to commitments while ever increasing the distance between myself and the object of my lover's desire.

I'm sure she has a different story to tell. For me this was a time of freedom. The very negotiation, our revolutionary political acumen, our philosophical dance, our verbal dexterity. Courting could not have been better. The woman loved me, this I knew. I loved her. But the excitement of our love required the potential traps and escapes for which our philosophical training had prepared us and which our politics demanded of us. I am older now, more encumbered, perhaps less free or temporarily just more lost. But I remember those scenes as sites of love and freedom. They still hold powerful liberatory potential. I used to joke that I should write down the typology I was developing in our lovers' tousling. I would surprise myself, both of us actually—though to her the proper term may have been more "exasperate"—with the arguments I could come up with to avoid actually embracing monogamy. "This would make a good article," we would joke, ever the aspiring academics. It's probably best I never did write any of it down at the time. It likely would have spoiled the joy. Or, like those dreams one has, vivid and fantastical, colors only muted and meaning lost when you wake up and try to explain them to someone.

Here I sit, years later, to write of marriage and monogamy. Commanded by some power greater than myself. Teaching the stuff? Always a powerful force in having one confront what one really means. A Fromm-like reversal of a flight toward freedom? What appears to be an irrational rejection of the seduction of capitalist possession? An incomprehensible impulse to restore my self and the world to sanity? Who can say?

My issue in those days was not a roving eye. I had no particular need for sexual liaisons with other chicks. In all this time I have resisted the tidal force of marriage and still hold out on an acceptance of two matters of my final categorical inventions: the philosophical and political aspects of monogamy. Recalling the broad strokes of the typology now, I talked of three types of monogamy: the practical, the philosophical, and the political. For me, at the time, the emotional was obvious in the types themselves, needing no independent standing. Perhaps this was blindness, perhaps insight. The types then had points, and factors to the points, though I no longer remember all the specific details. Regarding practice I talked about the differences between de facto practical monogamy and a conscious commitment to such. I actually used those words. Can you imagine two philosophers courting? Of course, a third form of practical monogamy is when one makes a commitment to practice but doesn't actually do so in their lives. This difference between promises and action form part of a core of what we will see are the inherent contradictions within the institution.

On the two grand types, the political and the philosophical, I thus far still refuse to cede ground. I'm not the kind to draw lines in the sand, or in my urban landscape, on pavement. It's not that I gain strength from intransigence: who does really, especially in love, politics, and philosophy? Emotionally it remains my truth. Logically the argument stands. Here is a version of our conversation about monogamy which I am now (and in life for many becomes) linking to a critical analysis of marriage. Like any narrative, I don't claim that it is at all an actual rendition. Memory grounds us, but it never promises truth. Yet truthful it is, many years, experiences, and books read later. No, it is not the argument I devised over time in our lovers whispers, tuggings, and orations. But it does them justice, I hope, all the same.

Queers Gone Awry

Critiques of marriage and monogamy may sound antiquated to some. They recall early twentieth-century anarchist, Marxist, and other utopian visions, early second wave feminist radicalism . . . and even pop versions of mid-century acclaim for a sexual revolution.[5] Since the 1970s, we began to see such critiques coming from a problematically sexist portion of the men's movement including a growing articulation of these institutions as harming men's and fathers' rights.[6] These debates have been mainly put back onto the table of public discourse with GLBTQ (contemporary shorthand for Gay, Lesbian, Bisexual, Transgendered, and Queer) claims to a "right to marry."[7] In a legislative move designed to "protect the freedom to marry," in response to GLBT activism, the U.S. Congress and

supporters publically reaffirmed the inherent heterosexuality of the institution of marriage. In 2003–2004 the U.S. Congress held hearings on a
proposed constitutional amendment to ban "same-sex marriage." At the
state and local level of politics, activist groups, courts, and elected officials
are ensconced in the struggle over whether to extend the rights effected
in conferring the legal status of marriage to those not involved in hetero-
sexual-sexual relationships. From Taiwan to Canada, same-sex marital
unions have become quite the item. The more recent focus of GLBT
organizations on marriage as a right is inherently connected to action and
theorizing contesting "legitimate" family functions with so-called new
practices of queers adopting children, transracial adoption, and often
surrogacy and gamete (meaning both egg and sperm) transfers for single,
queer, same sex, and unmarried heterosexual partners. Unfortunately, much
of the revived discussion of these "current events"—type of political issues barely scratches the surface of critical inquiry. The new discussions
initiated by sections of GLBT-based movement generally forget or gloss
over the radical challenges of not only early sexual revolution theories
from Marxists, anarchists, and feminists, but even from the life and history of queer folks and our theorizings.

Among U.S. Jewish institutions, the question of "gay marriage" and
the legitimacy of same-sex partnerships has been a hot topic for many
years. Although rabbis may be vested with state power to marry a couple
legally under U.S. law (where separation of religion and state is a slippery
slope), there remains a difference between a marriage that is deemed legal
Jewishly and in terms of civil law. A couple may get married in the United
States but not have a "Jewish" wedding, or a rabbi may marry a couple
with legal standing in the Jewish circles they deem authoritative without
that authority accepted by the state. Individual rabbis and Jewish institutions have come to any number of different decisions regarding same-sex
marriages. In Jewish law one does not even need a rabbi to perform a
marriage ceremony, though it has become customary. Before there were
many rabbis available to officiate at same-sex weddings, lots of queers
took advantage of this loophole and had friends or colleagues officiate.

Here is a brief overview of the variety of Jewish policies regarding
"same-sex marriage." A large number of Jewish institutions in the United
States support moves for civil recognition of same-sex unions. At the
same time, some movements will not perform Jewish ceremonies for same-
sex couples. One rabbinical seminary has not authorized "gay" weddings
across the board, but allows individual congregations and rabbis to make
their own choices. Some congregations stipulate that their rabbis cannot
perform same-sex marriages, although the movements of which they are
members allow it. Other congregations will allow their rabbis to perform

the ceremonies, but will not allow them to take place on the premises of the synagogue. At one seminary where same-sex unions were deemed legitimate years ago, the concern of queers is the pressure to assimilate to straight standards in this supposedly most open environment. There, more radical queer challenges to heteronorms are still beyond the pale. If you are monogamously partnered and happy to call yourself some version of married you will be accepted. Queers there have noted that they too have now become part of the "pressured to marry club," marginalizing singles within their community. When the seminary made problematic new rules requiring that all students preparing for rabbinical ordination must not be intermarried (Jew-speak for someone married to a non-Jew—another hot topic at seminaries), given their equal status, this ruling extended to same-sex couples as well.[8]

But this being a Christian country, U.S. legal battles rage on regardless of the varied politics of same-sex unions within the Jewish community. Even if an ordained rabbi performs your same-sex wedding, outside of Massachusetts at present, this does not entitle you to any of the rights of marriage in U.S. law. (This is somewhat similar to the politics of abortion. Abortion is not illegal in Jewish law, and yet Jews must live within the Christian constraints expressed in supposedly secular U.S. law.) To be fair, many ministers will also perform such ceremonies, despite the fact that U.S. policy makers ground their efforts to preserve the heterosexual character of the institution in Christian morality.

Thus, we find the mass (meaning not explicitly Jewish) current debates regarding marriage—siding with either protecting the venerated institution from defilement, or with allowing same-sex and transgendered individuals to marry under U.S. law—tend to be state focused. Large sections of the GLBT community and its supporters are working on an application and introduction of legislation and or seeking redress and change through the courts. It is not that I take a public stand against these valiant efforts or many individual campaigns to raise awareness, collect data, and otherwise effect public opinion or pressure policy makers. In fact, I also might argue differently for such rights within Jewish law than within U.S. law given that the historical contexts and political implications are different.

Readers may recall that in what is often referred to in the United States as the first wave of feminism there was a tension between those working on a wide array of justice issues and those who came to see suffrage as the primary aim of the movement. Although certainly many working-class women did support suffrage, over time, and given the elite status and therefore access of many of the suffrage-first supporters, activity to secure the vote for white native born women came to take over the movement as a whole. This was not only a phenomenon confined to that specific historical moment. The state-focused and more limited version of the broad, creative radicalness of the movement at large got narrowed then and also narrowed many people's capacities to theorize beyond a state-centered strategy towards overcoming sexist oppression. This is usually the version of the legacy bequeathed to history: that the first wave of feminism concerned suffrage, forgetting the deep searching and experimentation on myriad issues. We can see something similar happening before our eyes in queer politics. The mass media and large GLBT organizations have "chosen" to focus on the "right to marry."[9]

Is this the most significant issue, or one with the most far-reaching effects, for the array of queers right now in history? Debatable, but doubtful. Does this work generally draw on the lessons of the wide variety of ideas and life choices of queer people in their diversity over time? Debatable, but doubtful. Yet, this is where much attention is being paid. Even with this intense flurry of activism, I can at least assert that we need not lose a critique and perhaps can develop an engagement with the state in such a way that we can also maintain and foster fecund spaces for deeper examination and challenges to prevailing norms and presumptions regarding marriage and monogamy. My view is that Marx and some other fabulous thinkers can help us to do just that.

Let's Talk About Marriage

Really, the first question we ought to be asking is: What is marriage? *Webster's Third New International Dictionary, Unabridged* (that my mom bought me as a gift for starting college—oh, if she had any inkling of how I would end up using that incredible tome) tells us that it is:

> 1 a (1): the state of being united to a person of the opposite sex as husband or wife. b: the mutual relation of husband and wife: WEDLOCK c: the institution whereby men and women are joined in a special kind of social and legal dependence for the purpose of founding and maintaining a family—see MONOGAMY, POLYGAMY (2): an act of marrying or the rite by which the married status is effected: WEDDING; *esp*: the wedding ceremony and attendant festivities or formalities—compare BEENA MARRIAGE, union (4): MARITAGE (5): the combination of a king and queen of the same suit (as in pinochle)—see ROYAL MARRIAGE

My dad used to play pinochle. He rode the commuter train into Manhattan with the same group of friends from our neighborhood (and others that got on at later stops) for nearly thirty years. They would sit in the set of five seats that face each other next to the train's door. Every morning when they boarded the train they would take down the large cardboard advertisements hung on the walls, turn them over and use them as both card table and score card. (One of them might very well have been a Levy's ad!) At 7:00 A.M., they screamed, fought, and cheered all the way into the city. They played for small sums of money. My dad was much beloved and respected generally by these men. Even so, the joke was he lost money for his teammates too often; they began to pay him NOT to play. Who knew that every morning this group of same-sex partners was striving for a royal marriage. . . . In the frenzy of overworked and sleep deprived identification with the cards, I wonder who thought of themselves as king and who queen.

Back to *Webster's* . . . I admit I had to look up BEENA MARRIAGE. The book says that it is "a marriage in parts of India and Ceylon in which the husband enters the wife's kinship group and has little authority in the household." I remain unclear why this is to be compared to the ceremony, festivities, or formalities. In the West, what some Easterners call BEENA MARRIAGE seems to refer to the phenomenon of a henpecked husband, not managing to be master of his fate and captain of his landlocked ship. Perhaps we are asked to compare it since marriage is without a doubt a patriarchal institution, but appealing to women as a female financé and her mother are expected to plan all the festivities and the man generally gets moved around from place to place like a dummy, by which I mean a mannequin. I had to look up various other words that came up in that trail on which defining marriage sent me. Curious indeed, this definition of marriage. Some might even call it queer. When/if queers are ever legally allowed to marry en mass, would anything change in the definitions found in all the dictionaries in the world beyond noting that the union is between people of the opposite sex? Its hard to tell, and *Webster's* doesn't give us much guidance.

Webster's never really does define what it is about the state of being or social and legal dependence that makes marriage different from other states of being or dependence. Funny that in our day we follow the practices of bourgeois marriage, though Liberalism would admit to no dependencies for one worthy of the citizenship needed to engage in the legal rite and relation. In the antebellum U.S. South, slaves could not legally marry.[10] They were seen as dependents, not as having the requisite autonomy and self-sufficiency for acquiring this coveted legal status. In Nazi Germany Jews were forbidden to marry: not human enough to be granted the privilege. I said in my introduction that this exploration is not about religion, but we can't avoid the topic here completely. For example, strange that as a rite, certain religious leaders recognized by the state are empowered with creating/conferring the legal status. Plenty of Black ministers during slavery and queer rabbis and other clergy have performed "marriage ceremonies." Depending on the historical context, however, if the festivities are to honor slaves or queers or Jews, the law does not recognize their right to the rite. And as a rite, with "the wedding ceremony and attendant festivities or formalities" few other religious rituals simultaneously create so obviously and incipiently, through their very performance, hegemonic forms of hetero-normative identity, ideology, and institutions.

I actually know and respect many GLBT folks individually and in organizations working on the right to marry. They have considered much and I don't mean my comments to sound like cheap shots. Ending discrimination is without a doubt significant. But when we think about what we really want to be free to do, with whom and in what ways, how does monogamous marriage really get us to a place of freedom instead of also just constraining us in new ways within the confines of a long-standing existing institution? Women and queers seeking inclusion into their religions' infrastructures have faced similar challenges and the answers are not easily found.

There are other contradictions in the neat *Webster's* world, played out every day in our rather messy lives and law. I can't stand those definitions that use the word (or forms of it) in the explanation. If a student of mine tried to define marriage by referring to marrying, married, or maritage you know they'd flunk the quiz. *Webster's*, like ideology itself, often gets away with a good deal of confusion and lack of clarity. It's partly how ideology works. You can't be husband and wife without entering the state of being united in that way. And don't you hate those definitions (oh, or do I mean aspects of ideology!?) that work as tautologies? In some cases this "unity" is itself called a family. In other cases, the "unit" is not complete without others. Generally most folks of reason would not consider a marriage dissolved that did not yield children. Or perhaps the question is: how long must these two folks be married without children before they would no longer be considered married? In some cultures, a union that does not produce biological offspring is open for a divorce claim, or the husband's taking on additional wives. We consider ourselves, under Liberalism, more "enlightened." Definitely reflecting the cultures of "lighter"-skinned folks in Western modernity, we consider such traditions as oppressive and archaic. Thus, also in the contentious debates about the possibility of queers marrying, some U.S. lawmakers have been careful to say that heterosexual couples who do not have children can still be considered married. On the other hand, in arguments against queer marriage, or conferring this coveted legal status on a couple in which at least one of the partners is transgendered (even post-operatively so), many public officials and the courts do still say that marriage is about having children and if two people cannot produce children (implying in a combination of their biological matter and gestational services), then they do not have the right to marry.[11] In the face of queer challenges, bourgeois marriage is being forced to face its contradictions— dutifully reported, though unselfconsciously, by *Webster*'s first definition.

Okay, enough already with Mr. Webster and his teams of ideology reflectors/producers. My other source of information in trying to answer the question "what is marriage anyway" has been endless queries with experts on the ideology and practice. Of course, I mean ordinary people. Giving students assignments with this question has been especially helpful. My most radical students in queer theory seminars often offer the most thoughtful replies. Here is what I have drawn from the array of responses I've received over some years of pestering students and others with this question:

> Marriage is a legal status naming a one-to-one union between a man and woman, sufficiently publically identified as heterosexual. What differentiates this union from other unions that an individual man and an individual woman willing to be publically identified as heterosexual may enter, is that it is based on common life goals and romantic love, with a promise for lifelong companionship, sex, more love, physical touch, cohabitation, and children. This union is unusual in its religious sanction and linearity. By linearity, most explain that they mean marriage is a legal status, naming a union distinguished from most others in that it is understood within a particular and culturally recognized linear progression of relations, involving the above mentioned aspects, and seen as a transitional moment in that progression which then trumps all prior moments of relationship.

I think that real people do much better than generations of *Webster* teams.

I also always ask people what they think are the component aspects of marriage (beyond the definition they come to). The responses include the following understandings: Acquiring formal benefits and rights. It connotes success in life. Marriage validates relationships and also validates sex. It gives an identity particularly to women as it also gives freedom to women. Marriage anticipates a guaranteed companion, and suggests characteristics between these companions such as trust, liking each other, friendship, stability, and security. One other aspect I find worth mentioning is that "you get a family," meaning from becoming joined to the family of the person you have taken on as your partner in the union.

When I'm really grooving I ask one more question: to try to name explicitly what are marriage's strengths, or what is so appealing about it. I always ask people to be serious in their responses, not ironic or critical or too casual. I don't think you will find this part surprising, but I do think it is important for an analysis to have it clearly articulated. I have consistently heard one form or another of the following: Marriage extends one's social contacts. Offers you the myth that life will be perfect. That you can commit to others based on love. That there are expectations and you will have an end of life mate. You will have something you can belong to. You will find completion through another. Marriage makes for one's identity. Compared to your family of origin, this time you can make a family based on choice. Marriage is a rite of passage one goes through in order to be considered an adult. Its strengths are its traditions themselves. You get a wedding. The financial incentives and it gives you a right to inherited property. You get to know that you are worthy because you are your partner's only true love and the focus of their sexual desire.

This brings us to a discussion of monogamy. I would say that for most ordinary people, marriage is the explicit or public aspect of the dyad, and monogamy the more implicit, or more private aspect. Nowhere in the "I do" version of a marriage ceremony is a practice of exclusive sexual relationship discussed. We do not "promise to love, honor, cherish, and *only have sex with*" so and so. Monogamy is somewhat implied in parental concerns that their children settle down, though the phrase also implies a host of other disciplining behaviors necessary for the functioning of a capitalist system. Some say monogamy became more popular, and is really the only feasible form of marital relation, under capitalism. No longer living in community and networks of mutual support closely related to the products of our labors and satisfying at least subsistence needs, how many men can really afford to "keep" more than one wife and one set of kids. With the soaring divorce rate and the new version of having multiple families, you can ask the men and sometimes women who *are* asked to support more than one set of (ex)spouses and kids how costly this is. Although in both precapitalist and capitalist economies men's capacities to serve as heads of household and for a few who actually manage to build their financial base over time, the under—and usually un—paid work of wives and children are required. In this sense, one might argue that in capitalism, just as in feudal or agricultural economies, the more wives and kids the better. However, the introduction of wage labor, and the processes of separation and privatization of the nuclear family probably contributed most to the economic incentive to prioritize monogamy over male polygamy. It also helped to create the very notion of European mainstream Christian identity as civilized as opposed to the "backward" habits of the uncivilized. Polygamy was of course common for Christianity's own religious patriarchs (who were also dark-skinned by the way). However, modern mainline Christianity increasingly responded to the "needs" of a developing capitalism by forgetting, or apologizing, for these facts as it came to sanction only monogamous relations as marital relations.

The above discussion on the definition, component aspects, and strengths of bourgeois marriage all hinge on an inherently related institution called "monogamy." Historically and today in many cultures, marriage had nothing to do with the notion of monogamy. Even in certain periods when, or places where, bourgeois marriage is the norm and people married with a legal commitment to monogamy, it was simultaneously expected that husbands (and very occasionally wives) have affairs and/or frequent brothels, or otherwise pay for the services of sex-workers (of either one's same or different sex/gender). The fact that you individually may have a fully articulated and mutually fulfilling nonmonogamous marriage, or that you or your spouse may have broken your promise of lifelong sexual and emotional fidelity does not challenge the critical understanding that monogamy as an ideology and institution is indispensable to the practice and function of bourgeois marriage.

A View of Monogamy from an Anarchist Watchtower

Life is certainly stranger than fiction. Or maybe the point is that we ought not really distinguish between the ideas held by actual people and those found in and between the lines of little paperback books on those small roundabout displays. I have to interrupt this discussion to tell you that I myself have just been interrupted by two twelve-year-old South Asian females, dressed in formal attire. They rang my doorbell in the Bronx where I live at present to ask me if I would accept their publication on Loyalty. It is put out by the Christian group Watchtower and discusses various forms of loyalty and how one might achieve this moral goal. The interesting thing is that although the booklet and the twelve-year-olds are easily recognizable, and self-defined, as part of a strategy of Christian fundamentalist proselytizing, I have noticed that many people from all walks of life discuss marital fidelity in much the same ways as did my visitors and their booklet. Monogamy's strength is characterized similarly to the description of the appeal of marriage. Not just by all the average people I pepper with the questions, nor just by my idealistic and generally quite progressive students. The benefits of monogamy seem to mirror the benefits of marriage discussed above as a foundational aspect of LOYALTY promoted by the Watchtower girls.

Wedded to the promises and attraction of marriage, publically at least, most people assume monogamy to be the most appealing aspect of long-term sexualized relationships. To many ordinary folks, monogamy suggests the loyalty and fidelity they need in order to pursue intimate relations over time. Moreover, by "settling" into a defined monogamous relationship, people often feel a burden has been lifted, and now they can attend to other significant life matters. Somehow, feeling assured that our partner's sexual activity is directed only toward us, this gives us a feeling of security, it frees us of anxiety and other energy-draining emotions, leaving us with more energy to put into other aspects of our life plans. We feel more able to open up physically and emotionally with our partner. We feel we can now "depend" on them in a way we could not before the commitment to practicing monogamy. And we feel we have succeeded in at least this one sphere of living. Of course, in this day, many tout the health benefits of monogamous relationships given the prevalence of life-threatening sexually transmitted diseases. People can let their guard down, and not worry as much about the complicated business of safe sex and latex love. Acknowledging some of the strengths people find in monogamy, let us turn to our old friend *Webster's* for a more clinical view.

In *Webster's*, my trusty ideology gauge, monogamy is defined as:

(1): single marriage : a: one marriage only during life—compare DIGAMY b: marriage with but one person at a time—compare BIGAMY, POLYGAMY (2): the condition of having a single mate at any one time.

Well, I was surprised. I love my *Webster's*, don't get me wrong. But it is truly unusual for me to turn to a dictionary in this way in the first place. I'm not a linguist, nor do I have Mary Daly's skills to turn the dictionary into a most fascinating source for radical lesbian feminism. I also find it tedious when students use a verbatim dictionary definition in those early sections of their papers where I have warned them to make certain to "define your terms." For whatever reason I was drawn to my *Webster's*, I'm glad I followed that inclination. No mention of sex here at all. Come on. How is a person supposed to learn the rules of civil life if you can't even get the honest lowdown from *Webster's*? How many dykes out there used the dictionary as their first source in identity exploration by looking up the word "lesbian?" You hope it's instructive, it is often degrading, but just as often even the dictionary is titillating for youngsters in its dry, distanced, science-like manner. (I'll give you a sneak preview: Coming Soon—A Definition for Deuterogamy.) I'd say *Webster's* avoiding the use of the word sex when defining monogamy, and relying on the term mate as its most lightly veiled replacement, exposes the depth of the way the institution of monogamy is an ideological function. Sex is not noted in the definition of marriage, although it is only marriage which is taken in religion and law to sanction sexual activity. We are supposed to "know" what the terms mean, "know" they are about forms of sexual relationships without *Webster* or anyone else ever really spelling these things out for us. That is certainly part of the problem with our lacking a healthy, dare I say expressive if even the dictionary dares not express, sexual social more.

A few more things to notice about *Webster's*. In common usage to be single is not to be married, so it is difficult to say single marriage. But more so, have you ever heard of digamy? Surely I looked that up too. It's from the Greek for adultery—from di meaning two and gamma—gamous really—relating to our understanding of marriage. I'm no Greek scholar, but its interesting that there is a Greek letter called a digamma which "fell out of use," but was referred to by that name because it resembled "two capital gammas placed on top of each other." (How sexy.)[12]

I find it interesting that digamy comes from the concept of adultery, but adultery refers to sexual liaisons with those other than one's legally defined spouse while that person is still one's spouse. In our culture, the way people avoid looking loose, or becoming adulterous—meaning nonmonogamous while married, since adultery only applied to a legally recognized marriage—is having the first spouse done with (either by death or divorce . . . it doesn't say if the two have had sex before the spouse has been done with) in order to have two legal marriages recognized serially. The definition for adultery does explicitly mention sexual intercourse. (That's where patriarchy and Bill Clinton get it from. Clinton wasn't adulterous because he supposedly was more creative and did not have sexual intercourse.) But adultery is only mentioned in the fine print. It is here in the reference to deuterogamy that we find our only other hint of sex. Deuterogamy's first definition is simply DIGAMY. Its second and final definition reads: "secondary pairing of sexual cells or nuclei that replaces direct copulation in many fungi, algae, and higher plants." Typical, just when you think you're getting to a discussion of sex, it is again deferred. This time by definition, as those cells and nuclei don't even get any, directly. This makes sense as deutero comes from the Greek for "to lack, miss" or for second.

Average folks usually describe monogamy as not having sex with people other than your legally recognized spouse, since the official history of sex is that it occurs only in marriage. These days, since so many people are having sex while not married, people also mean not sleeping around when you're dating, or seriously involved in a romantic relationship with someone to whom you have committed exclusive sexual activity.

I helped to found and then coordinated a group its members referred to as the Jewish Queer Think Tank. For a year or so we looked into issues of sexually intimate relationships including marriage, monogamy, anonymous sex, commitment ceremonies, and beyond. With much diversity amongst us we are all also self-conscious Jews living within Jewish and various intersecting communities, and we tend to rely on our Jewishness as one amongst many groundings as we try to make meaning and social change in the world. Much of what I bring to this work has been shaped in important ways by the work we did during that period and since. The conversations and work we did together were extremely refreshing, especially because aside from Watchtower, not many people are writing on monogamy these days.

Over time in the JQTT, we discussed some of these issues in a variety of forms and fora. One issue we looked into is why society has stigmatized gay male cultures practicing anonymous sex with numerous partners. Some of the sweetest, traditionally inclined members shared their personal experiences with gay male sex clubs and the benefits of anonymous sex. Monogamy over time can often be somewhat stifling sexually. Or there are also many reasons we get involved with partners and our sex lives together may not turn out to be all that interesting or gratifying. Anonymous sex can help one explore one's sexuality and take risks that ideologically society suggests is the function of monogamy. We also came to question why society would presume an equation of religious or other profound fulfillment and exclusive sexual activity over time. What is it about the temporary or momentary that is necessarily antiprofound or antispiritual? I will discuss Martin Buber's ideas below, but in fact many theologians assume that religious and deeply spiritual experiences are often fleeting. To institutionalize spiritual inspiration is to deaden it. If you stop to think about it, if you are not thinking about sex specifically, we usually talk about profound *moments*, *flashes* of insight, religious ecstasy which overtakes us *suddenly*. Why would we assume that the deep meaning of sex in our lives would necessarily negate these views?

In the JQTT, we also discussed a common practice among lesbians which is often lovingly called "serial monogamy." Not all dykes are by any means attracted to monogamy though it is a culturally identifiable practice to: have a deep and intense intimate sexually monogamous relationship, have that relationship end, and at some later point enter into another deep and intense intimate and monogamous relationship. One of the significant cultural contributions of thinking about these forms of serial monogamy among many lesbians is that often the ended relationships are not viewed specifically as "failures." A marriage that ends is called a "failed marriage." Someone who has been divorced and remarried numerous times is often expected to explain themselves, if not assumed to be simply problematic. This is not my view, but is often what I hear from others in the marriage market. A fellow radical who found himself in this (the divorced and thrice re-married) category offered me the wonderful phrase "monogafied" to explain those relationships which achieve sexual exclusivity. And yet among lesbians we often assume our partners have had previous other significant relationships. Often our past lovers remain within our friendship circles or even among our closest friends . . . often enough because there was much that was "right" and successful about those relationships and those aspects of relation live on. (This is one of the reasons lesbians love Plato's notion from the *Symposium* that "an army of lovers cannot fail"!)

It is not easy to find current explorations and especially critical analyses of the phenomenon. Laurie Zimmerman, an old friend and fellow anarchist, now a Reconstructionist rabbi, and also member of the JQTT pointed me in the direction of a webzine article on the topic by her friend Peter. Peter Staudenmaier is also an anarchist, thinker, and activist. In his piece, "Slipping The Ties That Bind," Staudenmaier enters the discussion by introducing the phrase *compulsory monogamy*. He situates compulsory monogamy along with patriarchy, heterosexism, and capitalism "as one interlocking structure, where each component reinforces the others, to the detriment of us all." Interestingly, Staudenmaier breaks down monogamy into basically three manifestations which resonate with those I imagined in conversations with my partner over a decade ago. He names monogamy as an ideology and as an institution in much the same ways that I meant as inherently related politics and philosophy.

As an ideology, Staudenmaier clarifies that monogamy is based on the idea of perfect mates, who fulfill all of our dreams, and when we find them we get to just live happily ever after. These ideas are big business; Staudenmaier referred to them as comprising a Hollywood and Disney paradigm. He points out the contradiction of scarcity—fullness operating within this paradigm. Utilizing an economic framework, he identifies the promotion of emotional-erotic scarcity. This sits well within a capitalist system of grab and hold, aggressive acquisitiveness, romantic competition, and the commodification of pleasure whose producers, I would argue, then need disciplining and products need policing. At the same time, monogamy as an ideology relies on a notion that there will be complete one-to-one compatability, promising the satisfaction of all of our desires. Here the presumption is that we can expect to find one person who fulfills a variety of human needs: that attraction, emotional, and sexual needs will all be satisfied by one person in our lives.

The combination of these elements within capitalism promotes exclusivity. The process of commodification turns desire into a static entity rather than a dynamic force. Monogamy relies on and produces a sexual-emotional possessiveness, where people often end up coming and staying together out of fear and insecurity. As part of the so-called private realm supporting bourgeois economic relations, monogamy is often praised for being ethical, promoting honesty, and emotionally cleansed engagements with others. But Staudenmaier points out that monogamy actually functions as a way to bypass the challenges of human relationships and desire. He explains the process as being "an emotional shortcut by offering people a prepackaged set of easy answers and thus relieving them of the burden of making difficult choices."[13]

Extending Staudenmaier's insights, we can see here how monogamy functions more deeply, ideologically as a form of alienation. The dominant ideology casts individuals as autonomous, self-reliant, capable, and acting on their own behalf. Yet in neither of the two primary public realms, politics or economics, do individuals generally ever get to explore their own aspirations, move along to their own rhythms, or help set communal rhythms. In politics we have elected, appointed, or other elite "experts" who explore situations and make decisions for us. In the workplace, and in the intricacies of a functioning economy, average workers up to most management even do not have all that much say in deciding the direction of their lives and fates. Religion functions as one realm in which individuals have been trained to seek refuge from these aggressive, competitive, and alienating modes of social organization. Within the institutions governing other significant "personal" relations we see something similar.

Within bourgeois ideology, monogamy is presented as an ethical framework, and I would add as a positive form of focusing, of organizing and disciplining, sexuality. What is the payoff for such structuring? Counter to the public discourse of freedom from external constraints, monogamy offers a private discourse of freedom through relationship. But egotism and individualism still reign here, even though things *appear* relational. Relations are focused on a single other, never really transgressing the individualist paradigm. In the all or nothing fashion of our winner take all political system, and our either/or economic system, monogamy promises sexual and emotional riches; without it one is barren, impoverished, depraved. Independent women and various queers know these stereotypes all too well. What appears to be an *institution* of generous mutuality between partners is based on a presumption of jealousy and control. These issues are not simply operating between individual partners, but work systemically. Monogamy is a form of systemic control which—through the mutually constitutive institutions of patriarchy, racism, heterosexism, and capitalism—produces a possessive version of desire that must then submit to social restraint and regulation.

Monogamy, Marriage, and "Other" People's Problems

With respect to monogamy and marriage, critical race theory also helps us to see how the social categories of racial distinctions have been created and maintained as a mechanism to assist in the development of disciplined masses necessary for capitalist forms of production. Monogamy and its moral righteousness become comprehensible through differentiating certain segments of the population as its opposite, and therefore less assimilable into the economic structure. To mark what for shorthand we will call certain ethnic/racial groups as lewd and lascivious is a way not only to excuse their poverty and exclusion from the workforce. This marking also holds out the promises of the benefits of fidelity and appropriate sexualities at the same time as it keeps people practicing out of the ever present warning of the ruin that awaits if one falls off the wagon and becomes "like them."[14]

Further, when "free" women—when considered citizens—lost their citizenship if they married non-U.S. nationals, we see at work multiple hierarchies based on the intricacies of gender, nation, race, sexuality and property rights in U.S. laws of intimate association. Not only was this a directly gender-based distinction, (men did not lose their citizenship by marrying foreigners). The laws were applied differentially among women on a race-based axis. For example, white women who married Asians lost their citizenship but could regain it if widowed or divorced. However, U.S. born Asian women who married Asian men lost their citizenship but could *not* regain it if widowed or divorced.[15] Jewish women also faced challenges in this arena, and here gender, religion, race, and politics come together in specific ways to mark Jews. At a time of unprecedented immigration from Eastern Europe, with many poor and radical Jews seeking to immigrate to the United States, politicians sought to limit the flow of immigration by framing Jews as a stain on the national character and a drain on the economy. Some high-profile battles over these issues specifically targeted Jewish women with radical political ideas.[16] By 1930, Herbert Hoover moved to stem the tide of immigration by disallowing women citizens to bring over their foreign husbands. Polish men were disproportionately targeted in this effort, meaning the largest source of

radical Jewish adult male immigrants. Disciplining desire through discriminatory legislation in the realm of monogamous marriage has long
been coterminous with patriotism toward the nation and proof of one's
capacities of loyalty to race, class, religion, and caste.[17]

Linking monogamy as a discipline with racist and other discriminatory markers of capitalist development is key to understanding some
significant aspects of the history of the current same-sex marriage debates.
A ban on marriage between same-sex partners is neither the first, nor
only, marriage ban in the United States. For example, one cannot marry
someone who is a close relative. Since marriage laws are set at the state
level, just how close a relative must be to be denied the right to marry
differs, depending on the state and has differed over time across states.[18]
There are also laws against marrying a minor, though again they differ
across states, historical period, and depending on if one is male or female.
In some states, pregnancy status can often mitigate against an age-based
legal restraint. Additionally, there are laws against marrying people with
certain disabilities. For example, as recently as 1980 thirty-three states
had laws prohibiting people diagnosed as "retarded" from getting married.[19] Historically, taking blood tests before being allowed to marry also
had legal implications and licenses could be denied prospective marriage
partners depending on various aspects of their health and "general moral
fitness."[20] The most widespread set of laws limiting whom one may marry
regards marriage across racial lines, as confusing as their social constructions are, which have at times been co-created with some slippage between religion and race.

During the early years of European colonization in the Americas,
white male settlers often married Native American women, and during
the westward expansion white men often married Mexican women. Even
after the United States annexed Mexican territories, neither Native
Americans nor Latina/os were therefore included in antimiscegenation
laws.[21] It was, however, during the original colonial settler period that the
first antimiscegenation laws were passed. In 1661, the Maryland law's
concern was in policing sexual contact between white women and Black
males—here race, gender, and free/slave status are all at play. For white
men, later antimiscegenation laws helped protect their "all white" heirs in
inheritance, since the—usually forced—unions of white male slaveholders
and their female slaves could never be legitimated through marriage, the
intergenerational economic benefits of "pure" whiteness could be ensured. White men who wanted to marry such women might have tried to
have them "pass" as white, if the women were light enough, and then
legitimate the bond with marriage.[22]

As in the case of cross-racial adoption where the subject position is
white, the same may be said for cross-racial intimacies. In the debates

over cross-racial adoption, readers may remember, the parents are presumed to be white and the children Black (or occasionally other children of color particularly Native American, or in international adoptions where the children come from non-European countries).[23] In the case of the history of policing marriage boundaries in the United States, antimiscegenation laws were concerned with whites and their liaisons to people of color, not with liaisons amongst differing groups of folks of color. For example, different states had varying laws and practices against white/Black marriage, white/Indian marriage, white/Mexican and white/Asian marriage, though not against, for example, Mexian/Asian or Native/African marriages.[24]

The first antimiscegenation laws aimed at Asians targeted Chinese men who were brought to the United States to fill the great need for hard labor during the U.S. expansion westward. Conscious of the threat to racialized conceptions of nation building, these Chinese men, brought here to literally build the new nation, were excluded from basic rights of citizenship and the recognition of intimate bonds. Lawmakers wanted to discourage white women from marrying these Chinese men. (Further, remember that in keeping the Chinese men from being able to become citizens, it also meant that a U.S. woman would lose her citizenship were she to marry a Chinese laborer.) In an effort to keep their numbers down, the Chinese Exclusion Act of 1882 (reiterated in federal law through 1904) also ensured that these laborers would not be able to bring their wives and families to these shores (Barringer, Gardner, and Levin 1995). Laws discriminating against Chinese women did so out of fears regarding prostitution (Hing 1993, and Cott 1998). Though the United States came to limit the influx of Chinese laborers, cheap labor was still in demand. The Japanese who were then brought over to fill the gap were merely included in the earlier antimiscegenation laws designed for the Chinese as the language used categorized these groups both as "Mongols." The Japanese male laborers were, however, eventually more able to come with wives than the Chinese had been. When U.S. whites decided that the numbers of Japanese workers here were becoming threatening, Japanese migration was curtailed and Filipino workers were brought over.

As mentioned above, Latina/os were not included in U.S. antimiscegenation laws. Despite the Spanish linkages in Philippine culture and historic ties between U.S. Chicana/os and Filipina/os, with a rising number of immigrants, (U.S.)American laws were changed to include Filipina/os under antimiscegenation rulings. The "trouble" with Filippina/os and existing antimiscegenation laws was that this group was "proven" not to be "Mongolian." Thus, antimiscegenation laws were extended to include "Malayans." Further, although Filippino/as were technically under U.S. jurisdiction at the time, logic supported excluding them from marrying whites since enough of public opinion had supported such practices with others living in U.S. territories such as Native Americans and those of African heritage.[25]

As with social, also class-based, bias and laws against marrying Jews, some of these practices regarding "interracial" marriage were at least partly fueled by religious prejudices of the U.S. Christian mainstream. The disciplining necessary of the working class under capitalism in the West has been seen as a central portion of the purview of Christianity,[26] at least in the case of the Chinese, Japanese, Native American, and Indian populations on these shores. Religious difference from Christianity was co-created as a racial difference from developing conceptions of whiteness while simultaneously marking/generating class-based hierarchies. A 1705 bill regarding slaves and servants identifies Jews, Muslims, and other infidels prohibiting them from purchasing Christian servants or marrying white Christians, while the Supreme Court later ruled that Jews and Arabs were racially distinct from "Caucasians."[27] As another example, anti-Indian sentiment was co-created by prejudice against Hindus. Among those involved in antimiscegenation legislation there was then a dispute over whether Asian Indians (popularly categorized as Caucasian, though not "white") fell into the category covering other Asian groups. Eventually with the Supreme Court decision of *United States v. Thind* in 1923, it was concluded that the ban on intermarriage with whites would apply to Indians as it did to other Asian groups (Moran 2001, 30).

Heartlessness Begets Heartlessness

Why would we think that any dominant system, and in our case a system grounded in alienated forms of relation, could actually produce and sanction major institutions that truly challenge itself? Why would we think that bourgeois marriage and the other relation-based institution upon which it relies, monogamy, could deliver on promises of modes of being in relationship that really counter its inherent modes of estrangement? Efforts at heart, at bringing the heart to fullness, at working from the heart, at being recognized for the richness of one's heart, are so very difficult within a hegemonic set of alienated human relations. We distinguish from the public realm specific arenas in which we are allowed to feel and seek deep expression and self-direction. And yet, the very institutions set up in which we are told we can finally explore and walk a path guided by what our hearts tell us, instead distances us from those very same aspects of instinct and spontaneity that come from the heart. A brief look at Audre Lorde's essay on the erotic as power seems fitting here.

In an oft reprinted essay on the "Uses of the Erotic," Lorde talks about the erotic as a nexus of powers, a life force bridging the emotional and rational. She reminds us that "in order to perpetuate itself, every oppression must corrupt or distort those various sources of power within the culture of the oppressed that can provide energy for change. For women, this has meant a suppression of the erotic as a considered source of power and information within our lives" (1984, 53). Not to take away from the import her essay has had for multicultural feminist movement, I have found it interesting to also think about Lorde's insights in the context of this argument and relevant, even if often in different ways, for queers and everyone. She reinterprets the erotic from its pornographic deadness under hetero-capitalist patriarchy as an empowering aspect of spontaneous aliveness. She sees the erotic as spiritual, political, and potentially subversive. The bourgeois institution of marriage, what Staudenmaier names "compulsory monogamy"—along with racism, patriarchy, and compulsory heterosexuality—aims to tap into this nexus of powers in order to constrain and direct these various forces in ways that serve the structural needs of capitalism. All the richness of Lorde's poetic and revolutionary vision are trampled on by the march of opiate-like expectations and promises.

Lorde understands the erotic as "a measurement between the beginnings of our sense of self and the chaos of our strongest feelings" (1984, 54). Significant is her capacity to keep bringing us back to feelings, and feeling our feelings as a pathway to satisfaction, to excellence, fulfillment, and of course to social change. The forms of channeling—of what she calls—the erotic under hetero-capitalist patriarchy must take on and redirect such forces. The more we are able to actually stay in touch with, and know how to trust, our feelings, seeking relationship, and a life with meaning, the less we are able to allow for the layers of alienation, static-ness, hierarchy, and disempowerment within and beyond the spheres of our lives and the relations that arise in intimacy. The workings of the ideologies and institutions of both monogamy and marriage function to alienate us from these very life forces within ourselves, between us, and collectively.

A socialist, Lorde writes that "the principle horror of any system which defines the good in terms of profit rather than in terms of human need, or which defines human need to the exclusion of the psychic and emotional components of that need . . . is that it robs our work of its erotic value, its erotic power and life appeal and fulfillment." She continues that this "system reduces work to a travesty of necessities, a duty by which we earn bread or obligation for ourselves and those we love" (1984, 55). In our work lives, mechanization, technocracy, being overseen, competition, and various other means breach the sharing of joy and completion of a job between workers. Desire is constructed to an appropriate demand as consumers, divorced from the desire to honestly gauge the relations between satisfaction in ourselves, in relation with others, through work and shared projects. Our desire directed, our needs trained to serve production, we learn to fear the kinds of power in ourselves and in relations which Lorde discusses. This fear helps to keep us "docile and loyal and obedient, externally defined, and lead[s] us to accept many facets of our oppression" (1984, 58). The confines of institutions such as marriage and monogamy require a "looking away" from each other and from our own selves in order to keep the gaps shakily bridged between our full expression and fulfilling their narrow ideological expectations. "In the face of a racist, patriarchal, and anti-erotic society," affirming lesbian eros and other forms of life affirmation "can give us the energy to pursue genuine change within our world, rather than merely settling for a shift of characters in the same weary drama" (1984, 59).

With varying degrees of consciousness, instead, we think that by making a lifelong commitment to one person, putting our emotional, sexual, and friendship eggs in one basket, we will find peace, happiness, and fulfillment. But these visions prey on fears inherent within our systemic modes of ageism. We abandon our elders but somehow believe that by marrying someone and maintaining a monogamous relationship you will be cared for in your old age. You will not be alone. You will have a companion until you are parted by death. Generally those who think this way do not acknowledge that even if this were based on any kind of reality, one's chances of having a companion until death are about only 50 percent to begin with. It is perhaps not surprising that it is women who live out the antithesis of this most frequently, since they tend to outlive men and their male partners by a good many years. Who is taking care of them? Where is their end of life companion?

Again in the face of actual evidence, people think that getting married will land them security. Approximately half of all marriages end in divorce. We really must ask how any semirational person could think that marriage will provide one with lifelong anything. The amount of cheating, lying, secrecy, and general deadness in supposedly monogamous relationships belies the myth of trust which people idealize.[28] Disruptions, dishonesty, and life's impredictability all weigh-in against the promise of stability offered by monogamous marriage. We are presented this slim area of life and told here we have choice, here we will finally belong to something, here we will get to feel complete, have our self-worth validated. The institutionalization of love and intimacy within the confines of monogamous marriage instead tends to require a sacrificing of the self, of a fluid exploration and expression of desire. Pressures to marry and stay that way, to bear children, to marry certain kinds of people and raise certain kinds of children all run counter to the idealization of choice and family formation by choice rather than by birth. Finally, marriage and monogamy with all their "promises" hold such appeal only due to the lack of connection, belonging, fulfillment, choice, self direction, and self-esteem possible within such a hierarchically structured social fabric fraying everywhere for its lack of heart.

Are these just holes in an otherwise worthy set of interlocking institutions? If people just believed more, were less afraid to commit, were better able to keep their promises could the ideal be restored? This view is what the crackdown on the poor, on single motherhood, and what the protection of marriage are expressing. The institutions remain venerable but the flesh is weak, the social weave is unraveling. We need to reaffirm the promises of the practices, discipline the flesh, and strengthen the fragile bonds of human relations. In its own way, identifying the failure of the ideology to fulfill its promises, the dominant view is to bolster the institution. In response, GLBT organizations tend to say it is not us queers who are causing this weakening in the institutions. In fact, we so believe the promise we want to be allowed into its halls. Another view is that these "failures" are not to be remedied . . . not because we have gone too far astray in our capacity for ethical living, but because the problems are inherent in the institutions themselves.

In *The Human Condition*, Hannah Arendt talks about unpredictability and the power of promises. Since the story of Abraham and the concept of the Covenant, in Western legal tradition "promises" in the form of contracts are a common public form of achieving stabilization. In Arendt's view, promises are a human response to the unpredictability and unreliability of the human condition. We cannot "guarantee today who [we] will be tomorrow" (244). We cannot "foretell . . . the consequences" of our actions. We cannot "rely upon," or have "complete faith in" ourselves. Promises function as an alternative to domination in an attempt to cope with this existential condition. They do not solve the anxiety and the problems that arise in consequence there of, but function as "a medium . . . into which certain islands of predicatability are thrown and in which certain guideposts of reliability are erected." To Arendt there is great power in people coming together and acting in concert. But this power "disappears" when they are no longer present together. Promises, and contracts as an example, step in to hold together what would otherwise be lost when not being lived in the present. Arendt discusses these favorably as public modes of self-determination as opposed to being subject to tyranny. They work, in her schema, to the extent that "they are not applied to action from the outside, from some supposedly higher faculty or from experiences outside action's own reach." In her writing, there is a tension regarding the qualities of these forms of promises. On the one hand there is the stability offered by promises, their capacity to take us out of the unending cycles of nature that would not allow human society to build on itself. On the other hand, as promises take us out of the cycles of becoming, we also truly need new beginnings to offer us the possibilities of the very same characteristics just named—the capacity to move in history.

So what is a promise to another really? How can one presume to "commit to" a future arrangement? Does any of this make any sense? Generally promises appear to provide us with some grounding, trust, that people seem to need to build their capacity for intimacy and getting on with their lives. Yet promises (as in the phrase "promises, promises") are a deflection from action, from living, and from being in the moment. This is certainly so in the concept of "committing to some future action"—as the "vow of marriage"—and making a commitment to be monogamous are usually understood. The promise does not make the action happen. Lives in which we are capable of listening to and caring for ourselves, being honest about our desires and expectations can make actions happen, because they are actions themselves. Lives lived in dignity, lives lived in relation, and lives spent attempting mutuality at least make possible the qualities of intimacy most people seem to be searching for in the extraction of so many promises. The promise itself cannot make the desired intimacy occur. It takes lives, lived in the present and honesty with the self in relation that create opportunities for connection.

Arendt writes "the moment promises lose their character as isolated islands of certainty in an ocean of uncertainty, that is, when this faculty is misused to cover the whole ground of the future and to map out a path secured in all directions, they lose their binding power and the whole enterprise becomes self-defeating" (244). I am arguing that marriage and monogamy as institutions calcify the dynamics of relation. They become ideologically co-produced as the congealed answer to riding the waves of the torrid oceans of life. Under threats of poverty and war, hurricanes and cancer, incest and domestic violence, self-doubt and work as drudgery, capitalism capitalizes on intimate fears of the isolation, loss, and insecurity it taps into, necessitates, and simultaneously creates to offer back a promise of intimacy. Let us explore this a bit further.

Martin Buber views all life as relation and understands this universal experience as having two expressions, I-Thou relations and I-It relations. I-Thou relations come by way of grace, they cannot be planned or controlled. As in my reference to Buber above in the comment on anony-

mous sex, they exist only in the present, the future an abstraction which
cannot be claimed as a truth but instead which needs to be lived. I-Thou
relations can only come to be in a context of change and movement,
making direct relation possible as it also makes it generally fleeting.
I-Thou relations cannot be adjudicated, regulated, or even just exist; they
must be lived and re-lived in spontaneity. Efforts to institutionalize the
creative powers of I-Thou relationships necessarily, then, create I-It relationships. Work to systematize or guarantee the expressive richness of
I-Thou relations creates relations of any I to an It instead of to a Thou.

Staudenmaier's discussion of compulsory monogamy and Lorde's critique of the suppression of the erotic share a concern for the *institutionalism*
of I-It relations as Buber would call them. (This does not mean Buber is
simply "against" all *institutions*.) In these two forms, intimacy and relation
are framed in such a way that I-Thou relations are barely possible. Both
Staudenmaier and Lorde yearn for the freedom of an I in the primary word
combination I-Thou. They seek possibilities for becoming bound up in
relation in the manner of Buber's articulation of the I-Thou. They do not
want to have to turn away in order to accept an ideological mythic vision
in the place of knowledge and relation. The myth of monogamous marriage is that of sameness (in this sense also as with the "as if" adoptive
family), of expecting your own reflection in the mirror of the other. For
Buber this characterizes the I-It, the objectification and commodification of
the other in expecting deep relation through replicating the self in our idea
of our mate. But this is the ideal of monogamous marriage.

In *I and Thou*, Buber writes: "Just as prayer is not in time but time
in prayer, sacrifice not in space but space in sacrifice, and to reverse the
relation is to abolish the reality, so with the man to whom I say *Thou*. I
do not meet with him at some time and place or other. I can set him in
a particular time and place; I must continually do it; but I only set a *He*
or a *She*, that is an *It*, no longer my *Thou*" (9). In the expectations and
promises of monogamous marriage the present is lost, and relation becomes an object with a pretense to the future as real. For Buber this is
a stultifying of the present. It is not the aliveness promised by the ideological vision, but instead "cessation, suspension, a breaking off and cutting clear and hardening, absence of relation and of present being" (13).
Presented as a retreat from the world, the private realm of monogamous
marriage is a deeper form of the deadening we undergo in the public
modes of economic and political relations.

Buber may not have directly discussed these institutions and I cannot presume he would agree with my critique here, but I do find his
description fitting when addressing a sphere of ideas "in which [man]
finds refuge and repose from the oncome of nothingness. On the thresh-

old he lays aside his inauspicious everyday dress, wraps himself in pure linen, and regales himself with the spectacle of primal being, or of necessary being; but his life has no part in it" (13). Buber acknowledges that "To proclaim his ways may even fill him with well being," but it has "nothing in common with a living mankind where Thou may truly be spoken" (13). Resonating with what I am suggesting dies in the idealized promise necessary to perpetuate the institution of monogamous marriage, Buber reminds us that "the noblest fiction is a fetish, the loftiest fictitious sentiment is depraved" (13).

Of all the great aspects of romantic love, supposedly sanctified and made pure in monogamous marriage, invoking Buber I would challenge them as usually fictions. A lived out pretense to unconditional and everlasting love is a relation of an I to an It. The hyperbole of a love that is blind is more than hyperbole, it is a form of compartmentalism and not being direct. The notion of stability and security most strive for by entering into these institutions is more a dwindling of the life force of a love that exists only as long as it "meets me through grace."[29] In the legislating, in the presumption of agency and will in our society in which we plan through stopping time and turning living into yet another object, we have already lost what the idealized promise seems to offer.

To bring this discussion back into a Marxist framework, we return to the concept of alienation. Situated as a balm for the alienation-degradation, loss of self, of freedom, and of the space to carry out a unique life style—inherent in the nondemocratic relations publically with respect to both politics and economics is the privacy of the home and constitutive of "private" institutions of monogamy and marriage. Bourgeois ideology suggests that these provide refuge from the atomistic and antagonistic modes of relation in public. These private institutions are held out as counter to, or even as anti-, spaces. However, if we look to the relations inherent within them, rather than functioning as counters to alienation (and oppression and even violence) the institutions of the so called private realm are created with the same ideological assumptions and power dynamics of all modes of bourgeois society. Monogamy and marriage resemble and manifest, rather than invert, the public institutions. Most people are rarely able to make decisions, or are not involved in the decision making, which concern our own lives, the lives of those for whom we directly care, and our vision of relations with our neighbors around the nation and the globe. Our bosses and bureaucrats, media moguls and elected officials make decisions on our behalf. The private is promised as a place where we can be engaged in decision making. Even were this true, it is not a real antidote to the nondemocratic relations we suffer elsewhere. However, politics and economics, the complex relations within families and among generations in ways constituted for most people in an array of communities under capitalism guarantees that we are no more likely to find (or recognize) the personal space and abilities to exercise our capacities to explore our needs and aspirations—either on our own OR in relation.

In his master work on alienation, Bertell Ollman makes the analogy "in capitalism, the state is an abstraction in political life on the same plane that value is in economic life; the one is the abstract product of alienated political activity, just as the other is the abstract product of alienated productive activity" (1971, 216). I would like to push this analogy further. One could say that monogamy is the abstract product of alienated sexual/emotional desire, experience, and activity. Marriage is the abstract product of sexualized kin experiences. These institutions require alienated forms of relation and loss of self in terms of our sexuality and needs for intimacy. As Ollman clarifies, "'patriotism' best expresses the detached impersonal kind of belonging that is associated with the state" (217–218). In patriotism, the state is binding individuals to the social whole in links of alienated relation to an abstraction—the illusory community of the state. This same phenomenon, patriotism, is experienced by ordinary folk as a full, deep feeling of a real bond to fellow citizens and the social whole. My argument is that marriage works similarly for many people not only having real ties (if they are lucky or creative, to real people in the "union" or family unit more broadly), but also for most people in alienated form (regarding what is experienced as real in the IDEA of marriage and for many "family"). Marriage and monogamy promise deep and lasting ties, and human fulfillment in relation. Yet, as structured, both marriage and monogamy require varied and complex alienated forms of relation, of hypocrisy, of narrowed and disciplined desire, of denying the self, and of abstraction in the place of human connection.

Parting Thoughts

Marriage takes on a life of its own. Instead of remaining committed to the ideals and lofty aims of love for another and care for one's highest self, which many enter into the institution with the best of intentions, an alienated form of "Shalom Bayit/peace in the family," "for the best interests of the children," sacrificing for the family unit come to be the private form of the general interest not really serving the individuals involved (Ollman, 1971: 220–222).

This we can see in all the times we hear people say that they want to be in a relationship and are looking for someone that they can fit into their preconceived notion of the other with whom they can live out their fantasy of relation. Or statements people commonly make such as "I'm ready/want/need to have a family," thus trying to fit their children—if they are lucky or rich enough—into their cookie-cutter idea. It is usually when people start pining for children that they "need" to find a spouse as the piece of the puzzle that they think gets them to the kids/family they want. As a stereotype, this may seem common to heterosexual women, though it is also as common for many queers and for straight men. The statistic that older widowers remarry within a year of their wife's death is illustrative of this point. The phenomenon may suggest that "marriage just works for them" and does not at all imply that their bond to the first—or even second, and so forth—wife is not honest. It may also at the same time suggest that marriage as an idea expressed in the institution seems to work for them—regardless of the particular women in the picture. The adult children of the first marriage are likely to see this in a veiled form of its critical perspective (1) more so than they may have been able to see it in their father's marriage to their own mother, (2) though not realizing the implications of their pained response to what they call their father's replacement as a critique of the institution more broadly. Both of these are likely to be the case because the children of the father's first marriage have the benefit of feeling their mother's union with the father to have been the "real" one. The discourse of reality or what seems natural to them obfuscating the ideological construction of marriage in general. The second marriage is the deutero, the first one was the true one.

Although I am resisting "concluding" (too linear, like the expectations of the linear progress expected in the ideologies and institutions of marriage and monogamy themselves), I can make a few parting observations. Lest I leave readers with the impression that there is an easy answer once we have critiqued marriage and monogamy as alienating, and setting us up inherently for I-It relations. To offer such a cast . . . (I could say castrating but I won't) castigating exposure of these institutions which promise I-Thou relations, but fail I would not want to pose as someone who presumes that a simple alternative of I-Thou's exist.

It ought to be pointed out here that people who act in seemingly countercultural ways may not necessarily be countering the norms of marriage and monogamy. The pressures of the ideologies involved (like some Catholics who leave the Church yet remain forever oppressed by its teachings) just flipping the terms, not transforming them. Those who divorce often, avoid marriage or other intimacies, sleep around (either against their promises of monogamy or without forming any supposedly monogamous attachments), or create nonmarital intimacies in a manner as marriage (as many straight couples have done and certainly as queers are increasingly doing) may just as likely be keeping the presumptions of marriage and monogamy intact, their actions not necessarily radical. To be in flight from the oppressive aspects of marriage and monogamy may not yield revolutionary life paths and/or unions, just other versions of fraught and stuck lives.

As Kathy Ferguson has pointed out, the networks of care required to make possible the thinking and practices of revolutionary work also create their own forms of dependency and impositions on autonomy. This is not only so in the politically accepted Liberal versions where mythic forms of separative individualism cast any relations at all as a breach in one's autonomous life path and ensconce one in the tangle of dependence. Of course, the elite men (and slowly over time some others) who appear to fulfill this mythic form are engaged in endless webs of relation and dependent on innumerable others (to cook their food, clean their clothes and other possessions, care for their children, plan their dinner parties, etc). Ferguson's insight also comes from her study of the life and work of incredible anarchist women, particularly Emma Goldman, who explicitly construct their lives to make their politics. In anarchist and various other radical modes of praxis, autonomy is not separative but itself relational, recognizing and attending to the multilayered weave of dependencies as assisting each one of us in our individual experiments with freedom. In this way of understanding the self, we are constituted as unique through each peculiar navigation within shifting sets of relations (both current and historical). As Marso (2003) on Goldman points out, even here, radical work and the work of living out radical lives requires relationships that cannot, at least under capitalism and probably under most circumstances, avoid some struggle with enmeshment in which one loses one's self or dependence that brings also loss of self-reliance and a distracted process of developing our unique capacities. Even for radicals, and in radical theories of relation, there may remain tensions between freedom, mutuality, reciprocity, dependency, and loss of self.[30] Thus, my critique of the shortcomings of the ideologies and institutions of marriage and monogamy is not meant to suggest that we can simply banish the challenges of relationship by banning these specific institutions in a world currently constituted.

It is my argument here that society sets us up systematically through our ideology and institutions to be in I-It relations. A central medium through which it does so is by posing those institutions as fulfilling aspirations for I-Thou relations.

In *I and Thou* Martin Buber writes: "I can neither experience nor describe the form which meets me, but only body it forth. And yet I behold it, splendid in the radiance of what confronts me, clearer than all the clearness of the world which is experienced. I do not behold it as a thing among 'inner' things nor as an image of my 'fancy,' but as that which exists in the present. If test is made of its objectivity the form is certainly not 'there.' Yet what is actually so much present as it is? And the relation in which I stand to it is real, for it affects me, as I affect it" (10). This is not something we can count on.

I know too many people are being denied their rights. But we have seen and hopefully learned from the state-centered strategy time and again in the history of social change movements: we cannot simply produce what we want through the courts and legislation. In institutionalized form it is surely dead. The mark is missed. We quest, but follow a path back to our own loneliness. It is not necessarily the quest I call into question here. It is not necessarily the relations we quest for that I call into question here. It is more their illusory form that troubles me. The ways in which we bound ourselves up by questing in alienated forms to the abstractions of our times.

Epilogue

Justice and La Vida Jew . . . in Technicolor Queer

The pounding of the jackhammer next door has continued on and off for years now. The solidity of New York bedrock and the tenacity of local organizers has drawn out the process of clearing away that sweet patch of wooded hill on the lot adjacent to our apartment. Today, I notice the workmen measuring, prepping a preliminary layout for a foundation.

I'm coming to think that being flamboyant is possibly a usual experience for many families. Being with kids, their fabulous selves and their crazy energy, just makes one *so* noticeable. More, Paris and Toni, each in her own way, loves being a diva. The drama queen persona appears to come easily to them as well.

My daughters are growing, thank goodness. It's getting harder to picture that toddler incarnation of Paris looking in the mirror. She's become a fast runner, a graceful dancer, and a caring friend. Toni is now old enough that she argues with the ferocity of an old Jewish Marxist, though she's still young enough that we often can't decipher what she's saying exactly. She's got the body language and attitude down. We hope that one day such aggressive intensity is backed with love and pursues justice. Each day is a gift. However cranky the kids may get, however exhausted Dawn and I may be as workers and parents, weary as citizens and strung out as partners, it is helpful to remember that each day Paris and Toni make it through safely is a blessing. When the day ends and the children are somewhat clean under all that grime, basically fed, with some semblance of ego intact, have experienced joy, laughter, comfort, and love, it is a beautiful thing.

The kids have completed their universal pre-K (one of the treats of living in New York City as New Hampshire does not even offer kindergarten). The girls' pre-K was an Amalgamated labor co-op, previously also part of the Workman's Circle (a Jewish socialist organization). The Amalgamated Nursery School is still going strong—though it has not been a Workman's Circle project for many years—and is part of a highly developed coop system and set of values that keep this neighborhood in tact. We finally found a decent enough public school for K-5th grades. There's little money for supplies or programming. Phys-ed is a chaotic romp within a barricaded Bronx city block. Still, we feel lucky.

In contrast to Paris' two-year-old discovery of the self-identification "Paris is a Jewish Girl," by now the girls realize that not everyone is Jewish. In fact, although we moved back to New York City in large part to be within a broader and more diverse Jewish community, most people the girls encounter in their daily lives are not Jewish. Living in a racially, economically, and culturally diverse neighborhood within a Christian country means that by ages three and four, we had met the Christmas challenge.

In our neighborhood and with their schools and activities, the girls have met a few other Jewish children—mostly Euro-heritage but actually of all and mixed races. The majority of their daily classmates are nonwhite and non-Jewish. In their day care and public school settings, they have been the only Jew where there have been either no or a few white non-Jewish children. Their schools have made attempts to celebrate Kwanza, Hanukkah, and other non-Christian holidays. But the lure of Christmas always wins out. Toni can be heard humming "Jingle Bells" to herself any time of year. When we introduced the girls to the fact that some people are Christians and that is why they celebrate Christmas, they became fairly obsessed and conducted interviews at the slightest hint of Christmas decor. A visit with Jewish friends in New Hampshire one spring, who had a decorated ball reminiscent of a Christmas ornament, produced the familiar question: "Are you Christian?" Mostly people are somewhat perplexed. The Jews don't know where the question comes from. The Christians aren't used to being named Christian, like whites tend not to think of themselves when "race" is discussed.

Even with the Christmas challenge, we find Jewish life different here in New York in a way that works better for our family over all. Yes, it is certainly far from our perfect Jewish multiracial, queer/queer friendly, spiritually inclined, feminist and general political activist utopia. But still: more options, more diversity, more Jewishly situated political work to be a part of, more Jewish cultural events and creative expression, more synagogues/*havurot*/*minyanim* to share. Sheer numbers and the flavor of New York make a big difference, even though there is much to be said for the wonderful, close-knit, and necessarily intentional Jewish communities in rural settings such as we had in the seacoast area of New Hampshire and Maine.

Being in New York also gave us the opportunity to continue with the legal aspects of our adoption process. New York is one of a handful of states that allows for "second-parent same-sex" adoption—meaning two parents of the same sex may adopt children together. The girls have been issued yet more iterations of their "certificates of live birth." The narrative of the legal fiction takes a new turn with each one. One state named one of us the legal father. An interesting gender identity. For a brief period we were actually "co-parents." Another state had deleted the automated slots for "mother" and "father" on the standard-issue birth certificate and hand wrote in "co-parent" and "co-parent." Unfortunately, they spelled my name wrong on that document so we had to have them reissue. The new birth certificate, though, came back to us with the spelling correct but the official "mother" and "father" slots reinstated. I had been concerned that the misspell might cause us trouble in a bureau-cratic bind (recall that a mere ampersand once had lawyers call my par-entage into question). The handwritten sections might have also, but we were just delighted to be "co-parents." And we didn't know that "fixing" the misspell would mean other "fixings" and we would lose our "co-parent" status. Now we're back to being two generally identified women who are the legal mother and father of these two wonderful girls. Politi-cally I find all this fascinating, to say the least. It is also my life, so living it is a little more complicated.

Whatever the changes in our legal status as parents to the children and partners to each other, we still need to carry with us copies of all our legal documents when we travel. Can't risk being denied access in the event of an emergency, being held in detention for kidnapping, and the myriad delays and annoyances that inevitably arise. There are many people who may see four humans but refuse to see the family before them. When some Black women realize we're a family, they find it perfectly normal to chastise us for: a crooked part of the hair, the shades of the girls' clothes (I don't bother to explain: hand-me-downs are like family, you take what you get), a potential *future* lapse in lotioning elbows and knees. When white folks decide that the kids are sisters, our most frequently asked question is: Are they twins? Paris has always been at least a head taller than Toni. People hold deep and largely unconscious ideas about what a family looks like. We know this in part from those on the street who stop our children for fear that they are lost, not recognizing that the adults standing right next to them are their parents.[1] There are also the new travel laws, requiring single adults to provide proof that the other parent is cognizant, and approves, of the travel (for getting passports or during international travel). We were told by a customs agent that these laws were designed to protect mothers, as renegade fathers were whisking their kids off to places such as Mexico to arrange legal custody against the mothers' wishes. Single parents who travel with their kids are presumed guilty until proven innocent. We happen to be two parents. But when a customs agent does not see a man in the picture, we are required to demonstrate proof of our legal bonds. Over and over we must actively legitimate this family without a father space. Presumed guilty. What we need to prove, really, and if we will ever succeed, continue to elude me.

And as the girls grow, and our geographical coordinates shift, so do our racial identities—or our "racial assignments" as Karen Brodkin phrases it. Many will look at me and for the moment of our interaction my whiteness will not be a question. Many will look at each of my daughters, and for that moment presume their Blackness without hesitation. Yet this is not and will not always be so. Some of the kids' peers appear to need to work harder than others, trying to make sense of our color differences or the girls' two mommies. Especially as educated parents, our nonBlackness occasionally effects the associations of "Blackness" people would have otherwise likely made with Toni and Paris. Time will tell how well we light-skinned moms will have prepared them to navigate their brown-skinned selves in a country filled with much ignorance and too much race hatred. At the same time, as they grow I wonder who will ostracize them for not being Black enough? In what contexts? In what ways will it matter . . . to them, to us, to others any of us may care about?

I've said earlier in this text that when the kids were infants and toddlers in nothern New England people generally did not question my maternal tie to them—meaning they assumed a bio-tie. When we came to New York, my whiteness became more pronounced. But as the girls grow a bit, Dawn has noticed more changes. She agrees that when I'm on my own or with her in New York City, people generally do presume me as white/Anglo. (The clerk in a store will almost always switch from speaking in Spanish to the customer before me, to English when it's my turn at the counter.) When I'm with the kids, she finds that people often treat me differently racially; they must presume I'm mixed race and that the kids are my bio-kids. I see what she means. She can literally be standing *with* the kids and some figure on the urban landscape look right past her concerned about the children. I walk up and get the question: "Are they yours?" This is not the time for a dissertation on the fact that the kids are their own persons, they are not "mine," and so forth. (The girls love the gay acappella group The Flirtations' version of Khalil Gibran's "Your Children are not your children." . . . as early as four and five when

they learned it, we wondered if they were trying to tell us something!)
This is the time to say "yes," casually, and wave a protective hand around
their bodies and general "aura" space. Folks still exhibit some anxiety, a
lack of assuredness, with me but you can also see, palpably, the person's
relief at recognizing an adult who may have a bond even with Dawn
physically right there. Other times I feel like Dawn does anyway. People
not seeing me, and/or not seeing me in relation to the girls.

Still, time passes and usually we are just us. Two moms, two kids,
the world mapped on our faces and history marching on in our varying
skin shades. Often enough, it's clear that either of us adults are the ones
to be shushed, scolded, or the object of *kvelling*: for letting the kids jump
on this, run around that, for being their beautiful selves. Some folks can
see family whatever the package. Our job is to do the best we can with
our love and political consciousness of the moment, to raise these kids
aware of and hopefully able to move in such a world while we help them
be/become as grounded as any parent might hope their kids can be. Our
situation calls upon us to grow these kids up with a capacity for self-
definition, self-love, love for others, a deep appreciation for intimate bonds
of various stripes. Knowing they have an address, as Isaac Bashevis Singer
puts it, even as at that address there are many doorbells. Growing with
a capacity to journey in life with a love for and of the world, to paraphrase
Hannah Arendt.

The world will sometimes work with us in these efforts, sometimes
against us, often both at once. This time it's not to sell bread. No yummy
Levy's rye at stake. In recent years, there were two public service campaigns to raise awareness of anti-Jewish hatred. One was spearheaded by
Russell Simmons (hip-hop music star and founder of Def Jam Records),
and Rabbi Marc Schneier (founder of a New York-based organization
devoted to improving "Black-Jewish" relations called the Foundation for
Ethnic Understanding). The 2005 "I am a Jew" campaign invited various
internationally famous non-Jewish celebrities to make public service clips,
translated into various European languages for the international MTV/
Entertainment Tonight set to help curb the rise of anti-Semitism particularly in Europe. "I am a Jew" came on the heels of a similar 2004 campaign run by the U.S. Jewish organization, the Anti-Defamation League.

ADL's brainchild was "Anti-Semitism Is Anti-Me." With a poster
series of trendy snapshots of the well-known Lutheran minister Reverand
Kathleen Rusnak (with collar), an Asian-presenting young boy, and
supermodel Naomi Campbell with the written message "Anti-Semitism Is
Anti-Me." Here the intention was a great solidarity-like link that anti-
Semitism is an attack on other groups, especially other minorities, as
well.[2] I remember seeing the ads on the sides of telephone booths around

Manhattan and thinking all at once, "What's that about? Interesting. Cool. How Levy's can you get? Will the iconic gorgeous Black woman in the future ever be presumed to be Jewish?" I recall thinking to myself: "what an age that there is an iconic gorgeous Black woman," and, simultaneously, "Oy, is this the only way Black will be beautiful?" But that's me. Recall Toni Eisendorf as a youngster reading Levy's ads: They *opened* a universe for her. What could it mean for Toni and Paris to see Naomi Campbell on a "Jewish" poster?

I wanted to write a book which drew on Jewish life in order to develop mutual construction identity theory. I wanted to be able to talk about politically charged aspects of our identities such as race, class, ethnicity, nationality, gender, sexuality as a Jew. To include Jewing within the fabulous work folks have been doing race-ing class, gender, and sexuality. To Jew the class analysis of race, gender, sexuality. To sex Jewishness in its raced, gendered, and classed manifestations. To engender different constructions of Jews as they are classed, and raced, and sexed. To show how studying Jews will be invaluable if one wants to explore how race and class, gender and sexuality are continually co-created. To clarify that you need to understand at least a little bit about the simultaneous processes of racing, classing, sexing, and gendering if you are interested in examining things/people Jewish. To share my view that awareness of *la vida Jew* is essential in efforts to confront injustice in its many forms. I am a philosopher, and find the best way to engage the philosophical questions of concern to me is to take them up in lived context. These days, raising two young children in a queer, multiracial Jewish family formed through adoption . . . family-related challenges take up much of my lived context.

Same-sex marriage, queer parenting, single-headed households, adoption, multiracial families, surrogacy and gamete transfer, abortion, contraception, sterilization, teen pregnancy. With countless poor people, full-time jobs that don't sustain workers, the child care crisis, the proliferation of guns, ongoing street crime, through-the-roof corporate crime, wars, tsunamis, hurricanes in the U.S. South, eco-devastation, sexual violence, and affirmative action programs unraveling, you'd think people might have other things to work on. But debates on "the family" may be found daily in the popular press, with new books published every season. Within the American Jewish community "the family" tops the list amongst communal concerns. Yet, almost no scholarly work on the Jewish politics within these debates exists. Further, the Jewish communal conversation is taking place *along side* the larger U.S. one, not generally *within* it. We need to begin to build a bridge between the two sets of conversations, especially given the dearth of Jewishly identified Jewish voices within the larger ones. As people of color, gays and lesbians, queers and transfolk, bi and multisexuals, feminists, liberals, conservatives, and people from a variety of positions in the United States have been presenting differing views, Jewish perspectives need to be heard. To enter this conversation with the insights of Jewish experience, Jews must be able to speak from the diversity of Jewish life that directly relates to these communities and the general legislative arena. I hope that with this work I have been able to offer some contribution.

People say, "just because you're paranoid, doesn't mean someone isn't after you." Just because the right is obsessed with "family" issues does not mean that there aren't significant links between the family debates and other social justice issues. Mainly, because the trope of justice (or lack thereof) is part of the family debates as it is part of everything. Mainly, because within an array of pressing social justice issues, seeing how these issues play out on the stage of the family drama is crucial to challenging them on that stage and in conjunction with the challenges we launch in other arenas of our public and private lives.

Notes

Chapter 1: Whitens Whites, Keeps Colors Bright

1. This is not the common interpretation of the boundedness of identity. See Bickford, "Anti-Anti-Identity Politics," 1997.

2. See Brettschneider, *Democratic Theorizing From the Margins*, 2002 for an extended discussion on my views here, and Brettschneider, *Race, Gender, and Class*, 1999 for an encapsulated version in a Jewish context.

3. See Walker, *Black, White, and Jewish*, 2001; Azoulay, *Black, Jewish, and Interracial*, 1997; Blustain, "Are You Black or Are You Jewish?, 1996; Krakauer, "Casting Miss Saigon's Baby," 1991; Patton, *Birth Marks*, 2000; McKinley, *The Book of Sarahs*, 2002; Chau, "More than Chicken Chow Mein," 2004; Radin, "Better Off Than You Would Have Been," 2004; Ross, *Oreo*, 1974; Propp et al., for writing by some who have been through this before us as the kids noted here. There are also many examples of those who grow up to explore this phenomenon in the arts. For example, in 2005 Rain Pryor, Richard Pryor's daughter, took her one woman show "Fried Chicken and Latkes" about being Black and Jewish on tour.

4. This point is palpable in Hart's *The Identity of Mixed Race* (2001) study on Black Jews in the United States. Her work revealed that participants felt the need to educate people regarding African-American and Jewish diversity in order, in part, "to begin to establish a place for Black Jews that would be recognized by society." This was so because the issues of identity-based ambiguity Hart found among participants stemmed from their experience of people's lack of information of the very existence of Black Jews (99). See also Conaway, "Journey to the Promised Land," 2004; Herron, "Pastel Meetings," 2003; Gray, *My Sister, the Jew*, 2001; Yolanda Shoshanna, "Am I My Sister's Keeper?," 2004.

5. Although we carry nine books by Julius Lester, we do not carry his *Lovesong: Becoming a Jew* 1988. Regarding "celebrity" or well known Black Jews, for example, we also carry a number of holdings including films, audio recordings, and books by and about Sammy Davis, Jr. (i.e., 1965), Lani Guinier, or Walter Mosley though they appear in no Jewishly related searches.

6. Berger notes that as late as 1942 there was still a functioning Black Jewish community in St. Thomas (1978, 12).

7. Hatzaad Harishon was an organization to help with the problematic reaction of the mainstream U.S. Jewish community to Black Jews and growing congregations of Hebrew Israelites (Berger 1978, chap. 15: 166–171). Of interest

147

to archivists and others, the short-lived group published its own newsletter. The Synagogue Council of America also made an effort to deal with the disenfranchisement of, and bias against, Black Jews with regard to the larger Jewish community in the United States. In 1970, the organization created a Committee on Black Jews, which also organized a well-attended conference in the spring of 1973 (Berger 1978, 180–182).

8. Chireau, Yvonne and Nathaniel Deutsch, eds., *Black Zion*, 2000.

9. We carry Tudor Parfitt's work (the 1993, not the 1987). As yet another aspect of the racial politics discussed here, our library carries two works by Howard Brodtz, one on African-American history and social conditions and one on racial issues in South Africa. We do not carry Brodtz's 1964 work on Black Jews in the United States. See also Boykin , *Black Jews*, 1982; Ben-Jochannan, *We the Black Jews*, 1993, and *Our Black Seminarians*, 1998; Freedberg, *Brother Love*, 1994; Gelman, *Adat Beyt Moshe, the Colored House of Moses*, 1967–1971; Landing, *Black Judaism*, 2001; Lounds, *Israel's Black Jews*, 1981; Berger, *Black Jews in America*, 1978; Gerber, *The Heritage Seekers*, 1977; Wynia, *The Church of God and Saints of Christ*, 1994; and Kinda, *La Bagola*, 1930. For works on Jews in Africa see for example: Onolemhemhen and Gessesse, *The Black Jews of Ethiopia*, 1998; Parfitt, *The Thirteenth Gate*, 1987, and *Journey to the Vanished City*, 1993.

10. We also carry Herron, *Nappy Hair* (1997), who self identifies as Black and Jewish . . . and how many others who are not recognized/erased?

11. Azouley, *A Jewishness After* (2001) notes this problematic as well.

12. A sampling of the large body of literature on Black-Jewish relations may be found in: Adams and Bracey, eds., *Strangers and Neighbors*, 1999; Weisbord and Stein, *Bittersweet Encounter*, 1970; West and Salzman, *Struggles in the Promised Land*, 1997; Salzman, ed., *Bridges and Boundaries*, 1992; Rogin, *Black Face, White Noise*, 1996; Pogrebin, *Deborah, Golda and Me* (1991), ch. 14: 275–311; Newton, *Facing Black and Jew*, 1999; Melnick, *A Right to Sing the Blues*, 1999, and *Black-Jewish Relations on Trial*, 2000; Lerner and West, *Jews and Blacks*, 1995, and *Jews & Blacks*, 1996; Kaufman, *Broken Alliance*, 1988; Harris and Swanson, *Black-Jewish Relations in New York*, 1970; Friedman, *What Went Wrong?*, 1995; Budick, *Blacks and Jews in Literary Conversation*, 1998; Berman, ed., *Blacks and Jews*, 1994.

13. The essays in the special *Identities* issues on Jews (Goluboff, ed. 2001) discuss, at least from within the academic discipline of anthropology, how liberal Jewish scholarship helped construct this cluster of identity constellations regarding "Blacks" and "Jews" as distinct categories.

14. See for example Funderberg, *Black, White, Other*, 1994; Patton, *Birth Marks*, 2000; Zack, *Race and Mixed Race*, 1993; Korgen, *From Black to Biracial*, 1998; Root, *The Multiracial Experience*, 1996. This pattern is replayed in slight variation in works such as McKinley, *The Book of Sarahs*, 2002; Lazzare, *Beyond the Whiteness of Whiteness*, 1996; McBride, *The Color of Water*, 1996; and Rothman, *Weaving a Family*, 2005 where the racial dichotomy within the family is noted within the bi-polar Black-White system of signs and yet the "white" mothers in these texts are Jewish. The richness of, for example, James McBride's identity is lost in this ambiguity in that he both differentiates himself from "whites" at the same time notes that in his experience Jews are not exactly the same as white folk.

The "Jewishness" and/or not simplistically blackness then of the Black children often remains underexamined. See also Jones, *Bulletproof Diva*, 1994. On the other hand, in a study of multiracial Black Jews specifically, meaning where the Jewishness of the participants was not a by-product but a subject of inquiry, Hart, *The Identity of Mixed Race*, 2001 describes, "Most participants with one White parent collapsed their Jewish and White identities together. They saw their White and Jewish identities as blended, and spoke primarily of being Jewish. Similarly those participants of mixed Black and White heritage spoke largely of feeling Black. White identity was rarely discussed" (91). Note to readers: not all the participants were Jewish through their "white" parent, some were African-heritage on both sides or if mixed were Jewish through their African-heritage parents.

15. For more information, see the work of Stars of David, the Multiracial Jewish Network, the special focus issue in adoption of *Lilith* (Schnur, ed., 1998), and Krakauer, "Casting Miss Saigon's Baby," 1991.

16. I refer here to Leslea Newman's *Heather Has Two Mommies* (2000). Not only did the book sell well, the phrasing of the title itself was taken up in popular language. Interestingly enough, Newman is also Jewish and much of her other work is explicitly on Jewish themes though these works did not become as famous as the white/race-culture "neutral" story in *Heather*.

17. Mayer, Kosman, and Keysar, *The American Jewish Identity Survey*, 2002, 20–25 report that there are one hundred seventy thousand people in the United States who are not of Jewish parentage but of Jewish Religion (their method of identifying "converts" or "Jews by Choice"). Kosman, Mayer, and Keysar, *American Religions Identification Survey*, 2001, 38 estimate that 8 percent of U.S. Jews are not defined as "white" (in the language of the report: 92 percent "White," 1 percent "Black," 1 percent "Asian," 5 percent Hispanic," 1 percent "Other"). In another counting, Tobin, Tobin, and Rubin, "The Growth and Vitality of Jewish Peoplehood," 2005 estimate that there are approximately four hundred thousand Jews of color in the United States, such as Asian/Latina/African-American Jews. This accounts for approximately 7 percent of the Jewish community in the United States. This figure is not meant to indicate the 1.7 million people of color in the United States who also have a familial or ethnic connection to Judaism, or an ancestral connection but may not identify "Jewish" as their primary religious/ethnic affiliation. Further, the figure four hundred thousand does not include the at least 8 percent of U.S. Jews currently identified as Sephardi (a much lower percentage than might otherwise be noted as the data is not easily gathered, and many people are not aware of, or do not use, this term to self-identify). The figure also does not include those Jews identified as Mizrachi in the United States amounting to approximately one hundred thousand people. In addition, there are currently approximately one hundred thousand Jews in the United States who have migrated from Latin America not included in the above. Thus, the studies estimate that at least 20 percent of the Jewish community in the United States today is nonwhite/non-Ashkenazi.

18. There have been many playful/serious attempts to reinterpret the meaning of W. E. B. Du Bois' notion of the color line as it has played itself out in U.S. politics. Of relevance for this study, see for example, Dalmage, *Tripping on the Color Line*, 2000.

19. The "one-drop rule" historically refers to a racist system of human classification whereby those with the power to (whose act of naming themselves created and institutionalized their power to) call themselves white said that anyone who had ever had an ancestor who was "Black" was then essentially Black. (See, for example, Davis 1991 and Wright 1994.) This system was reinforced by the U.S. courts as recently as 1983. An important insight is found with this chapter's grounding in my family constellation and its focus on the complexity of Jewish identity. What is significant about the one-drop rule is not only that it has been applied inconsistently, that it essentializes identity and does so through recourse to the facticity of biology, but that it also has been historically understood as created by and reinforcing racism. This is due to the politics involved in why and when whites have invoked it and its usually negative consequences for those named Black as well. By contrast, many Jews (a similarity may be found among certain indigenous peoples in the United States) have used an equivalent search for a Jewish heritage as part of the resistance to the dominant powers of majority groups in their attempts to eradicate Jews. (See Azoulay 2001, and Kessel 2000.) Black Jews' quest for history exposes these multiple modes of inquiry.

20. Interesting note: our landlord is a recent immigrant, light-skinned Irish man who would now be considered "white" in U.S. racial codes, but if he had immigrated a century ago would not have been classified as "white." On the creation of whiteness and the shifting racial positioning of the Irish and other European immigrants in the United States see for example: Allen, *The Invention of the White Race*, 1994; Jacobson, *Whiteness of a Different Color*, 1998; Curtis, *Apes and Angels*, 1971; Ignatiev, *How the Irish Became White*, 1995; Knobel, *Paddy and the Republic*, 1986. On the newer area of white studies see Lipsitz, *The Possessive Investment in Whiteness*, 1998; Delgado and Stefancic eds., *Critical White Studies*, 1997; Nakayama and Martin eds., *Whiteness*, 1999; Williams, *The Constraint of Race*, 2003.

21. On class and the making of racial categories, see for example Roediger, *The Wages of Whiteness*, 1991–9; Brodkin, *How Jews Became White Folks*, 1998; and Steinberg, *The Ethnic Myth*, 2001.

22. See for example: Tevajieh, "Out of Africa," 1993; Esses, "A Common Language Between East and West," 2003; Khazzoom ed., *The Flying Camel*, 2003; Agosín, *A Cross and a Star*, 1995, *Always From Somewhere Else*, 1998, *Passion, Memory, and Identity*, 1999a, *Uncertain Travelers*, 1999b, *Taking Root*, 2002; Agosín and Horan, eds., *The House of Memory*, 1999; Agosín and Gordenstein, eds., *Miriam's Daughters*, 2001; Daniel and Johnson, *Ruby of Cochin*, 1995; Delman, *Burnt Bread and Chutney*, 2002; Stavans, *The Scroll and The Cross*, 2003; Silliman, *Jewish Portraits*, 2001; *Bridges* 1997–1998, 2001; Kaye/Kantrowitz and Klepfisz, eds., *The Tribe of Dina*, 1989.

23. There have been numerous other ethnic tensions among Jewish groups which themselves have at different historical moments taken on racialized overtones. Tensions between Iranian and different groups of Arab Jews have occasionally fallen into this paradigm. The differences between those called "white" or "black" Jews among the Bene Israel and differently among Cochin Jews of India have such a history. Relations between Eastern and Western European Jews, in

the East between Litvaks and Galitcianas, among the Gora and Kala of Bene Israel in India were at different historical moments as significant in the lives of these group of Jews as any intergroup differences one might imagine. (On tensions amongst the differing ethnic groups of India's Jews see Boykin 1982, and also Daniel and Johnson 1995.)

24. When literary scholars have done work on the creation of whiteness in England, for example, they do not always fully investigate the implications of the fact that many of the Jews in England in the nineteenth century (a crucial period in the development of these racialized classifications) were Sephardi. (See Kaufman 2001 and for an historical view see Faber 1998.) This is significant because they propose to be untangling a tangle of those, from this historical vantage point in the United States, who would be deemed as already white. Even these Jewish scholars have adapted Western Christian racial categories in these examples. In Jewish racialized terms, Ashkenazi Jews did not begin to migrate to England in large numbers until later towards the twentieth century (though for the dominant English, by the time the racialized classifications had come into use, even Eastern Europeans were considered racially distinct, darker and inferior).

25. Sandra Patton (2000) chooses the term routes, rather than roots, to explore such concepts as lineage and kinship to avoid the essentialist assumptions in the myth of biological roots, and to demonstrate that all of us have come to be where/who we are through travels/movement, not given/nature.

26. The Inquisition not only was carried out centrally in Spain, but also significantly in Portugal and Italy as well. Those that fled went back into African and Middle Eastern lands, for example, to Algeria, Lybia, and Tunisia, and particularly into lands within the Ottoman Empire such as Morocco, Kurdistan, Turkey, and Greece, including Balkan nations such Bulgaria, Yugoslavia, and Romania. "Sephardi Jews" are often said to speak Ladino, a mixture of Spanish and Hebrew. However, depending on the countries they fled to after the Inquisition, their languages also included various Arabic dialects, Greek, Latin, and Turkish, with Kurdish Jews speaking *Targum* derived from a variety of Kurdish, Persian, Turkish, Hebrew, Arabic, and Aramaic linguistic traditions. These communities cross with those that may be referred to today as Mizrachis, eastern Jews, while many Jews from the Middle East and North Africa never were in Spain at all and always had living communities in these geographical areas. Similarly, there were also non-Sephardi Jewish communities living in the Balkans since Roman Imperial times. The Inquisition also further extended to lands of Spanish and Portugese conquest in the New World, forcing many conversos, or anusim (since converso refers to someone who has converted, many prefer the term anusim, meaning the forced ones) to move north into territories that eventually came under U.S. jurisdiction many also mixing with the African-heritage and indigenous populations in these locales. (See Faber 1998; Holzberg 1987; and Miles 2005, and Ruggiero 2005 more generally.) Today numerous communities of crypto-Jews in the U.S. southwest are coming out/coming to the attention of the larger Jewish community and sometimes with great tension. (Popper 2005; Gitlitz 1996; Prinz 1977; Matza 1997; Bridges 1997–8, passim and for additional resources and research centers, Sieglitz 1991; Wise 1992; Kessel 2000; and Melammed 2002, and 2004.)

27. For examples of works on Jews and multiculturalism, see Brettschneider 1996a, 1996b, 1999, 2001, 2002, 2004; Brettschneider and Rose, eds. 2003; Kaye/Kantrowitz and Klepfisz 1989; Kaye/Kantrowitz 1992; Boyarin and Boyarin eds. 1997; Biale et al., eds. 1998; Pegueros 2004; Levine 2003; and Prager et al., 1993.

28. Figures from Tobin, Tobin, and Rubin, "The Growth and Vitality of Jewish Peoplehood," 2005 suggest that approximately 93 percent of the U.S. Jewish community is Ashkenazi. It is difficult to say exactly what this means for critical race theory, however, when white Christian-born folks like my partner Dawn as well as many other white, and Asian, African-American, Native American, Latina/os Jews, and Jews who are any combinations of this list (whether by birth, adult conversion, or childhood adoption), may be classified in U.S. racial terms in any number of ways and may also practice Ashkenazi Judaism.

29. Interestingly, Jean-Paul Sartre, neither Black nor Jewish, has written two of what are considered pivotal texts on racial politics: *Anti-Semite and Jew* (1948), and *Black Orpheus* (1963). Although the French racial formation of Jews has been very different than that in the United States, in *Black Orpheus* his rendering is consistent with the ellipses to be discussed here. Sartre writes: "A Jew, white among white men, can deny that he is a Jew, can declare himself a man among men. The Negro cannot deny that he is a Negro nor claim for himself this abstract uncolored humanity" (1963, 15). In this passage, not only has Sartre made all Jews white, but he has placed all Jews only in white-dominated cultures.

In Nella Larsen's pivotal fictional piece on passing (originally published in 1929), when the two main characters find each other again after a long absence, along with another light-skinned woman with whom they grew up, they discuss passing and what became of various old friends. Clare says of those who pass "Everything must be paid for" and then inquires about a man from the old neighborhood, Claude Jones. Larsen continues the narrative: "At that Gertrude shrieked with laughter. 'Claude Jones!' and launched into the story of how he was no longer a Negro or a Christian but had become a Jew.

"A Jew!" Clare exclaimed.

"Yes, a Jew. A black Jew, he calls himself. He won't eat ham and goes to the synagogue on Saturday. He's got a beard now as well as a moustache. You'd die laughing if you saw him. He's really too funny for words. Fred says he's crazy and I guess he is. Oh, he's a scream all right, a regular scream!" And She shrieked again (1986, 169).

Clare originally joins in the laughter, but becomes subdued when Irene protests that perhaps the man "might possibly be sincere in changing his religion" and that his transformation might not be "for gain." It is not immediately apparent why this was supposed to be so hilarious. Further, if the man calls himself a black Jew, why is it presented that he is no longer a "Negro?" He is not even presented as having attempted to pass as a "white" Jew.

30. As an interesting contrast, compare the Larsen and Sartre to a comment made by Frederick Douglass: "The Jews who are to be found in all coun-

tries, never intermarrying, are white in Europe, brown in Asia, and black in Africa." (From "The Effect of Circumstances upon the Physical Man," July 12, 1854—cited in Berger 1978, 4.) Though I assume some Jews around the globe have intermarried—or Jewish women raped—Douglas at least has a sense of world Jewry and its racial diversity. If he calls European Jews white, however, I wonder how he understands Jews, race, and power in the United States in 1854 and later? (1854 is a period before the large influx of European Jews making them the majority ethnic group within the U.S. Jewish community by the early 1900s. Douglas died in 1895, after the main wave of German-Jewish immigration, only at the very start of the larger Eastern European migration.) See also Levine's discussion, "Multiculturalism, Women's Studies," 2003.

31. Goldman, "Who Knew?," 2004 notes that when U.S. Jews took up a celebration of the three hundredth anniversary of the twenty-three Jews' landing in New Amsterdam, the theme was explicitly about a male legacy. Fifty years later, with the assistance of the Jewish Women's Archive, the 2004 celebration was infused with somewhat more of a feminist sensibility (See jwa.org).

32. See, for example, Isaacs 1996.

33. This is so for James Baldwin as well. A similar concept is elaborated in his earlier article (1984, 90): "The price of the ticket was to become 'white.' No one was white before he/she came to America. It took generations, and a vast amount of coercion, before this became a white country. It is probable that it is the Jewish community—or more accurately, perhaps, its remnants—that in America has paid the highest and most extraordinary price for becoming white. For the Jews came here from countries where they were not white, and they came here in part *because* they were not white; and incontestably—in the eyes of the Black American (and not only in those eyes) American Jews have opted to become white, and this is how they operate." Kaye/Kantrowitz, *The Issue is Power*, 1992 is excellent on these issues. But the whiteness you see or not depends on your social location. It seems that some White Supremacists actually know the word Ashkenazi (by which they mean "European"), and to them even Ashkenazi Jewish immigrants never became white. In fact, according to one web source, it is Ashkenazi Jews who are most threatening to the supposed racial purity of "white America."

34. See the work of Swirl, Inc. on census politics. http://www. swirlinc.org/ CensusFAQs.htm (6/22/05). Contributing to critical race theory as an African-American Jew, Azoulay 2001a and b discusses some of the reasons to mistrust a "multiracial" box on the U.S. Census.

35. Though Christine Jorgensen was not the first person to undertake sex re-assignment surgery, her experiences are the first widely publicized in this vein in the United States. See Meyerowitz, *How Sex Changed*, 2002 who offers interesting insights into these simultaneous moves of breaking bounded identity expectations as the new identity forms come to be reessentialized. For an analysis of an aspect of this phenomenon relevant for the U.S. Jewish community significant for this historical moment, see my argument in Brettschneider 1996b. As an explicit example of shaking up boundaries through a process of reessentializing, it is also interesting to note that in the development of the Levy's campaign discussed below (credited in the history of advertising for "jolting readers out of their

preconceptions" Nathanson-Moog 1984, 20), Levenson 1987 relates that the up and coming advertising genius, Bill Bernbach, taken on by Levy's was the one responsible for changing the name of Levy's Real Rye to Levy's Real Jewish Rye at this time. Whitey Rubin of Levy's was confused by this suggestion, fearing anti-Semitic backlash. Levenson writes that Bernbach replied: "For God's sake, your name is Levy's. They're not going to mistake you for High Episcopalian" (12).

36. Given my concern here about theorizing race, class, gender *and* sexuality, Karen Brodkin's work would have benefited greatly if she had been able to hold sexuality and sexual orientation in the complex more fully with her integrative critique of the race/ethnicity, class, and gender of a shifting Jewish identity in the United States.

37. Those from North Africa today may not be designated as "Black," but instead as "Arab," though at that historical point, those of African descent were lumped together as a group as Black. Other groups such as Mexicans in the southwest, however, held differential racial assignments given the hierarchical structures internal to their communities when the territories they lived in became part of the United States. So certain Mexicans, if wealthy, landowning, or otherwise in prestigious power positions, might have been classified as "white" whereas Mexican physical laborers and the poor were classified as nonwhite. James Boykin quotes Joel Hawkins, a Black Jew, about his differing racial assignment depending on geography. Hawkins first recalls an experience in Texas: "One day . . . I went on a picnic with a Jewish congregation there. Remember they still lynched people then, the sign at the picnic ground said 'whites only,' but I went in and we had a fine picnic. There I wasn't considered black because I was a Jew. When I returned to New York, I went to Sabbath services at a white synagogue and afterwards the rabbi said 'I think you would be happier with the Black Jews in Harlem than with us here in Queens.' Strange but in New York I wasn't considered a Jew because I was black" (1982, 56).

38. For additional aspects of class analysis of the situation of Jews, see, for example, Yeskel in Brettschneider, "Beyond the Taboo," 1996b, and in Balka and Rose, *Twice Blessed*, 1989; Rose, "Class as Problematic in Jewish Feminist Theology," 1999; Klepfisz, *Dreams of an Insomniac*, 1990b; Kaye/Kantrowitz, *The Issue is Power*, 1992; Kaye/Kantrowitz and Klepfisz, *The Tribe of Dina*, 1989; Lerner, *The Socialism of Fools*, 1992, and in the pages of *Bridges* especially issues vol. 2, no. 2 (Fall 1991), and vol. 3, no. 1 (Spring, Summer 1992). See Gilman, *The Jew's Body*, 1991 for an historical analysis where Eastern European Jews stand in for "lower class," for Western Europeans, and particularly Jews in Western Europe, who are themselves engaged in the re-creation of racial designations of Jews.

39. *Identities* special issue (Goluboff, ed. 2001).

40. In addition to the paradigms offered by Brodkin, these government programs, enabling the creation of a Jewish middle class and suburban landscape, are best understood as situated between a history of restrictive anti-Jewish geographical covenants in the United States and the dismantling of Jewish communities in urban areas for the benefit of bankers, real estate brokers, and other white/non-Jewish interests to the express detriment of Black communities and

(also with significant *cost* to) Jewish ones. (See Levine and Harmon 1992 and also Massey 1993.)

41. See Gladwell, "Examined Life," 2001.

42. For example, her history and therefore her theoretical structure remains primarily an east coast version. Her argument would have been enhanced if she had been more self conscious of how she was using the Jewish, also meaning predominantly east coast, case study to tease out a theory of racial formation. In a strange way therefore, that I am certain the author did not intend, Brodkin replays the "Jew as model minority myth" which so disturbs her. This is not Brodkin's problem only. It is a problem for all U.S. Jews, particularly with the conservative (and conservatizing) model minority template in our collective, or hegemonic, Jewish self-consciousness. How to write about Jews as important in their own right, and as important for the lessons Jewish experience offers to others is a difficult enterprise. In large part, it is difficult because the line is all too slippery between the legitimacy of a case study approach and the way that the particularity of the case study then sets up the frameworks of itself as inappropriately paradigmatic.

43. As examples, to ignore the section of Jews who *had* become wealthy, to not make more explicit that her use of socialist to cover communists or anarchists and other radicals would not have made as much sense to the people she is writing about. To fold Jewish gangsters, the Jewish petty bourgeoisie, and aspiring capitalist assimilationists into a collective socialist identity was unnecessary for her argument about the primacy of radical politics and a communal ethic of care and reciprocity among Eastern European Jews at the turn of the century. Similarly, it is not only unacceptable to ignore the existence of those currently self-identifying by the term "Jews of Color" (also meaning historically non-Ashkenazi/ Euro-American Jews), but the analysis developed by Brodkin will benefit from understanding how intra-ethnoracial tensions among Jews, given Ashkenazi/Euro-American hegemony, work in the assignment/identity dynamic.

44. This provides a small counterpoint to Brodkin's generalized analysis of a shift in the ethno-racial assignment of Jews at mid-century which actually relies on an east coast, particularly New York urban geographical specificity. See also, for example, Rogoff, "Is the Jew White?," 1997. As a personal example: although within my biological Jewish family, I am relatively light-skinned, when I lived in northern New England I was often not assumed to be white and most people seemed to assume my African-American children are my biological relations. This is especially apparent due to the comparative experience Dawn had with our daughters: up north she was stopped quite frequently by strangers inquiring about her relation to the girls and whether they were adopted. When I was out alone with our daughters up north people did not stop me or question our relationship in this way at all. As a geographical contrast, in New York City, I am assumed to be white, and strangers are more likely to identify my family as interracial.

45. The National Jewish Population Survey for 2000–2001 (with later revisions) reports that the median household income for "core population" U.S. Jews was $54,000 as compared to $42,000 for the U.S. median. Jewish households

with incomes over $75,000 is higher than average at 34 percent compared to 17 percent of total U.S. households. Jewish households with incomes under $25,000 is 22 percent, significant *and* slightly lower than the national average of 28 percent. Also 7 percent of Jews live below the official poverty level; again an important fact while slightly lower than the national average at 11 percent. As is common for most communities, the percentage of single Jewish mothers living below poverty level is higher than the community norm at 8 percent with 12 percent of Jewish children living in low-income households. Other demographers "count" Jews differently and would likely show a different, probably somewhat lower, median income level. (See also Popper 2004.)

46. Hettie Jones, "How I Became Hettie Jones," 1990 writes: "As an outsider Jew I could have tried for white, aspired to the liberal, intellectual, potentially conservative western tradition," but clearly "chose" otherwise. See also Adler, *Heretic's Heart*, 1997 for an interesting memoir of a Jewish feminist activist in the United States.

47. See Singer, "Red-Diaper Daughter," 1992. I also want to draw a connection between the work of Yeskel, "Beyond the Taboo," 1996; Kaye/Kantrowitz, *The Issue is Power*, 1992; Brettschneider, *Democratic Theorizing*, 2002 (chap. 2); Svonkin, *Jews Against Prejudice*, 1997, and others and Schultz's unrecognized contribution. The Red Scare decimation of Jewish and other communist, socialist, and anarchist organizations made it nearly impossible to do mass-based politics on class and economic issues. Schultz shows how Jewish women and men took on other aspects of economic and other inequalities in their post-McCarthy civil rights work. As time passes there are more and more Jewish efforts to deal directly with economic and class issues that do not call themselves socialist, but use terms such as "economic justice." Yeskel's work with United for a Fair Economy (see Yeskel and Collins 2000), The Jewish Fund for Justice, the Shefa Fund, Jews for Racial and Economic Justice, the Network of Jewish Social Justice organizations, and the (now defunct) New Jewish Agenda, are examples of more recent efforts by Jews—and particularly by many Jewish women (from street activists to wealthy donors)—which bring together issues of class and race justice with insights from years of Jewish feminist activism.

48. Yeskel, "Beyond the Taboo," 1996; Klepfisz, *Dreams*, 1990b; and Kaye/Kantrowitz, *The Issue is Power*, 1992, and in a different but related vein, Dekro in Brettschneider, "Facilitating Multicultural Progress," 1996b.

49. Rose, "Against Marriage," 1996; Tucker, "Passing," 1996; Schimel, "Diaspora, Sweet Diaspora," 1997; Blumenfeld, "History/Hysteria," 1996; Rosenberg, "Trans/positioning the (Drag?)," 2003; Beck, *Nice Jewish Girls*, 1984; Balka and Rose, eds., *Twice Blessed*, 1989; Alpert, *Like Bread on the Seder Plate*, 1997; Kaye/Kantrowitz, *The Issue is Power*, 1992; Klepfisz, 1990; Kaye/Kantrowitz and Klepfisz, *The Tribe of Dina*, 1989; Alpert, Levi Elwell, and Idelson, *Lesbian Rabbis*, 2001; Aviv and Shneer, *Queer Jews*, 2002; the special issue of *Response Magazine: Queer Jews* 1997; Tessman and Bar-On, eds., *Jewish Locations*, 2001; Boyarin, *Unheroic Conduct*, 1997; Boyarin et al., *Queer Theory and the Jewish Question*, 2003; Seidman, *A Marriage Made in Heaven*, 1997; Levinson, "Cultural Androgyny," 2000; Satlow, "Try To Be a Man," 1996; Seif, 1999; Olyan, " 'and

with a Male," 1994; Litwoman, "Some Thoughts on Bisexuality," 1990; Artson, 1990–1991); Fonrobert, "When Women Walk," 2001. Kessler, "Let's Cross That Body," 2005 does an excellent job of developing, utilizing, and advancing mutual construction identity theory in this context; Brown, *Mentsh*, 2004; see also Gross and West, *Take Back the Word*, 2000 for some interesting Jewish contributions.

50. In her exploration of Jewish children hidden by Christians during the Holocaust, Barbara Kessel quotes from an interview in which Abraham Foxman notes that it was more dangerous to try to save boys, and that one method of attempting to keep the boys safer at this particular historical moment was to raise them as girls (2000, 43).

51. See Siculair, "Gender Rebellion in Yiddish Film," 1995–1996, and Boyarin et al., eds., *Queer Theory and the Jewish Question*, 2003.

52. Gilman, *The Jewish Body*, 1991 is especially helpful on this in historical perspective.

53. Boyarin, *Unheroic Conduct*, 1997 is an excellent work in this area.

54. See for example, Hyman, *Gender and Assimilation*, 1995 and Glückel of Hameln, *The Memoirs*, 1977.

55. See Cohen, *Tough Jews*, 1998; and Zerubavel, *Recovered Roots*, 1995.

56. For an early analysis of this phenomenon, see Rich, "Disloyal to Civilizations," 1979 in which she links compulsory heterosexuality with racism and shows that feminist, antiracist, and lesbian activism is considered "disloyal to civilization" (meaning white male supremacy in the Christian West).

57. In 1963 it was reported that in nearly half of the "Negro-white intermarriages in New York" the "white" spouse was Jewish, and most often female. Reported in Berger, *Black Jews in America*, 1978, p. 122—see also p. 126—and his discussion of the *Commentary* article published by editor Norman Podhoretz 1963 regarding the idea of his daughter's marriage to a "Negro" and the debate that ensued (122–123). See also McKinley, *The Book of Sarahs*, 2002. For additional discussion of this phenomenon at the time, see for example Gordon, "Negro-Jewish Marriages," 1964, and Gibel's response, "The Negro-Jewish Scene," 1965; Cahnman, "The Interracial Jewish Children," 1967, and more recently Blustain, "Are You Black or Are You Jewish?," 1996. We are beginning to hear more from the children of these unions who have become political and public figures in their own right. Often referred to as "movement kids," they are the offspring of European Jewish and African-American Christian (some later becoming Muslim) civil rights workers. For example, Rebecca Walker (see 2001) is the daughter of an Ashkenazi/Euro-Jewish father and the well-known bisexual African-American author Alice Walker; Lisa Jones (see 1994) is the daughter of working-class Ashkenazi/Euro-Jewish Hettie (Cohen) Jones (see Hetti Jones 1990) and middle-class Christian-raised African-American LeRoi Jones who changed his name to Amiri Baraka. See also Azoulay 2001 for critically situating the erasures of Jewishness that often accompanies this phenomenon. In popular culture of 2005 (Gross 2005), however, we saw a mix of these developments when the first clearly marked "Star Trek" Jewish presence leads to an intermarriage of a stereotyped "white" and materialistic Jewish woman marrying a Klingon (a people stereotyped as Black and Brutish), glossing over the possible feminism of the prior generation

(the character's mother—a 1960s generation product—is a rabbi). Gross, "To Boldly Go Where No Jew Has Gone," 2005.

58. For example: Butler 2000a, Feinberg, *Stone, Butch Blues*, 1993; and Bornstein, *Gender Outlaw*, 1995 are all Jewish. For other Jewish trans-writing see: Krawitz, "A Voice From Within," 2004; Kanegson, "A Young Man From Chelm," 2002; Michaels and Cannon, "Which Side Are You On?," 2002; Coleman, "Variations on a Theme," 2003; and Moriel, "Dana International," 1999.

59. The film *Ruthie and Connie: Every Room in the House* (Dickson 2002) is a documentary about the lives of two Jewish women from Brooklyn: each had married a man and raised children only to fall in love with each other and go on to make history. Ruth Berman was my mother's childhood girlfriend and dated my father before he and my mom got together. Ruthie and I met through our joint love of politics, our mutual membership in CBST-Congregation Bet Simchat Torah, the gay and lesbian synagogue of New York, and a variety of other points of synapse not long after Ruthie and Connie won domestic partnership rights for New York City employees. No longer close friends of my *parents*, life is full of unanticipated twists and they are now a central part of *my* constructed adult community.

60. As many even Christian religious and other figures have found out, men who work with society's needy and oppressed have been historically feminized in post chivalry—Christian Western constructions of masculinity.

61. See for example Daniels, *Exposing Men*, forthcoming, and Snyder, *Citizen-Soldiers and Manly Warriors*, 1999.

62. Williams, *Constraint of Race*, 2003, and Delgado and Stefancic eds., *Critical White Studies*, 1997.

63. The work of Jenn Chau, "More than Chicken Chow Mein," 2004 and at Swirl, Inc., is a great example of new modes of politics by and about mixed-race and mixed-heritage folks.

64. For a quick overview of data yielded by the new census see Thornton, "What the Census Doesn't Count," 2001. It is likely impossible to find "Americans" with "pure bloodlines," even if one could figure out what that might mean in the first place. The history of cultural, ethnic, and racial mixing through conversion, passing, practices of altering information in adoption records, people lying on sperm or egg donation applications, "mistakes" in the in vitro-insemination business, marriage, a variety of chosen sexual liaisons, and rape makes the notion of "pure" anything a racialized fiction. For additional comments on mixing in this context, see also Williams, *Seeing a Color-Blind Future*, 1997a, and Thornton, "Is Multiracial Status Unique?," 1992. There is a growing body of literature on the experiences of those from mixed families, those raised with a different racial identity from their bio-parents, and those who sometimes pass. As examples see Azouley, *Black, Jewish, and Interracial*, 1997; McLarin, "Primary Colors," 1998; Scales-Trent, *Notes of a White Black Woman*, 1995; Derricotte, *The Black Notebooks*, 1997; Larson, *Quicksand and Passing*, 1986; Kessel, *Suddenly Jewish*, 2000; Cross, *Secret Daughter*, 1996.

65. See Brettschneider, "To Race, to Class, to Queer," 2001.

66. The Balch Institute for Ethnic Studies exhibit dated the copyright on this Levy's campaign image as 1967 (see Nathanson-Moog 1984, 21), and the campaign then ran for many years (Levenson 1987, 12).

67. There were five images, all presenting as males and the rest as: a white boy (whose dress suggested his "Pilgrim" background representing "true/original" white Protestant "America"), an Irish cop (Catholics in U.S. stereotyping of the Irish), and an Asian older man.

68. Nathanson-Moog writes in the brochure for the Balch exhibit: ". . . by using clear-cut ethnic images of other groups . . . the negative stereotype of Jews as an exclusive, clannish lot is blasted apart. At the same time, the product, like the Jewish people themselves, insists on retaining its ethnic identity as 'real.' This ad models a process of ethnic identification which sells more than bread; it sells a perception of openness and mutual respect for differences" (1984, 21). The author appears unconscious of the contradictions here: that this version of multicultural difference requires clearly identified "others" and Jewish "authenticity."

69. It appears a magazine in the style of Schiffman, *Generation*, 1999, though perhaps for a half generation younger. See also the special issue of *Time Out*, "The New Super Jews," 2003; Belzer and Pelc, *Joining the Sisterhood*, 2003; the *Response* special issue on *Queer Jews* 1997; Aviv and Shneer, *Queer Jews*, 2002; and Ruttenberg, *Yentl's Revenge*, 2001, for other examples of work from the voices of/appealing to this Jewish generational/cultural style.

70. It is interesting to juxtapose Jones, *Bulletproof Diva*, 1994, African-American Jewish Herron's *Nappy Hair*, 1997, and, "Pastel Meetings," 2003, and *Lilith*'s special issue on hair 1995 with this spread in *Heeb*.

71. As another alternative, Nathanson-Moog, "The Psychological Power of Ethnic Image," 1984, suggests the "the psychological message of this ad translates as 'You don't have to be Jewish to love Jews'" (21).

Chapter Two: Jew Dykes Adopting Children

1. Wadia-Ells' *The Adoption Reader*, 1995 edited volume includes stories from the "three parties" in adoption with great depth and sensitivity. Also, it is important to note that the emphasis on mothers in the adoption process is decidedly a contemporary product and producer of certain political ideas and practices to be discussed below. For example, in Gager's, *Blood Ties and Fictive Ties*, 1996 discussion of adoption in early modern France, it is largely fathers who play a distinctive role and are the focus of legislative and propagandist discourse. Given the absence of fathers in most of the contemporary U.S. adoption literature, readers may find interesting Bayer's, "Close By," 1995 moving story of her adoptive and birth fathers, Jewish and Palestinian respectively.

2. I found this in my experience and research (verbally in discussions and interviews mainly), but I have not found studies documenting the phenomenon, or other "written proof" as there is so little formal research done in this area. In an article on the empowering of bio-families to call the shots in adoption

placements, however, Cynthia Crossen writes of the criteria used by bio-families to identify potential adoptive families: "Religion is a major factor, and so are the couple's lifestyle and stability" (1989, A12).

3. As of 1992 127,441 children were adopted in the United States. The National Adoption Information Clearinghouse (1996) reports that the largest group are adopted by stepparent or other relatives (nearly half). Approximately 37 percent were handled by private agencies or independent practitioners such as lawyers. Five percent were children adopted from other countries. In the following discussion, I am generally referring to what is commonly called "stranger adoption," or the approximately 42 percent of adoptions not done within the children's existing families (either by blood or marriage).

4. The Evan B. Donaldson Adoption Institute estimates that between 2 and 4 percent of families in the United States have adopted children. The 1990 National Jewish Population Study estimates that more than 3 percent of the children in Jewish homes had been adopted.

5. This does not mean that all Christians who relinquish their parental rights might not also have sincere religious convictions and also aspirations for their bio-offspring. When I discuss the challenges for Jews in adoption, aside from a few Jewish social workers in New York City who work on adoptions and thus know this already, people are *always* amazed. As but one example: In the fall of 2002, I was privileged to speak at and facilitate a session of the Jewish Gay and Lesbian parenting series that Miryam Kabakov organized at the Jewish Community Center of the Upper West Side. Those attending had various fears, concerns, and many questions regarding possibilities of family formation and potential discrimination. That being Jewish would play a part in the navigational routes through discrimination and privilege was a new idea to the attendees.

6. Shanley, *Making Babies, Making Families*, 2001 and Roberts, *Shattered Bonds*, 2002 differently take on some of the problematic issues involved with this "best interest" formula.

7. There are currently very few children born to Jews who are eligible for adoption in the nation as a whole. Many of these have special needs. The Jewish Children's Adoption Network (JCAN) places about one hundred children born to Jewish women in Jewish homes. About 85 percent of those placed have special needs, have been abused, neglected, or abandoned. (As reported in Star Tracks, the newsletter of Stars of David, vol. 16, no. 1 (2000): 5.) This demographic differs from the turbulent (pre- and post-) 1960s as Jewish sexual norms shifted, discussed in the previous chapter. In the early 1950s, at the start of the civil rights movement and the beginning of a surge of interracial/cultural dating (distinguished here from the ongoing historical legacy of white men raping women of color), there were apparently numerous interracial children born to Euro-heritage Jewish women (see Berger 1978, 122–126; Gordon 1964; and Gibel 1965). Many were placed with adoption agencies which found it difficult to place them. One agency reports trying hard to place such children with Negro-Jewish families, but with no success (Berger 1978, 115). Even into the 1970s it was reported that "about 14 percent of the Jewish foster children are nonwhite, or the products of racially

mixed marriages and potential Jewish foster parents often shun these children" (Cited in Berger 1978, 116.). See also McKinley, *The Book of Sarahs*, 2002.

8. This set of stereotypes has not always been operative. In fact, specifically prior to the popular racial reassignment of Jews as a community in a mid-twentieth century U.S., as discussed in the previous chapter, Jews had long been marked as predatory and dangerous to children (i.e., in popular Christian myths that Jews used Christian children's blood in the making of Passover matzahs). In modernity, the invention of the notion of sexual perversion relied upon the creation of groups then called perverse and predatory. Jewish men were often categorized this way, including in the United States particularly if they were associated with radical political causes (and certainly at the anxious moment of the community's racial reassignment). Examples of this may be seen in the trope of male sexual perversion regarding the lynching of Leo Frank in 1915 (see Oney 2003), or the case against Harvard scientist Gregory Pincus in the 1930s (see Reed 1983, and Ratcliff 1937), and on a more recently a feminized version of the demon Jewess, sexualized to cause a stain on the purity of the nation see Kitlinski, Leszkowicz, and Lockard, "Monica Dreyfus," 2001.

9. For a detailed resource, see Spiegel, *Bibliography of Sexual and Domestic Violence*, 2000. As individual examples, see Matousek, *Sex, Death, Enlightenment*, 1996 and Fries, *Body, Remember*, 1997.

10. According to the data collected by Adoption and Foster Care Analysis Reporting Systems (AFCARS) released by the Children's Bureau of the U.S. Department of Health and Human Services, as of January 2000 there were approximately five hundred twenty thousand children in foster care.

11. According to the AFCARS data, one hundred seventeen thousand of the children in foster care are eligible for adoption. The data on both the number of children in foster care and those available for adoption represent increases.

12. Jews and queers are often disqualified from denominational/Christian agencies, though adoptions through them tend to be less costly than other private means. Nondenominational private agencies and "independent" (such as through lawyers) are the most expensive methods of adoption. Adoptions, particularly of white newborns, can cost up to fifty thousand dollars. Adoptive Families of America estimates that nondenominational and other private adoptions tend to cost on average fifteen thousand dollars. Whereas working with public agencies is usually free, or requiring minimal fees, or adoptive parents may be eligible to receive subsidies

13. Adopting children is a competitive enterprise. In 1997, the National Center for Health Statistics reported that there are approximately five adoption seekers for every actual adoption. Perhaps not surprisingly, those most likely to adopt are white women with higher than average levels of income and education. More to follow below on the racialized bias regarding "adoption seekers."

14. We can see from Spelman, *Inessential Woman*, 1988, this ideological presumption appeals more solidly the closer one is to white and middle class. As Roberts, *Killing the Black Body*, 1997 demonstrates, for example, Black women have rarely had the same rights to motherhood as white women. See Cahill, Battle, and Meyer, "Partnering, Parenting and Policy," 2004 for how some of this dynamic plays out for Black lesbians.

15. See Simon and Alstein, *Adoption Across Borders*, 2000, 11. This was the common wisdom, though when queer women began to adopt under the "single woman" category in larger numbers, problems developed with "single women" adopting from there. For a discussion of a bizarre juxtaposition of the simultaneous levels of inclusion and exclusion of queers in the commodified adoption world, see Eng's, "Transnational Adoption and Queer Diasporas," 2003 discussion of the John Hancock ad showing a lesbian couple adopting a child from China, especially note 12.

16. The "structure" of families adopting children as collected by AFCARS is revealing: married couples 66 percent, unmarried couples 2 percent, single females 30 percent, single males 2 percent. These figures obscure the numbers of gay and lesbian singles and couples adopting as the majority adopt as "singles" to avoid naming a gendered partner.

17. Commission for Women's Equality of the American Jewish Congress, *Highlights*, 1993; Isserman and Hostein, *Status of Women*, 1994; Council of Jewish Federations Research Department, "The Status of Women in Lay and Professional Leadership," 1994; and Horowitz, Beck, and Kadushin, *Power and Parity*, 1997. For studies of Jewish women and work issues more broadly see Geffen, *Jewish Women on the Way Up*, 1987; Fishman, *A Breath of Life*, 1993; Denholtz, *Balancing Work and Love*, 2000; Hartman and Hartman, *Gender Equality and American Jews*, 1996; Cohen et al., "Creating Gender Equity," 2004; Cohen, "Listen to Her Voice," 2005; Ma'yan, "Power and Parity," 1998; and Sales, "Voices for Change," 1995.

18. See Moore, "Black Children Facing Adoption Barriers," 1984 as the main source for information in this section. An exception among the (even critical and "progressive") adoption literature generally cited, Simon and Alstein (2000, 41–44) mention this phenomenon though they do not critically integrate it in the argument of the book as a whole. Roberts 2002 provides the most thorough critical analysis of racism, changing government policy, and the development of new modes of adoption.

19. Which Evelyn Moore 1984 notes as well. In the film *Secret Daughter* (Cross 1996), June presents how she has been raised by friends of her parents' from the age of four. She finds out later in life that a child her bio-father has had with another woman after he and her mother split up has faced a similar fate. Their mothers are white, their shared father is Black. Neither white woman is able to integrate the child fully into her life, and each child is sent to live with middle-class Black friends. June is introduced to her new school principal as the daughter of the woman who is now raising her. June also actually sees her bio-mother on a regular basis, and the man her mother marries later. When she is with her bio-mother and the new husband in a mostly white world, they introduce June as their "adopted" daughter. See also Mays et al., "African American Families," 1998.

20. See for example Cahill, Battle, Meyer, "Partnering, Parenting, and Policy," 2004.

21. Ibid., p. 91

22. CBS News, "Born in USA, Adopted in Canada," 2005.

23. In an effort to change this phenomenon, the Institute for Black Parenting, as an example, became licensed as an adoption agency in 1988, charging no fees for services. The Institute for Black Parenting (IBP) was founded in 1976 as the social services and research component to advance and concretize the goals of the Association of Black Social Workers of Greater Los Angeles (A.B.S.W.—L.A.) by "strengthening" African-American families (www.institute forblackparenting.org).

24. AFCARS reports in 2000 that the mean length of time children spend in foster care is forty-six months. See Mallon, *We Don't Exactly Get the Welcome Wagon*, 1998 for a discussion of the experiences of queer adolescents' multiple-care placements due to (often explicitly violent) homophobia.

25. AFCARS 2000 reports that the average mean age of children waiting to be adopted is eight years, and over a quarter of the children are over ten years of age. This bodes ill for the children as the Voluntary Cooperative Information System reports that the younger the child, the more likely he or she will be adopted from foster care. For example, over half of finalized adoptions were of children between new born and five-years-old; The numbers go down to 7.7 percent of the children between thirteen and eighteen.

26. The average racial breakdown of children in foster care is: 43 percent African-American, 36 percent white, 15 percent Hispanic, 2 percent American Indian/Alaskan Native and Asian/Pacific Islander (4 percent unknown). The average racial breakdown of those in foster care needing adoptive families is: 51 percent African-American, 32 percent white, 11 percent Hispanic, 2 percent American Indian/Alaskan Native and Asian/Pacific Islander (5 percent unknown). (Notice that Jews are not a category.) Compare these percentages to the population at large. In the year 2000, the U.S. government census estimates that non-Hispanic whites comprise 74 percent of the population, non-Hispanic Blacks 12 percent, Hispanics 10 percent, non-Hispanic American Indian/Eskimo/Aluet 0.7 percent, and non-Hispanic Asian and Pacific Islanders 3.3 percent. The U.S. Census gathers no data on the percentage of the population that is Jewish.

27. By queer here I mean both gender nonconforming and gay, lesbian, and bisexual. Gerald P. Mallon 1998 documents the horrid conditions and abuse gay and lesbian adolescents experience in the child welfare system (by their families of origin, the staff, peers, and neighbors of group homes). He writes that most of these kids did not go into public services for homosexuality but that most had bad experiences once in care because of it. Mallon notes that whatever their sexual orientation, gender nonconformists tend to fare even more poorly than gays and lesbians (107) and that Jews are not represented in his sample "and similarly are underrepresented in the out-of-home-care systems of Canada and the United States" (11).

28. In *Reproducing the State* 1999, Stevens discusses the multiple designations of fatherhood, mostly biological and legal (through marriage to a child's biological mother). Her research demonstrates that the state privileges legal fathers over biological ones. This can make information on waiting children's bio-fathers more complicated to obtain. In 1994 the U.S. Immigration and Naturalization Service implemented a new law designed to protect the biological

fathers of children considered for intercountry adoption into the United States (now requiring approval of two parents whereas in the past the bio-mother's permission was sufficient). Simon and Alstein write: "The American statute assumes all births are legitimate births" and challenge the wisdom of the new legislation (2000, 30–31).

29. Rawlings, "Reconstructing Identities," 1999 has done excellent research on and analysis regarding the mutual construction of race, class, and gender in the ideological construction of focusing on mothers. She looks at African-American teen women's choices of who to impregnate them according to skin tone and asks whether such choices are adaptions or resistances to caste, classism, and racism.

30. For information on adoption with respect to hidden children see Kessel, *Suddenly Jewish*, 2000 and information through the Hidden Children Foundation of the Anti-Defamation League.

31. Many states also now have information available online as well. See Fogg-Davis, *Ethics of Transracial Adoption*, 2002, 43 for a discussion of this phenomenon wherein nonwhite children are classified as "special needs." See Roberts 2002 on how being Black is all too likely to land one in the system in the first place.

32. The United States is the largest receiving country of adoptees from other countries, actually more than all other nations combined and nearly double the amount from a decade ago (Pertman 2000b). The numbers of children adopted to U.S. adults from other countries in 1999 was 16,396 (as reported by the U.S. Immigration and Naturalization Services and the U.S. Department of State). The logic of the national distribution will be discussed below. The countries most frequently adopted from are Russia, Romania, then Guatemala, China, and Korea. International Concerns for Children reported in 1996 that on average, adoptions from Eastern European countries such as Russia and Romania are most expensive, then "Hispanic" countries such as Guatemala and Columbia, then Asian countries such as China, Korea, and Vietnam. U.S. adoptions from countries with Black populations such as Haiti, Ethiopia, or other African states cost on average one-half to one-third of those from other regions. For a history and an empirical study of transracial and intercountry adoption, given the U.S. debates over transracial placements, see Simon and Alstein, *Adoption Across Borders*, 2000.

33. Talbot's, *Attachment Theory*, 1998 story on the traumatic experience of orphans in and from Eastern Europe is a controversial classic in this discussion. It is important to note that in 2000 the United States ratified a new international law for international adoption called The Hague Convention on Intercountry Adoption (see Pertman 2000b). The treaty "establishes the first global standards intended to protect children from being sold and mandates cuts in bureaucratic red tape for finding them homes." *The Globe* reported that the treaty had "the support of an unusually broad coalition of groups." However, U.S. ratification of this international treaty was held up, for example, in the House by Christopher Smith (a Republican from New Jersey), because he wanted the legislation to explicitly "preclude adoptions by homosexuals, unmarried Americans, and people with 'promiscuous lifestyles.'"

34. See Simon and Alstein, *Adoption Across Borders*, 2000, 13–15. A paradigmatic historical example regards Catholics stealing Jewish children to save their souls during the Inquisition, perhaps the most high profile case involving a boy

named Edgardo Mortara (see Kertzer 1997). The more contemporary U.S. phenomenon is a spin on an earlier nineteenth-century domestic practice, perfected by the then new Children's Aid Society, of elite Protestants sweeping U.S. urban areas populated by poor, immigrant, often Catholic, Irish, Slavic, Italian, occasionally Black and probably Jewish people, in an effort they called "saving" and what the birth families deemed "stealing" children; they sent over one hundred thousand children to Protestant country settings on "orphan trains" (Gordon 1999). Given the historical moment, this was the domestic version of an economically based religious and racial cleansing in which the debate foreshadows also more well-known later domestic arguments about genocidal motives with regard to cross-racial adoptive placements of Black and Native American children.

35. See Deann Borshay Liem's 2000 documentary film as a Korean female adopted into a white family in the United States and David Eng's 2003 insightful critique of the film as a gateway for analysis of issues in transracial adoption involving Asian children. See also Simon and Alstein 2000 for a comparison of how Korean and Black transracial adoptionees have fared. An unusual aspect of the Simon and Alstein 2000 study is that it addresses Jewish adoptive families as well (see also Pfeffer 2002 and Rosenberg 1998). Despite the fact that many Asian-Americans would characterize their own experience as marginal, and their racial identity as nonwhite, in reproductive arenas the lines have been more blurred. As an example of this phenomenon playing out in other modes of family formation, Gillian M. Goslinga-Roy quotes from a white surrogate mother regarding her horror at the idea of gestating a Black baby, the woman says: "It feels foreign to me . . . I could carry a Japanese baby or a Chinese baby because they are white to me. Society sees them as white" and she placed a Black child in a wholly other category (2000, 16).

36. For an historical analysis, see Gilman, *Smart Jews*, 1996. See also Gladwell, "Examined Life," 2001.

37. This logic has contributed to the lucrative black market in stolen Native American babies being passed off as "white" to white U.S. prospective parents. A personal account of the involvement of Jews as consumers in this market is told from the perspective of a stolen child in Melanson, *Looking for Lost Bird*, 1999.

38. See Judy Ashkenaz's 1995 piece about a U.S. Jewish family adopting a mixed Spanish Indian child from Colombia and taking on issues involved in transracial adoptions with self-identified "white" parents and Native American children.

39. Whites adopting children who could not be passed off as white is a relatively new situation in adoption reflecting a slight shift in racism among the white majority in the United States. Since the civil rights movement, however, there also have been intense debates about whether transracial adoptions (to be discussed below) are good or bad. For central scholarly literature debating transracial adoption see: Fogg-Davis, *Ethics of Transracial Adoption*, 2002; Banks, "The Color of Desire," 1998; Bartholet, "Where Do Black Children Belong," 1991; Bowen, "Cultural Convergences and Divergences," 1987–1988; Howe, "Transracial Adoption," 1997; Kennedy, "Orphans of Separatism," 1994; Perry, "The Transracial Adoption Controversy," 1993–1994, and 1990–1991; Shanley, *Making Babies*, 2001; Landes and Posner, "The Economics of Baby Shortage," 1978; Carroll and Dockery,

"The Debate over Cross-Racial Adoption," 1995; Volkman and Katz, eds., *Special Issue on Transnational Adoption*, 2003. Some organizations involved in the legislative battle included the Children's Defense Fund, the North American Council on Adoptable Children, and Adoptive Families of America (Fogg-Davis 2002, 45).

Minority communities wanted an end to discrimination, but at various times certain sections publically opposed transracial adoptions. For example since the early 1970s the National Association of Black Social Workers (NABSW) has put forth the view that it is not in the best interests of the children and the Black community for Black children to be adopted by white people (see National Association of Black Social Workers 1972 and 1994). Many states do not do transracial adoptions—based not on the logic of the NABSW but on the logic of white supremacy. There have been laws passed (and some repealed) attempting to address racial discrimination in adoption. However, many agencies nevertheless practice discrimination as a matter of course. (As will be discussed below, adoptions involving Native American children are treated under separate laws than those aimed at ending discrimination against other racial minorities.)

40. See Williams, "Losing Isaiah," 1995; Bartholet, *Nobody's Children*, 1991, 11738n, and discussed in Fogg-Davis, *Ethics of Transracial Adoption*, 2002, 85–86.

41. "Although the term *TRA* [transracial adoption] generally describes adoptions involving adults and children of different racial classifications, the adoption of black children by white parents has defined the image of TRA in the public debate from the very beginning. This narrow popular image . . . is striking given that adoptions of black children by white parents account for only a small percentage of TRAs and an even smaller percentage of all U.S. domestic adoptions" (Fogg-Davis 2002, 3). This second fact is interesting, though later Fogg-Davis seems to use the quantitative infrequency of the practice to make troublesome conclusions regarding the qualitative aspects of TRA for parties of different races. For some history on transracial adoption see Ladner, *Mixed Families*, 1977, and Howe, "Transracial Adoption," 1997.

42. Interestingly enough, for example, Fogg-Davis is well aware of the political context of the equation of transracial with "black" in the adoption world. However, in her choice to call her book the *Ethics of Transracial Adoption* while still focusing explicitly and exclusively about the Black-white example she herself reifies these dynamics. (Note: although she discusses her rationale in the introduction, the politics of the title and content choices remain.) As another example, Simon and Alstein at least address issues of non-native adults adopting Native American children in addition to their discussion of domestic adoption of Black minors (they do not discuss domestic adoptions involving children from other minority groups), though they consider situations with Native Americans a "special" case as opposed to the African-American experience. Further, their treatment of intercountry adoption is broken down by region and they do not consider Africa at all.

43. Landes and Posner, "The Economics of Baby Shortage," 1978 are credited for having opened the practice to public discussion by proposing to remedy the "shortage" of healthy white babies by pricing them higher than nonwhite babies. This would encourage white adults to adopt nonwhite children because their adoptions were cheaper.

44. See Simon for a discussion of agency pricing schedules based on race (et al., 1994, 11).

45. I specify U.S. domestic adoptions purposely. Although many international adoptions are also "transracial," these are usually referred to by the euphemism "international." Note that the word race is not invoked. International transracial adoptions usually involve white adults adopting Latina/o or Asian children. As international adoptions rarely involve Black children, the term transracial is used less frequently.

46. Different studies report various percentages of transracial adoptions. To give readers an idea of the range, although I suspect numbers have changed in the last decade or two, a 1990 study reported that transracial adoptions made up 8 percent of adoptions in the United States, and the adoption of Black children by white mothers represents 1 percent (see Simon and Roorda 2000; Simon, et al., 1994, 3, and 1995). The Child Welfare League of America reported a slightly higher level than other studies at 4 percent, though states such as New York may have yet higher rates of transracial adoptions.

47. According to the latest National Surveys of Family Growth data (from 1995) in the comparison between white and Black women's preferences, fewer white women seeking to adopt would accept Black children than Black women who would accept white children, and almost none (1.8 percent) of the white women prefer Black children. Thus, the joke is not that minority adults would not prefer or accept children of other races, but that the system deems absurd having a white child raised by nonwhite parents, while it considers white people as potentially fit parents for minority children. (See also Williams 1997 and Fogg-Davis 2002 for discussions of the politics of this arrangement.)

48. Richard Posner (1992, 415) explains away the adoption market concept of goods being bought and sold by saying what is being negotiated is not human lives but parental rights.

49. See Smolowe, "Adoption in Black and White," 1995.

50. See Fogg-Davis, *Ethics of Transracial Adoption*, 2002.

51. According to the National Center for Health Statistics in 1999, there has been a decline in the numbers of women giving their children up for adoption. This is largely due to the dramatic drop in white women relinquishing their children (from 19 percent in 1965–1972, to 1.7 percent today). Relinquishment rates for Black and Hispanic women have remained basically constant. The rate for Latinas has been consistently at or under 2 percent. The current figures for Black women relinquishing their infants for adoption is less than 1 percent, meaning that African-American women actually relinquish their children for adoption less frequently than white women and Latinas.

52. Most whites want healthy white infants, and after finding them in "short supply," they want South American, Asian, or Native American before African-heritage children. It is assessed, therefore, that African and African-heritage kids are the most likely racial group to be discriminated against in adoption (Fogg Davis 2002,12; Courtney 1997).

53. See Bell Kaplan's 1997 discussion of the role of idealic motherhood in the choices of African-American single, teeenage mothers. She also comments on

the emphasis on these images specifically in glossy magazines geared toward a female, African-American clientele such as *Essence.*

54. See for example, Sanger, "Separating from Children," 1996 and Roberts 1997 and 2002, for a discussion.

55. On differential treatment of Black and white birthmothers in historical perspective, see Shanley, *Making Babies,* 2001, 16–17.

56. Biased presumptions remain within arguments by scholars who see themselves as making the most progressive arguments. For example, Fogg-Davis refers to the phenomenon of white-Black transracial adoptions as that some white adopters are "willing" to adopt Black children (2002, 4) and bases the premise of this theory on a response to the "gap" (5) that exists between these parents and children.

57. For example see the Maine statute (8205) on collection and disclosure of information in adoption cases.

58. See Fanshel, *Far from the Reservation,* 1972 and for a contradicting more recent study see Simon and Alstein, *Adopting Across Borders,* 2000.

59. GLAD is also behind the more recent move to allow same sex adults to share legal guardianship of children.

60. The Hebrew word for Egypt is *mitzrayim* linked to the word for "narrow straits." Jews have interpreted this as suggesting that the very name of Egypt for Jews is taken from a metaphor for slavery in its narrowness. Also, then that the exodus from Egypt and the difficulties which the biblical text notes of birthing the Jewish nation into freedom is presented in terms of the trauma of a biological/ vaginal birth, the Jews emerging from the birth canal (narrow straits) into the selfhood of a self-defined nation.

61. It would also be worthwhile to assess the imbrication of the policies in this section with the 1996 DOMA, Defense of Marriage Act. See Cahill, "Welfare Moms and the Two Grooms," 2005.

62. The primary goal in child welfare had long been reuniting bio-families. Whether this was wise or not is a long debate (see Roberts 2002). During the period in which I became involved in this sphere, new legislation was being developed to make it easier to formally cut bio-ties in favor of placing kids in adoptive situations. The experiences of queer youth have run counter to this historical pattern. Getting queer kids in the child welfare system back together with their families of origin was generally not an option. More recently, however, given years of GLBTQ activism there has been an effort on the part of some in the system to work on the homophobia in the family in order to open up the possibility of reunification. (See Mallon 1998, 98.)

63. For an analysis of the intersection of racism, new welfare and crime laws in this period, see Roberts 2002 and Williams, *The Constraint of Race,* 2003 chaps. five and six. Cahill 2005 would also likely add the passing of DOMA, the Defense of Marriage Act. Important analysis remains to be done by deepening this analysis including DOMA.

64. See Siegel, "Women in Prison," 1998; Roth, "Reproductive Rights of Prisoners," 1999; Davis, "An Interview with Angela Davis," 1998; and Sidel, "The Enemy Within," 2000.

65. By referring to "the public" here I do not mean to unintentionally reproduce a notion of the public devoid of minority women. To the contrary, we are seeing that it has sometimes been necessary for communities of women of color to accept the very same set of stereotypes about themselves and each other. See Kaplan, *Not Our Kind*, 1997.

66. For example, Simon and Alstein, *Adoption Across Borders*, 2000, 128–129 found that most of the Jewish families formed through TRA "discussed their plans to adopt a child of a different race or nationality with their rabbis, and, with one or two exceptions, received a positive and supportive response." Further, facing issues of cultural genocide themselves, and the specific situation of the hidden children of the Holocaust (Jewish children taken in by Christian institutions and families and either hidden or raised under an assumed Christian identity in order to save them from Nazi anti-Jewish policies) provide some of the cultural touchstones Jews refer to when explaining the NABSW rationale. See, for example, Kessel, *Suddenly Jewish*, 2000.

67. U.S. "Founding Father" and signer of the Declaration of Independence Benjamin Rush thought similarly. In what was considered by many at that the time a "progressive" stance, Rush sought to confront racism. In his view the problem for Black slaves was their blackness itself. He was interested in changing the skin color, hair texture, and other "features" of slaves. Making them white, physically to the eye (as if there is a real measure of whiteness to achieve) was Rush's suggested solution to the problem of racist discrimination.

68. The contemporary spin on eugenics via adoption (born-marginalized and therefore tainted children can be "saved" by being adoptively "born again" into white middle-class families) stands in direct contrast to the revolutionary adoption agenda of the late eighteenth century creation of the early French Republic. Although later rejected, the revolutionary agenda of modernist democracy forcibly included adoption as a means of democratizing the republic (a positively valenced notion at the time) by bringing democratizing elements (children of nonaristocratic backgrounds) into the sphere of the former ruling class. Similar to the U.S. case, adoption in revolutionary France was also a matter of poor children being adopted into richer families. Diverging from U.S. patterns, the French example from that historical moment was to change the elite for the better, not to yuppify/gentrify the ordinary and/or formerly outcast. (See Gager 1996, especially the epilogue.)

69. For example, between our search for our daughters, Paris and Toni, who were born fifteen months apart, we learned that many adoption agencies had abandoned their policies offering Black children at cut rates believing that such practices reinforced racism. Some have argued, however, that certain agencies have done so more for financial gain. As transracial adoptions become less stigmatized, agencies find they might be able to charge more money for children of color. At the same time as the "formal policies" might be changing in some areas, many of the same agencies still end up charging half or otherwise lower prices for Black children suggesting the disingenuousness of "looking good" formally, but still responding to a market in which they assess "people (meaning whites) won't pay full price for Black kids."

70. Although I cannot vouch for all of their practices and individual work-ers, organizations such as Jewish Family Services, which also has an Alliance for Adoption division, or other Jewish Family and Children Services with Adoption Resources offices, Stars of David (a national organization with local chapters makes available many resources on the web, on paper and including their news-letter Star Tracks), and the Jewish Social Service Agency (JSSA) are all helping Jewish families adopt and are increasingly open to queers and multiculturalism. The Jewish Multiracial Network is doing important work helping multiracial Jewish families, many created through adoption, build community and address bias. GLAD, The National Gay and Lesbian Task Force, other queer and ally groups, many local activists and legislators are working to end discrimination against queers in adoption and foster care and seeking to clarify the connections between these struggles and antiracist ones.

Chapter Three: Going Natural

1. Historians of the family have long argued that the nuclear family form now regarded as natural emerged in a long and sometimes fraught process of interaction with broader economic and social forces (see for example Hareven 2000, Kandiyoti 1998, Carbone 2000). On the difficulties of identifying general-izable patterns of family formation due to regional variation in family form see Wall et al., *Family History Revisited*, 2001. Anthropologists have long pointed to the enormous variations in kinship forms regarded as normative (Modell 1994; Stone 2001; Coontz 1992).

2. I'm not sure what a .2 gender is, but I would suggest that the one boy and one girl concept (even perhaps the gendered association of a dog for the boy and a cat for the girl) relates to a social imperative for heterosexual complementarity. See Alpert, *Like Bread on the Seder Plate*, 1997 for her introduction of the term heterosexual complementarity.

3. In any number of popular and scientific forums, science, biology, ge-netics, and reproduction are associated within the language of nature, religion/ Christianity, and sexuality. As one illustrative example: in 2003 the *New York Times* ran an article on a "landmark" discovery of the "natural" attractant of a sperm for an egg and another compound which "shuts down the sperm receptor and keeps it from responding to an attractant." This "attractant" was referred to as "the holy grail in reproductive biology." As will be discussed below, there is a fine line between the celebration of "new knowledges" which can enable society to en-hance or limit birthrates as part of an effort toward reproductive freedom, and the use of such "knowledge" to enhance the birthrates among certain segments of the population, and limit it among "less desirable" segments. More generally on nature, sex, and science, see Lancaster, *The Trouble with Nature*, 2003. For examples of works critical of "nature" in the vein I examine here more broadly, see Katz, *Invention of Heterosexuality*, 1995; Warner, *Fear of a Queer Planet*, 1993; Berlant and Warner, "Sex in Public," 1998; Warner, *Trouble with Normal*, 1999.

4. See E. Wayne Carp, "Orphanages vs. Adoption," 2002. Stranger adoption was able to become more common after 1920 with the invention of mass-produced infant formula (Crossen 1989, 1). Though new in the United States (which as the "U.S." has only had a modern history), adoption had a long history in the pre-modern era outside the United States (Boswell 1988, and Gager 1996).

5. Thanks to Adele Reinhartz who taught me this so many years ago. See Boswell, *Kindness of Strangers*, 1988 for an excellent discussion of this and related phenomena.

6. See E. Wayne Carp particularly, *Family Matters*, 1998, and also "Orphanages vs. Adoption," 2002. See also Gill, "Adoption Agencies," 2002; Nelson, *Little Strangers*, 2003; Berebitsky, "To Raise as Your Own," 1994 for an overview of changing adoption and foster care practices in the United States.

7. On the relationship between indenture and changes in foster care and adoption practices see Porter, "A Good Home," 2002 and Hacsi, "From Indenture to Family Foster Care," 1995.

8. For example, see Millen, *Women, Birth, and Death in Jewish Law*, 2004; Sered, *What Makes Women Sick?*, 2000; Wasserfall ed., *Women and Water*, 1999; Kahn, *Reproducing Jews*, 2000; Cardin, *Tears of Sorrow, Seeds of Hope*, 1998; Weissler, *Voices of the Matriarchs*, 1998, esp. chap. four; Gold, *And Hannah Wept*, 1998; Umansky and Aston eds., *Four Centuries of Jewish Women's Spirituality*, 1992; Adelman, *Miriam's Well*, esp. months adar aleph and tammuz, 1986); Resnick Levine, ed., *A Ceremonies Sampler*, 1991. Also see websites for Stars of David, and the Shomrei Mitzvot Adoption List on Yahoo.

9. On the stigma of childlessness and women's internalization of such, see Ratner ed., *Bearing Life*, 2000; and Sandelowski, *With Child in Mind*, 1993, in historical perspective in the United States see Marsh and Ronner, *The Empty Cradle*, 1996, in international perspective see Inhorn and Van Balen eds., *Infertility Around the Globe*, 2002, and for attempts at changing viewpoints see Cain, *The Childless Revolution*, 2001. For Jewish examples see citations in note above.

10. The connection between formal adoption and infertility was in part a product of institutional practices/deliberate policy interventions: as Gill points out, adoption agencies in the 1940s and 1950s "commonly imposed a requirement of infertility as a prerequisite for adoption" (2002, 169), requiring medical examinations for example. Simon and Alstein note that they found in the first part of their twenty-year study performed in 1972: "Unless couples could produce medical evidence that they were unable to bear a child, most of them were 'strongly advised' to have at least one child; and then, if they found that they were still interested in adoption, the agency would be willing to consider candidacy" (2000, 61). See also Johnston, *Adopting Fertility*, 1996.

11. As argued here, the foundations of such reasoning are grounded in social ideology predicated on racial, heterosexist hierarchy. This has not precluded occasional "others" from engaging in the practice. We see this increasingly as the market opens up to nonwhites, queers, Jews, those who share these identities and others formerly excluded from the institutions offering eugenic promises. Even some proponents of eradicating race matching in adoption who purport

to be antiracist still rely on a notion of nature that can be approximated with a fixed notion of racial meaning. (See Fogg-Davis for her discussion 2002, 57–58.) For a critical look at queers' entry into the terrain of family formation as consumer choice see West, "Universalism, Liberal Theory and the Problem of Gay Marriage," 1998.

12. See Fein, "Secrecy and Stigma," 1998, 30; Carp, "Orphanages vs. Adoption," 1998; and Kennedy and Davis, *Boots of Leather, Slippers of Gold*, 1993. This reinvigorated hegemonic ideal was mostly aimed at those marked as coming closer to the cluster of identity signifiers characteristic of elites. However, such ideological pressures create standards for many individuals and marginalized groups seeking dignity and an end to discrimination via the path of assimilation. Further, Fein writes: "In addition, social workers seized on a postwar embrace of psychoanalytic theories—which tended to view unmarried mothers as disturbed, adoptees seeking information about their roots as neurotic, and infertile people as unstable—as a rationale for keeping adoptive families and biological families apart" (1998, 30). Recall that this is the same historical moment discussed in chapter one of the simultaneous opening/shifting of identity categories (the popularization of sex reassignment surgery in this country, the shifting racial assignment of the U.S. Jewish community, fluctuating gender roles, class-crossing for some subsets of the U.S. population, etc.) previously assumed to be immutable as these categories underwent a reessentialization (a jettisoning of diversity within them) as a corollary transformation.

13. Fogg-Davis 2002 figures the racial difference in transracial adoptions as a "gap" (5), a "fissure" (17), or a "schism" (93) requiring her theory of racial navigation. Though she suggests that such facility with racial navigation would be useful beyond cases of families formed through transracial adoption, she also states: "In racially monolithic biological families, . . . no racial discrepancies exist in the family's racial continuity" (13). She does not adequately problematize or explain the meaning of a "racially monolithic biological family." As debates over the racial-coding in the U.S. Census demonstrate (Williams 1997a; Azouley 2001), such a presumption relies on a mythic notion of racial purity initiated within the aspiration and acquisition of white supremacy. See Lester, *Lovesong*, 1988 for a beautifully written and illustrative personal tale also of Jewish relevance. Fogg-Davis' rendition is therefore also inattentive to other aspects of intragroup racially related hierarchies such as those relating to skin shading, hair, lips, noses, eyes (and eyelids), ears, bone structure, height and weight, etc. (See Golden 2004 as an example.)

14. This is a huge debate, wherein the mechanisms for expanding the market for genetic testing and gamete transfers rely on questionable assumptions. Infrequently are the limitations of genetic predictability discussed by agencies. Zack, *Race and Mixed Race*, 1993, however, as an example, calls into question the predictability of genetically passing on any particular characteristic associated with race. Stevens, "Methods of Adoption," 2005 decodes the assumption of genetic transmission through the generations more broadly in this context.

15. Williams, "Spare Parts, Family Values," 1997b; Cornell, *At the Heart of Freedom*, 1998; Shanley, *Making Babies*, 2001; Stevens, "Methods of Adoption," 2005; Fogg-Davis, *Ethics of Transracial Adoption*, 2002; Roberts 2002; Carp, "Intro-

duction," 2002 and *Family Matters*, 1998; Herman, "Families Made by Science," 2001; Samuels, "The Idea of Adoption," 2001; Berebitsky, *Like Our Very Own*, 2000; Presser, "The Historical Background of American Law of Adoption," 1971–72; Zainaldin, "The Emergence of a Modern American Family," 1979; Ben-Or, "The Law of Adoption in the United States," 1976; Howard, "Transracial Adoption," 1984; Howe, "Transracial Adoption (TRA)," 1997; Perry, "The Transracial Adoption Controversy," 1993–94 and "Race and Child Placement," 1990–91.

16. See the edited anthologies on adoption studies by Carp, "Introduction," 2002, Wadia-Ells, *The Adoption Reader*, 1995, and Haslanger and Witt, *Adoption Matters*, 2005 for excellent introductions.

17. See Kennedy, "Orphans of Separatism," 1994 and Gill, "Adoption Agencies," 2002.

18. See Shanley, *Making Babies*, 2001 for a critical discussion of the "as if" family.

19. Here I have in mind such arguments as in Pertman, *Adoption Nation*, 2000a.

20. Butler, *Gender Trouble*, 2000a (i.e., pp. 171–180).

21. For now I will use "alternative" in quotation marks. As I will argue below, to see such families as "alternative" maintains the imaginative—inextricably linked to the juridical—centrality of bio-family formation.

22. Among critical and progressive thinkers seeking to end discrimination against adoptive families, it is becoming more commonplace to point out the problematics of the "as if" family. Important contributions to the discussion, these arguments show the direction of influential norms carried from the world of bio-family formations onto adoptive family formations. (See, for example, Shanley 2002 and Fogg-Davis 2002.) Drawing on these works, my argument here will also turn the discussion around and examine the ways that developments regarding adoptive family formations have come to influence bio-family formations.

23. Unless otherwise stated, the stats in this paragraph are taken from: Federal Interagency Forum on Child and Family Statistics, *America's Children*, 2001. (The sources for the statistics taken from this section of that document are the 2000 March current Population Survey and Fields and Kreider 2002.)

24. Fields and Casper, *American Families and Living Arrangements*, 2001, 14.

25. The 2000–2001 NJPS places the current intermarriage rate at 43 percent (page 16).

26. The stats in this paragraph are taken from a report released by the Centers for Disease Control and Prevention (CDC) 2001 based on data from the 1995 National Survey of Family Growth.

27. Stats in this paragraph are taken from Fields and Kreider, *Number, Timing and Duration of Marriages*, 2002. See also Marquis, "Total of Unmarried Couples," 2003.

28. U.S. Census Bureau Statistical Abstract 2001.

29. The stats in the rest of this paragraph are taken from: Federal Interagency Forum on Child and Family Statistics, *America's Children*, 2001 (whose sources are March Current Population Survey 2000 and Fields and Kreider 2002).

30. See Thornton, "What the Census Doesn't Count," 2001 and McMillan, "Down For The Count," 2001.

31. The 2000 U.S. Census was the first to provide an opportunity to mark the sexual orientation of household members (this after GLBT groups turned to census counting as a political issue). Thus, some measure was taken of those reporting same-sex dual headed households with children. See Marquis, "Total Unmarried Couples," 2003 and Bellafante, "Two Fathers," 2004 for some information yielded.

32. Landes and Posner, in the article in which they argue for the differential pricing of children in adoption to remedy the "shortage" of white babies and encourage the adoption of "overstocked" Black babies, rely on the "knowledge" that people calculate in aspects of family formation as they do in the market and elsewhere (1978, 344).

33. The traditional raced heterosexual expectation that the sentence will end with SWM (male) has been expanded into an array of initilized symbols in queer communities, websites, and publications serving those in s/m cultures, etc. Such ads make for interesting studies in examining the "political" nature of "personal preferences." As nonheterosexual couples and those involved in nonmonogamous relationships are increasingly choosing, and more legally able, to create families with children, the reader ought not discount the eugenic potential embedded in these mass-market dating cultures as well. (See for example Smith and Stillman 2003; Sue 2001; Bartholome, Tewksbury, and Bruzzone 2000; Gonzales and Meyers 1993; Goode 1996; and Smith, Waldorf, and Trembath 1990.)

34. Stevens, *Reproducing the State*, 1999, Walzer, "On Voluntary Association," 1998, 65, and Fogg-Davis, *Ethics of Transracial Adoption*, 2002, 97 are political theorists who at least momentarily pause to consider the political question embedded in the category "those whom we meet." In a more problematic vein, Irvine, *The Politics of Parenting*, 2003 pauses to consider this question within an argument *for* eugenics (see especially pages 29–32).

35. See Moran, *Interracial Intimacy*, 2001, 116–119 and in general on this point. See also Belzer, "Ira Glass, Where Are You?," 2003 for great article by a Jewish feminist sorting through the dilemmas of heterosexual dating and attraction and Fries, *Body, Remember*, 1997 for a Jewish gay disabled perspective.

36. See for example, Giddens, *Transformation of Intimacy*, 1992 and Coontz, *Marriage, a History*, 2005; on the development of romance novels for women see Modleski, *Loving with a Vengeance*, 1982. On the development of the use of Yiddish (as opposed to Hebrew) for nonreligious writing such as romance novels for a female audience see Seidman, *A Marriage Made in Heaven*, 1997; see also Tucker, *A Probable State*, 2000 and Miron, *A Traveler Disguised*, 1996.

37. Written before *Lawrence v. Texas* see Morris Kaplan, *Sexual Justice*, 1997 for an alternative reading of potential privacy rights that might avoid this problem.

38. See Simon and Alstein, *Adoption Across Borders*, 2000, 23–25 for connections between this move to strike down laws against racially mixed marriages and developments in transracial adoption.

39. Foggs-Davis briefly discusses the "morally suspect private racial preferences in . . . reproductive decision-making calculus" and discusses some literature on popular views against interracial dating to demonstrate that heterosexuals intending to create bio-families also make specific decisions regarding race-based generation (2002, 84–85). See also Foucault, *History of Sexuality*, 1990 for a discussion of the state interest in regulating and normalizing family formation through concerns with reproduction and Stevens (1999, 14), for an exploration of how state-sanctioned kinship rules (re)produce heteronormative affiliations of family, race, and nation through a notion of "reproculture" in which individuals imagine their connections to others and in time through biological ties. For some earlier Jewish queer writings on family see for example essays in Beck, *Nice Jewish Girls*, 1982, and the "Honoring our Relationships" part of Balka and Rose, *Twice Blessed*, 1989 (i.e., Ackelsberg; Herman; Horowitz and Klein; Holtzman; and Plaskow).

40. Jessica Radin (2004), an adult transnational and transracial adoptee, calls such logic into question. Radin was adopted from Thailand by a U.S. Euro-Ashkenazi Jewish single mother. With much love and appreciation for her adoptive route and family, her analysis of her journey also provides critical insight into this long held notion that adoptive children are "better off" than they would have been had they stayed with their bio-relations. See Roberts 2002 on this point as well.

41. For example see Belkin, "The Opt-Out Revolution," 2003 mainly in reference to heterosexual women. Gina Bellafante 2004 writes that gay male couples with children choose to have one partner stay at home more frequently than heterosexual couples or lesbian couples, and that their numbers are much higher than the numbers of male partners in heterosexual couples who stay home.

42. Blum, *At the Breast*, 1999. As an example of Jewish feminist scholarship on breast feeding see Labovitz, "These are the Labors," 2000.

43. For an overview of research into changing family size and normative kinship forms see Hareven, *Families, History, and Social Change*, 2000; Stone, *New Directions*, 2001; Turner, *Families in America*, 2002; Abbott, *Family Affairs*, 2003; Peplar, *Family Matters*, 2002; Weston, *Familes We Choose*, 1991; Lehr, *Queer Family Values*, 1999.

44. For example, Herbert G. Gutman reports that in New York City of 1905, "Two in five immigrant Jewish and migrant black households had unrelated boarders in them" (1976, 525).

45. See for example Cahill, "Welfare Moms and the Two Grooms," 2005.

46. See for example: Johnson, "Former Cocaine User Regains Child," 1999; Williams, "Losing Isaiah," 1995; Smolowe, "Adoption in Black and White," 1995; Berry, "Adoption, Race, and Red Tape," 1995; and Holmes, "Bitter Racial Dispute," 1995.

47. For example, Blum's 1999 work on breast feeding suggests a racial break in the glorification of these bodily modalities. Her research found that many African-American women felt the need to distance themselves from U.S. historic associations of Black women's bodies with "nature" manifest in lower rates (or shorter durations) of breast feeding and a less idealized view of the practice than has come to be popular again in a new cult of motherhood for middle-class white women.

48. Fogg-Davis refers to this tendency to equate choice with control in adoption. Although she argues that it is not enough of a reason to engage in race matching adoption practices, she does not sufficiently analyze the envy that those in the bio-baby business direct onto those in adoption, as if one can really control a process whereby they can ready make the children they think they want. She writes: "To have choices suggests some measure of control. Choosing an already born child, rather than giving birth to a child, suggests that prospective adoptive parents can exercise control precisely where 'nature'/biology would have held the reins" (2002, 91).

49. As examples, I realize that I open myself up to the criticism that these are exceptions and not expressing hegemonic contemporary ideas. I can only respond to such a challenge with two insights: First, I find these presumptions so pervasive that I could simply not possibly point out all instances of their manifestations. I have decided that these examples serve as just that, examples of the phenomenon. The critique that follows will not apply in all cases to every production in their genres, but is meant to be illustrative enough to enable readers to undertake similar critical examinations of other texts. Second, without concretizing the analysis offered above, I also realize that readers may remain skeptical of the critique, assuming my claims to be the exaggerations of yet another academic. In this case, therefore, I hope readers will find a brief discussion of some pop forms and one scholarly text instructive, not exhaustive.

50. See Butler, "Imitation," 1991, and *Bodies That Matter*, 1993, 125–126.

51. Specific examples of the following points on soaps are far too numerous to note here. Wanting to provide some justification for this notion, however, I chose to turn on the television at midday during a winter break—deciding in advance, I would sit through the first soap opera I found. The *Young and the Restless* was the winner. I was not disappointed. Not long into the hour came the scene of an older generation couple secretly discussing the young beautiful couple in the scene just prior. The older couple discussed when they would tell the young man that the woman was "really" his sister. See also Mumford, *Love and Ideology in the Afternoon*, 1995, particularly chapter five on paternity plots in soaps, and also Modleski, *Loving with a Vengeance*, 1982. The daytime soap opera remains alive and well, yet somewhat eclipsed in the 1990s by the daytime talk show (see Abt and Mustazza 1997, 5) and in the next decade by reality television shows.

52. There is much scholarship on the paradoxes of "democratization through exploitation, truth wrapped in lies, normalization through freak show" of the daytime talk show. (Gamson 1998, 19; see also Priest 1995 for a discussion of the marginalized using the medium as a tactic.) More specifically, on the ways that these shows appear to challenge heterosexual, racial, classed, and gendered norms but actually reinforce those very norms see, for example, Epstein and Steinberg, "All Het Up!," 1996; Shattuc, *The Talking Cure*, 1997; Manga, *Talking Trash*, 2003; and Grindstaff, *The Money Shot*, 2002.

53. Another text worthy of such critical examination is Fogg-Davis, *Ethics of Transracial Adoption*, 2002. Like Shanley, she often refers to bio-families as original to distinguish them from adoptive ones. Fogg-Davis purports, especially in chapter four with a thought experiment of racial randomization for adoption,

to help us uncover biased assumptions commonly held about racial homogeneity and other fictions of the "rightness" of genetic ties in families. However, her argument relies on an unnecessary distinction she argues exists between adoptive and biological families which itself reifies presumptions of the "naturalness" of bio-families and the "createdness" of adoptive ones. The main factor she focuses on is the mediation of the state in adoptive families. With quick references to the fact that bio-families are also created through webs of social factors, she dismisses such to emphasize the social factors of adoption and ultimately pushes bio-families back into a more private/prepolitical category. In chapter five, she offers a theory of natal alienation that, while it may hold some helpful insights, relies all too heavily on assumptions of the trueness of bio-relations over and against adoptive ones.

54. Searches over the years for articles in Political Science and related disciplines have not yielded much fruit. Among the few other chapters and books written by political theorists are Stevens, "Methods of Adoption," 2005; Cornell, *At the Heart of Freedom*, 1998; Foggs-Davis, *Ethics of Transracial Adoption*, 2002.

55. There have always been multiple family forms. See, for example, Seccombe, *A Millenium of Family Change*, 1992; Skolnick, *Embattled Paradise*, 1991; Wall et al., *Family History Revisited*, 2001; Weston, *Families We Choose*, 1991; Mallon, *We Don't Exactly Get the Welcome Wagon*, 1998, 114 (for a discussion of alternative families created by GLBTQ adolescents who have fled foster care and group homes due to abuse). Similarly, the family has long been a concern of modern government (Foucault 1990; Stevens 1999). I am arguing that the specific manifestations of this concern are particularly interesting in an era marked by neoliberalism and cultural conservatism.

56. Having said this, I also thank Shanley for her work on these new ethics. They may seem *to her* prompted by "new" issues for new kinds of families, but they have also long been needed for families in general and understanding why will further help us denaturalize the family.

57. The law usually presupposes this (see Stevens 2005 note 29 for detailed conditions in law and some challenges). However, Shanley is generally interested in problematizing, rather than accepting, such hegemonic conceptions.

58. This position is similar to that expressed by Cornell, *At the Heart of Freedom*, 1998, where she argues that the key legitimate area for state intervention in/regulation of family relations is to formalize adult responsibility for children. See Fineman, *The Neutered Mother*, 1995, and Stevens, *Reproducing the State*, 1999 for alternative views.

59. See for example Cahill, "Welfare Moms and the Two Grooms," 2005.

60. There is a long history to this fear of the possibility of making men/fathers irrelevant. With the development of reproductive technologies such as the pill or research on parthenogenesis, there was an outcry of this sort. See for example Reed, *Birth Control Movement*, 1983 and Pauly, *Controlling Life*, 1987. The story of Mary is confusing for (U.S.) Americans in its secularized version. Stevens (2005) proposes eliminating the subject position father altogether.

61. Thus, the move for adoptees' rights, and the "right to know one's origins" too often relies similarly on a reification of bio-ties. On adoptees' rights

controversies see Carp, *Adoption Politics*, 2004; Pertman, *Adoption Nation*, 2000a; Sullivan, "Bastard Chronicles," 2001 parts one and two; Samuels, "The Idea of Adoption," 2001; Fischer, "Emerging Role of Adoption," 2002; the special issue on Adoption Controversies of the Congressional Quarterly Researcher (Stencel 1999), and Saunders, "Lawmakers Consider Unsealing Birth Certificates," 2004. See also information on activist organizations such as Bastard Nation (www. bastards.org). For a discussion of some difficulties to the broadest adoptee rights claims, see Shanley, *Making Babies*, 2001, 21–24. A common sentiment is expressed in the following query posed in a book about people who were born Jews but did not grow up knowing this information: "Yes, I love my adoptive parents and we have a good relationship. They even helped me in my search [for bio-ties]. But I wanted to know what everybody else knows . . . the basic facts of my identity" (cited in Kessel 2000, 98). The affect here certainly radiates. Nevertheless, it is important to note that biology is seen to provide "the basic facts of . . . identity," and it is assumed "everybody else knows" such things. For a more critical view, see Patton, *Birth Marks*, 2000, and Stevens, *Reproducing the State*, 1999.

62. See examples of this language deployed in studies such as Brodzinsky, Schecter, and Henig, *Being Adopted*, 1992.

63. See Crossen, *Hard Choices*, 1989, and Fein, "Secrecy and Stigma," 1998. Adding to the sensationalized character of these new power relations in the market economy of open adoption are events such as the *20/20 Special* on ABC by Barbara Walters Friday 4/30/04. "Be My Baby: A Unique Look Inside the Open Adoption Process." Here we get to see, "live," these heterosexual married couples desperately trying to sell themselves to the perky white sixteen-year-old birth mother. Widespread controversy erupted over the promotion of the show as a reality TV show about competing for a baby (See, for example, Carter 2004 a and b). The anchors' and network's response was to apologize, change the promotion campaign, and claim it's good journalism not about marketing the baby. What was missed in much of the controversy was that, insensitive promotional material notwithstanding, the show *was* a report on competition and marketing in humans because that is what happens in the contemporary white world of adoption. For more on the commodification of mothering generally, see the essays in Taylor et al., *Consuming Motherhood*, 2004.

64. Williams, "Spare Parts, Family Values," 1997b comments on this from her own experience as well.

65. Fogg-Davis, *Ethics of Transracial Adoption*, 2002, 81.

66. See Dubowsky, "Jewish Dyke Baby-Making," 2002 as an interesting Jewish lesbian example.

67. The growing popularity of new technologies such as sonograms and genetic screenings help to create a history for the fetus in new ways. Now the fetus which a woman who hopes to raise as her child once born is created as already having a life and can be set in a context of relationships much as the "prelife" of many adopted children and gametes utilized in transfers. In the cases of adoption and gamete transfers, the market focus on social, health, and other histories and relations of particulars singled out for commodification create a "life

embedded in relations" before families have living children. Seen as more concrete than the commonly fantasized "who will my child be" version in pregnancies of those who hope to raise the children they birth, now with sonograms, genetic screenings, and so forth, those engaged in more traditional forms of bio-baby production can get a prelife for their gametes and fetuses with the array of characteristics one can "choose" to know. These procedures are, of course, incredibly costly. "Choosing" to get a prelife for your gamete or fetus is largely a privilege of the wealthy and those few who have excellent health insurance coverage. At the same time, the creation of gametes and fetuses as "having lives of their own" are central to both the antichoice movement and those seeking to limit the birthing potential of marginalized and criminalized women (see, for example, Ordover 2003; Rapp 1999; Morgan and Michaels 1999; and Berlant 1997).

68. The Jewish newspaper *The Forward* occasionally includes a special supplement on Genetics. Generally the articles focus on developments, usually covered in laudatory fashion, of "Jewish" genetic diseases, improved options of doing Jewish geneologies, and other "breakthroughs" in genetics with a Jewish connection. Often basic issues of debate are at least noted. On the particular point of genetic testing of embryos, insurance coverage, costs and controversies, see Zuckerman, "Procedure Offers Hope for Families," 2003 in that year's supplement. She presents the new research in terms of genetically altering an embryo tested and found to have a genetic disease can theoretically enable a family to "avoid the anguish of abortion" although the process of in vitro fertilization necessitated usually requires "fetal reduction"—basically aborting the "extra" embryos implanted. See Alpert, "What is a Jew?," forthcoming for a Jewish feminist discussion of some issues involved in the notion of "Jewish genetic diseases." For a discussion of the eugenic-market connection see Foggs-Davis, *Ethics of Transracial Adoption*, 2002; Shanley, *Making Babies*, 2001; Daniels, *Exposing Men*, forthcoming; Radin, "Market Inalienabiliy," 1987; Anderson, "Is Women's Labor A Commodity," 1990.

69. Lancaster, *Trouble with Nature*, 2003, and Roberts, *Killing the Black Body*, 1997.

70. See the play made into a film *Twilight of the Golds* (Marks 1997) portraying the struggle of a Jewish family playing the gene game with Brandon Fraser playing the role of the gay son. See also Ordover, *American Eugenics*, 2003.

71. See Sered, *Women as Ritual Experts*, 1996 on such customs among Mizrachi women in Israel.

72. Hartmann, *Reproductive Rights and Wrongs*, 1995; Chatterjee and Riley, "Planning an Indian Modernity," 2001; Kaler, "Who Has Told You To Do This Thing?," 2000; Abrams, "Popular Politics," 2000; Silliman and King, *Dangerous Intersections*, 1999. On queer history and eugenics see Ordover, *American Eugenics*, 2003, and Kline, *Building a Better Race*, 2001. On related aspects of eugenics see Black, *War Against the Weak*, 2003; Roberts, *Killing the Black Body*, 1997; Inhorn and Van Balen, *Infertility*, 2002—and for related works including discussions of the relationship between the important work of Margaret Sanger on birth control see Ordover, *American Eugenics*, 2003; Reed, *Birth Control Movement*, 1983; Cuddy and Roche, eds., *Evolution and Eugenics*, 2003; Kennedy, *Birth Control in America*, 1970, esp. 108–125; and Gordon, *The Moral Property of Women*, 2002.

73. For an international analysis see Hartman, *Reproductive Rights and Wrongs*, 1995. For an historical analysis in the United States see Roth, "The Reproductive Rights of Prisoners," 1999; Roberts, *Killing the Black Body*, 1997; Ordover, *American Eugenics*, 2003; Gomez, *Misconceiving Mothers*, 1997. For news regarding this in my own backyard, so to speak, see Vega, "Sterilization Offer to Addicts," 2003.

74. Roberts, *Killing the Black Body*, 1997; Strathern, "Displacing Knowledge," 1995.

Chapter Four: Questing for Heart in a Heartless World

1. In Tucker ed., *Mark-Engels Reader*, 1978, 54.

2. This analysis is very much indebted to the insight Rich, *Of Woman Born*, 1976 offers into motherhood as both an experience *and* an institution.

3. Readers may hear an echo of Horney's, "Problem of the Monogamous Ideal," 1967 incredible essay on marriage and monogamy. I will not comment here on her examination in terms of the psychological bases for the problematics she delineates, but her views may still be seen as quite radical, for example, in their situation of marriage and monogamy as social institutions, her defiance of arguments relying on a recourse to "nature," her identification of a root problem the idealization of the experiences due to the functions as institutions, and the possessive nature of jealousy. Special thanks to Lanie Resnick for the lessons on Horney.

4. When I first conceived this chapter, I did not have in mind at all Christopher Lasch's work similarly titled: *Haven in a Heartless World*. Lasch does argue that the very system that sets up the need for the family as a private haven is what threatens this last heavenly stronghold against the conflict of the public world. He also presumes the family was once such a haven, become increasingly at risk and a host of other sentimental notions which differ from that which the reader will find in this chapter

5. See, for example, first-wave feminists: Victoria Woodhull's 1871 speech on "The Principles of Social Freedom" in which she discusses marriage and free love (pages 1–43 in Stern ed. 1974); and later de Cleyre's 1908 "They Who marry do Ill" (in Glassgold, ed. 2001, 103–113); and Emma Goldman's (in Goldman1969) anarchist essays. For other anarchist statements see Bakunin's 1866 Revolutionary Catechism: "N" (in Dolgoff 1972, 93–94).

Examples of radical early second-wave feminist writings include Cronin's 1973 article "Marriage"; Germaine Greer's 1971 chapter "The Middle-Class Myth in Love and Marriage" (198–218); and some of the historical documents collected in Morgan 1970 such as "Women: Do you know the Facts about Marriage?" (601–603); and among the WITCH documents such as the 1969 "Confront the Whoremakers at the Bridal Fair," (610–613). See also Echols' *Daring to Be Bad*, 1989 discussion of the era.

6. See Ehrenreich's, *The Hearts of Men*, 1983 classic critique, and Messner, *Politics of Masculinities*, 1997. For some of the original expressions of this view see Brenton, *The American Male*, 1966 (with his "every day is mother's day" attitude, pp.

134–141 and in general), Goldberg, *Hazards of Being Male*, 1976 (whose perspective on marriage is expressed clearly in the book's promotional materials: "Today one great difference between men and women is that women at least *know* they are oppressed."); see Farrell, *The Liberated Man*, 1974; Kaye, *Male Survival*, 1974; Nichols, *Men's Liberation*, 1975; Williams and Williams, "All We Want is Equality," 1995; Crowley, *Politics of Child Support in America*, 2003, 160–193. For updated information on men's and fathers' rights, see http://www.themenscenter.com/National/national 06.htm(7/5/05).

7. Queers hold an array of views on the matter of "legalizing same-sex marriage." A spate of works published in 1996 lay out some of this terrain: Vaid, *Virtual Equality*, 1996; Sullivan, *Virtually Normal*, 1996; Eskridge, *The Case of Same-Sex Marriage*, 1996; Osborn, *Coming Home to America*, 1996. Lehr, *Queer Family Values*, 1999 includes this discussion nicely within a larger frame of "queer family values." For later and other arguments, see Rauch, *Gay Marriage*, 2004; Warner, *The Trouble with Normal*, 1999; Duggan, "Holy Matrimony," 2004; and Calhoun, *Feminism, the Family, and the Politics of the Closet*, 2000 chap. 5. Also of particular interest in concert with chapter three above, Carbone, *From Partners to Parents*, 2000 discusses same-sex marriage in the context of a foundational shift in U.S. family law from attention to the partners in a marriage to attention to parents' relationships to children. In the Political Science literature, see the Symposium in *PS* 2005 (Segura; Lewis; Hillygus and Shields; Liu and Macedo; Gerstmann; Riggle, Thomas, and Rostosky; Smith; Egan and Sherrill, Haider-Markel and Joslyn). For a Jewish bisexual's critique, see Rose, "Against Marriage," 1996.

8. See Alpert (forthcoming); and Alpert, Levi Elwell, and Idelson eds., *Lesbian Rabbis*, 2001.

9. Though many a leader in these movements will understandably add that a more fitting description is that they were pushed into working within this issue arena over time as opposition mounted and the dynamics of politics "created" marriage as a distinct social justice issue area. Richard Goldstein (2003) wants to make a radical argument for gay marriage. Although he makes some good points, ultimately his stance is unpersuasive, not distinguishing clearly enough between queer critiques offered and explicit resistance to changing U.S. law. A helpful work which does take into account a broader constellation of race and class diversity among same-sex partners seeking marriage rights and the benefits to an array of populations is Cahill, *Same-Sex Marriage in the United States*, 2004.

10. See for example, Tannenbaum, *Slave and Citizen*, 1946, 85. For information on marriage between free Blacks and Black slaves see Gutman, *Black Family in Slavery and Freedom*, 1976; Stevenson, *Life in Black and White*, 1996; Malone, *Sweet Chariot*, 1992; Hudson, *To Have and to Hold*, 1997.

Scholarly debate regarding the desire to make slave marriage customs legal and whether such a move interrupted power dynamics of slavery or reinscribed them hauntingly recalls similar debates about making same-sex unions legally valid as marriages (see Will 1999).

11. See Jones, *What's So Queer About Marriage*, 2004.

12. Though *Webster's* makes it sound like the first definition of monogamy is about "one marriage only during life"—no, that's the definition itself—set off from bigamy and polygamy which are about having multiple spouses at the same time. And definition "*a*" is distinguished from definition "*b*" which suggests you can have more than one marriage "during life," but they must be entered into serially, unlike bigamy and polygamy. But faithful *Webster's* defines digamy as coming from the Greek for adultery but meaning "a legal second marriage after the termination of a first marriage" (as by death or divorce of the spouse). So the antonym for monogamy is not properly digamy—called also *deuterogamy*; distinguished from *bigamy*. There are those nondefinitional tautologies again.

13. Valerie Lehr 1999 takes a similar approach, arguing that (1) "if we accept social structures, such as monogamous marriage, as simply natural, we lose the opportunity to engage in the processes of reflection and self-construction. That is, we lose the possibility of enhancing our freedom" (21); and with regard to the specific push for same-sex marriage rights, (2) "the extension of rights depoliticizes issues that need to be subject to public debate and discussion," and thus the current form of seeking freedom in an extension of rights "foreclose[s] serious questioning of values" and institutions (14–15).

14. See Roediger, *Wages of Whiteness*, 1991 for more on this concern.

15. See the Expatriation Act of 1907 and for commentary: Cott, "Marriage and Women"s Citizenship," 1998; Nicolosi, "We Do Not Want Girls to Marry Foreigners," 2001.

16. As in the cases of Rebecca Shelley and Rosika Schwimmer both of whom were active pacifists and feminists. See Bredbenner, *A Nationality of Her Own*, 1998, 183–194.

17. Toward the end of the nineteenth century, white men could marry Black women foreign nationals, thereby making the Black women U.S. citizens. At the same time, Native American women, who married white men, were seen to be giving up their Native status under tribal law (Cott 1998, 148–49, note 53).

18. Cuddle—Cousins United to Defeat Discriminating Laws through Education—is an organization making appeals to overturn incest taboo-based marriage laws. This organization grounds its organizing strategy on work against earlier antimiscegenation laws and more recently the ban on gay marriage. See www.cuddleinternational.org and also on this issue Ottenheimer, *Forbidden Relatives*, 1996.

19. See for example Shapiro, *No Pity*, 1993, 197, and Pietrzak, "Marriage Laws and People with Mental Retardation," 1997.

20. In February of 1900, for example, the Journal of the American Medical Association took a stand pointing out the problems with Colorado's then current attempt to restrict marriage on such a basis with violation of the proposed act punishable with four to seven years in prison (Reiling 2000, 980). Medical exams often still test for rubella, venereal diseases, sickle cell anemia, and AIDS (Cornell University-Legal Information Institute, 7/12/05). In Massachussettes, for example, the law prohibiting marriage certificates if the parties have certain communicable diseases was in effect until January 27, 2005 (see the General Laws of Massachusetts "Notice of Intention of Marriage" (http://www.mass.gov/legis/laws/mgl/207-

28a.htm accessed 4/26/05). For history of the role of science in the denial of the right to marry within the context of a critique of U.S. eugenics, see Black, *War against the Weak*, 2003.

21. Moran, *Interracial Intimacy*, 2001, 42–43. On Native-white miscegenation laws, see for example Berger, "After Pocahontas," 2003 and Woods, "A 'Wicked and Mischievous Connection,' " 2003. The citizenship status of white men who married Native American women and resided in Indian territory subject to tribal law did come into question (see Cott 1998, 1441 footnote 4).

22. See, for example, Harper's autobiographical *Iona Leroy* 1988. On miscegenation laws more generally see: Pascoe, "Miscegenation Law, Court Cases," 2000; Johnson, *Mixed Race America and the Law*, 2003; Kennedy, *Interracial Intimacies*, 2003; Moran, *Interracial Intimacy*, 2001.

23. This analogy of the institutions of interracial marriage and adoption is not coincidental. In fact, their histories have long been intertwined, and in ways that continue to effect challenges in current adoption practices. See for example Kennedy, *Interracial Intimacies*, 2003, and Moran, *Interracial Intimacy*, 2001. This does not mean, however, that mixed race individuals and those in cross-racial adoptive families understand their life experiences and needs as necessarily allied. We see this dynamic played out in the growth patterns and tensions faced within organizations of and for those in mixed-race communities, such as Swirl, Inc. and the Multiracial Jewish Network. (See, for example, Chau 2004 and Radin 2004.)

24. In cases across minority communities, in their own particular ways, people have often noted the difficulty in holding a multiracial identity. For example, in the story of her becoming an African-American Jew who feels most comfortable praying in a Sephardi (rather than Ashkenazi) synagogue, Conaway, "Journey to the Promised Land," 2004 discusses how her family's African-American identity has trumped its Native American identity.

25. See for example, Volpp, "American Mestizo," 2003, and UCLA Asian American Studies Center, "Anti-Miscegenation Laws," 1976.

26. Explorations of this notion are originally indebted to Max Weber's *The Protestant Ethic and the Spirit of Capitalism*.

27. See Azouley's discussion of these interlocking phenomena (1997, 33–34 and in general). The U.S. ban on Jews employing Christian servants or marrying white Christians is similar to the way the Nuremburg Race Laws of twentieth-century Germany are conceived: Jews become prohibited from employing Aryan women as household help and marrying or having sexual relations with Aryans. (See Proctor 1988, 131–132, and The History Place 3/30/05.)

28. For example, although the history of adultery is long presumed to be that of married men having sexual relations with women other than their wives, a 1983 (Blumenstein and Schwartz, 274) study suggests that 68 percent of husbands and 57 percent of wives had engaged in such with those other than their spouses. Predictions were that these numbers would rise, with a ten-point spread between male and female adultery practices (Lampe 1987, i.e., 212).

29. I do not discuss this as a repudiation of the everyday. Nor does the fact that life cannot be lived in a continual I-Thou justify aspiring to (settling for, idealizing, or institutionalizing) the I-It. See Feld, *A Spiritual Life*, 1999, and Lester,

Lovesong, 1988 for examples in a Jewish context of attempting a life in which the I-Thou is brought into/experienced within the ordinary, without being apologetics for the way that life is lived within the realm of the I-It most of the time.

30. See also Heyward, *Touching Our Strength*, 1989.

Epilogue: Justice and La Vida Jew . . . in Technicolor Queer

1. Many others have commented on similar circumstances. See for example McLarin, "Primary Colors," 1998; Scales Trent, *Notes of a White Black Woman*, 1995; and Derricotte, *The Black Notebooks*, 1997; and see Rush, *Loving Across the Color Line*, 2000.

2. See Greenberg, "Hip Hop Moguls," 2005.

Bibliography

Abbott, Mary. 2003. *Family Affairs: a History of the Family in 20th Century England*. London and New York: Routledge.

Abrams, Paula. 2000. "Population Politics: Reproductive Rights and U.S. Asylum Policy." *Georgetown Immigration Law Journal* 1: 881–905.

Abt, Vicki and Leonard Mustazza. 1997. *Coming After Oprah: Cultural Fallout in the Age of the TV Talk Show*. Bowling Green, OH: Bowling Green State University Popular Press.

Adams, Maurianne and John Bracey, eds. 1999. *Strangers and Neighbors: Relations Between Blacks and Jews in the United States*. Amherst, MA: University of Massachusetts Press.

Adler, Margot. 1997. *Heretic's Heart: A Journey Through Spirit and Revolution*. Boston: Beacon Press.

Adler, Rachel. 1998. *Engendering Judaism: An Inclusive Theology and Ethics*. Philadelphia and Jerusalem: The Jewish Publication Society.

Adelman, Penina V. 1986. *Miriam's Well: Rituals for Jewish Women Around the Year*. New York: Bibliopress.

Agosín, Marjorie. 1995. *A Cross and a Star: Memoirs of a Jewish Girl in Chile*. Albuquerque, NM: University of New Mexico Press.

———. 1998. *Always From Somewhere Else: A Memoir of My Chilean Jewish Father*. New York: Feminist Press at the City University of New York.

———, ed. 1999a. *Passion, Memory, and Identity: Twentieth-Century Latin American Jewish Women Writers*. Albuquerque, NM: University of New Mexico Press.

———. 1999b. *Uncertain Travelers: Conversations with Jewish Women Immigrants to America*. Hanover, NH and London: University Press of New England for Brandeis University Press.

———. 2002. *Taking Root: Narratives of Jewish Women in Latin America*. Athens, OH: Ohio University Press.

Agosín, Marjorie and Elizabeth Horan, eds. 1999. *The House of Memory: Stories by Jewish Women Writers of Latin America*. New York: Feminist Press at The City University of New York.

Agosín, Marjorie and Roberta Gordenstein, eds. 2001. *Miriam's Daughters: Jewish Latin American Women Poets*. Santa Fe, NM: Sherman Asher Publishers.

Allen, Theodore. 1994. *The Invention of the White Race: Racial Oppression and Social Content, Vol. 1*. London: Verso.

Alpert, Rebecca. 1997. *Like Bread on the Seder Plate: Jewish Lesbians and the Trans-formation of Tradition*. New York: Columbia University Press.

———. Forthcoming. "Reconstructionist Judaism and Marriage Equality." Edited by Traci West. Westport, CT: Praeger.

———. Forthcoming. "What is a Jew? The Meaning of Genetic Diseases for Jewish Identity." Edited by Lori Zoloth and Elliot Dorf. Cambridge, MA: MIT Press.

Alpert, Rebecca, Sue Levi Elwell, and Shirley Idelson, eds. 2001. *Lesbian Rabbis: The First Generation*. New Brunswick, NJ: Rutgers University Press.

Anderson, Elizabeth S. 1990. "Is Women's Labor A Commodity?" *Philosophy and Public Affairs* 19, No. 1 (Winter): 71–92.

Anzaldúa, Gloria, ed. 1990. *Making Face, Making Soul: Haciendo Caras: Creative and Critical Perspectives by Feminists of Color*. San Francisco: Aunt Lute Foundation Books.

Anzaldúa, Gloria and Cherrie Moraga, eds. 1982. *This Bridge Called My Back: Writings of Radical Women of Color*. New York: Kitchen Table, Women of Color Press.

Arendt, Hannah. *The Human Condition*. 1958. Chicago: University of Chicago Press.

Ashkenaz, Judy. 1995. "Indians." In *The Adoption Reader: Birth Mothers, Adoptive Mothers and Adopted Daughters Tell Their Stories*. Edited by Susan Wadia-Ells, 141–149. Seattle: Seal Press.

Aviv, Caryn and David Shneer, eds. 2002. *Queer Jews.* New York: Routledge.

Azoulay, Katya Gibel. 1997. *Black, Jewish, and Interracial: It's Not the Color of Your Skin but the Race of Your Kin and Other Myths of Identity*. Durham, NC, and London: Duke University Press.

———. 2001a. "Jewishness After Mount Sinai: Jews, Blacks and the (Multi)racial Category." *Bridges: A Journal for Jewish Feminists and Our Friends* 9, No. 1: 31–45.

———. 2001b. "Jewishness After Mount Sinai: Jews, Blacks and the (Multi) Racial Category." *Identities* 8, No. 2: 211–246.

Baldwin, James, et al. 1969. *Black Anti-Semitism and Jewish Racism*. New York: R. W. Baron.

———. 1963. *The Fire Next Time*. New York: Dial Press.

———. 1984. "On Being 'White.' . . . and Other Lies." *Essence* April: 90–92.

———. 1985. *The Price of the Ticket: Collected Nonfiction, 1948–1985*. New York: St. Martin's Press.

Balka, Christie and Andy Rose, eds. 1989. *Twice Blessed: On Being Lesbian, Gay, and Jewish*. Boston: Beacon Press.

Banks, Richard. 1998. "The Color of Desire: Fulfilling Adoptive Parents' Racial Preferences through Discriminatory State Action." *Yale Law Journal* 107, No. 4: 875–964.

Barringer, Herbert, Robert Gardner, and Michael Levin. 1995. *Asian and Pacific Islanders in the Unites States*. New York: Russell Sage Foundation.

Bartholet, Elizabeth. 1999. *Nobody's Children: Abuse and Neglect, Foster Drift, and the Adoption Alternative*. Boston: Beacon Press.

————. 1991. "Where Do Black Children Belong? The Politics of Race Matching in Adoption." *University of Pennsylvania Law Review* 139: 1163–1256.

Bartholome, Adreanna, Richard Tewksbury, and Alex Bruzzone. 2000. " 'I Want
A Man:' Patterns of Attraction in All-male Personal Ads." *Journal of Men's
Studies* 8, No. 3: 309–321.

Bayer, Ruth Myra. 1995. "Close By." In *The Adoption Reader: Birth Mothers, Adoptive Mothers and Adopted Daughters Tell Their Stories.* Edited by Susan Wadia-
Ells, 251–260. Seattle: Seal Press.

Beck, Evelyn Torton. 1984. *Nice Jewish Girls: A Jewish Lesbian Anthology.*
Trumansburg, NY: Crossing Press.

Belkin, Lisa. 1999. "Getting the Girl." *New York Times Magazine*, July 25, p. 26.

————. 2003. "The Opt-Out Revolution." *New York Times Magazine*, October 26.
(accessed electronically at http://nytimes.com/2003/10/26/magazine/
26WOMEN.html?e=5070&en=4c4e8249 on 06/11/03)

Bellafante, Gina. 2004. "Two Fathers, With One Happy to Stay at Home." *New
York Times*, January 24, A1.

bell hooks. 1981. *Ain't I A Woman: Black Women and Feminism.* Boston: South End
Press.

Belzer, Tobin. 2003. "Ira Glass, Where Are You?." In *Joining the Sisterhood: Young
Jewish Women Write Their Lives.* Edited by Tobin Belzer and Julie Pelc,
177–188. Albany: State University of New York Press.

Belzer, Tobin and Julie Pelc, eds. 2003. *Joining the Sisterhood: Young Jewish Women
Write Their Lives.* Albany: State University of New York Press.

Ben-Jochannan, Yosef A. A. 1998. *Our Black Seminarians and Black Clergy Without
a Black Theology: The Tragedy of Black People/Africans in Religion Today.* Baltimore, MD: Black Classic Press.

————. 1993. *We the Black Jews.* Baltimore, MD: Black Classic Press.

Ben-Or, Joseph. 1976. "The Law of Adoption in the United States: Its Massachusetts Origins and the Statute of 1851." *New England Historical and Genea-
logical Register* 130: 259–73.

Berebitsky, Julie. 1994. " 'To Raise as Your Own': The Growth of Legal Adoption
in Washington." *Washington History* 6: 5–26, 105–7.

————. 2000. *Like Our Very Own: Adoption and the Changing Culture of Motherhood
1851–1950.* Lawrence, KS: University of Kansas Press.

Berger, Bethany Ruth. 2003. "After Pocahontas: Indian Women and the Law,
1830–1934." In *Mixed Race America and the Law: A Reader.* Edited by Kevin
R. Johnson, 71–80. New York and London: New York University Press.

Berger, Graenum. 1978. *Black Jews in America: A Documentary with Commentary.*
New York: Commission on Synagogue Relations/Federation of Jewish
Philanthropies of New York.

Berlant, Laura. 1997. *The Queen of America Goes to Washington City: Essays on Sex
and Citizenship.* Durham, NC: Duke University Press.

Berlant, Lauren and Michael Warner. 1998. "Sex in Public." *Critical Inquiry* 24,
No. 2 (Winter): 547–566.

Berman, Paul, ed. 1994. *Blacks and Jews: Alliances and Arguments.* New York:
Delacorte Press.

Bernards, Reena. 2001. "An Ethiopian *Gilgul* Come to Life: An Interview with Toni Eisendorf." *Bridges: A Journal for Jewish Feminists and our Friends* 9, No. 1: 21–25.

Berry, Karin D. 1995. "Adoption, Race, and Red Tape." *Emerge* (April): 40–46.

Biale, David, Michael Galchinsky, and Susannah Heschel, eds. 1998. *Insider/Outsider: American Jews and Multiculturalism*. Berkeley, CA: University of California Press.

Bickford, Susan. 1997. "Anti-Anti-Identity Politics: Feminism, Democracy, and the Complexities of Citizenship." *Hypatia* 12, No. 4 (Fall): 111–131.

Black, Edwin. 2003. *War Against the Weak: Eugenics and America's Campaign to Create a Master Race*. New York: Four Walls Eight Windows.

Blum, Linda. 1999. *At The Breast: Ideologies of Breastfeeding and Motherhood in the Contemporary United States*. Boston, MA: Beacon Press.

Blumenfeld, Warren J. 1996. "History/Hysteria: Parallel Representations of Jews and Gays, Lesbians and Bisexuals." In *Queer Studies: A Lesbian, Gay, Bisexual, and Transgender Anthology*. Edited by Brett Beemyn and Mickey Eliason, 146–162. New York and London: New York University Press.

Blumstein, Philip and Pepper Schwartz. 1983. *American Couples*. New York: Morrow.

Blustain, Sarah. 1996. "Are You Black or Are You Jewish? The New Identity Challenge." *Lilith: The Independent Jewish Women's Magazine* 21, No. 3 (Fall): 21–27.

Bornstein, Kate. 1995. *Gender Outlaw: On Men, Women, and the Rest of Us*. New York: Vintage.

Boswell, John. 1988. *The Kindness of Strangers: The Abandonment of Children in Western Europe from Late Antiquity to the Renaissance*. New York: Pantheon.

Bowen, James. 1987/8. "Cultural Convergences and Divergences: The Nexus between Putative Afro-American Family Values and the Best Interests of the Child." *Journal of Family Law* 26: 487–544.

Boyarin, Jonathan and Daniel Boyarin, eds. 1997. *Jews and Other Differences: The New Jewish Cultural Studies*. Minneapolis, MN: University of Minnesota Press.

Boyarin, Daniel. 1997. *Unheroic Conduct: The Rise of Heterosexuality and the Invention of the Jewish Man*. Berkeley, CA: University of California Press.

Boyarin, Daniel, Daniel Itzkovitz, and Ann Pellegrini, eds. 2003. *Queer Theory and the Jewish Question*. New York: Columbia University Press.

Boykin, James. 1982. *Black Jews: Ethiopia, India, United States*. Miami, FL: J. H. Boykin.

———. 1996. *Black Jews: A Study in Minority Experience*. Miami, FL: J. H. Boykin.

Bredbenner, Candace, Lewis. 1988. *A Nationality of Her Own: Women, Marriage, and the Law of Citizenship*. Berkeley, CA and London: University of California Press.

Brenton, Myron. 1966. *The American Male*. New York: Coward-McCann, Inc.

Brettschneider, Marla. 1996a. *Cornerstones of Peace: Jewish Identity Politics and Democratic Theory*. New Brunswick, NJ: Rutgers University Press.

———, ed. 1996b. *The Narrow Bridge: Jewish Views on Multiculturalism*. New Brunswick, NJ: Rutgers University Press.

————, ed. 1999. *Race, Gender, and Class: American Jewish Perspectives* 6, No. 4.

————. 2001. "To Race, to Class, to Queer: Jewish Contributions to Feminist Theory." In *Jewish Locations: Traversing Racialized Landscapes.* Edited by Bat-Ami Bar On and Lisa Tessman, 213–38. Lanhan, MD: Rowman and Littlefield.

————. 2002. *Democratic Theorizing From the Margins.* Philadelphia: Temple University Press.

————, ed. 2004. *Nashim: A Journal of Jewish Women's Studies and Gender Issues Special Issue: Tense Dialogues: Speaking (across) Multicultural Differences in the Jewish/Israeli/International Feminist World* 8 (Summer).

Brettschneider, Marla and Dawn Rose, eds. 2003. "Meeting at the Well: Multiculturalism and Jewish Feminism." A special section of the *Journal of Feminist Studies in Religion* 19, No. 1 (Spring): 85–128.

Bridges: A Journal for Jewish Feminists and our Friends. Special Issue: Writing and Art by Jewish Women of Color 2001. 9, No. 1.

Bridges: A Journal for Jewish Feminists and our Friends. Special Issue: Sephardi and Mizrachi Women Write About their Lives 1997–8 7, No. 1.

Brodkin, Karen. 1998. *How Jews Became White Folks and What that Says About Race in America.* New Brunswick, NJ: Rutgers University Press.

Brodzinsky, David, Marshall D. Schecter, and Robin Marantz Henig. 1992. *Being Adopted: The Lifelong Search for Self.* New York: Doubleday.

Brotz, Howard. 1964. *The Black Jews of Harlem: Negro Nationalism and the Dilemmas of Negro Leadership.* New York: Schocken Books.

Brown, Angela, ed. 2004. *Mentsh: On Being Jewish and Queer.* Los Angeles, CA: Alyson Books.

Buber, Martin. 1958. *I and Thou.* Translated by Gregor Smith. New York: Collier Books.

Budick, Emily Miller. 1998. *Blacks and Jews in Literary Conversation.* New York: Cambridge University Press.

Burns, James MacGregor, J. W. Peltason, Thomas Cronin, David Magleby, and David O'Brien. 2002. *Government by the People*, Brief 4th Ed. Upper Saddle River, NJ: Prentice Hall.

Butler, Judith. 1991. "Imitation and Gender Insubordination." In *Inside/Out: Lesbian Theories, Gay Theories.* Edited by Diana Fuss, 13–31. New York: Routledge.

————. 1993. *Bodies That Matter: On the Discursive Limits of "Sex."* New York: Routledge.

————. 2000a. *Gender Trouble: Feminism and the Subversion of Identity.* Tenth Anniversary Edition, 13–31. New York: Routledge.

————. 2000b. "Ethical Ambivalence." In *The Turn to Ethics.* Edited by Marjorie Garber, Beatrice Hanssen, and Rebecca L. Walkowitz, 15–28. New York: Routledge.

Butler, Shakti (Director). 1988. *The Way Home.* Presented by World Trust/New Day Films. Hohokus, NJ.

Cahill, Sean. 2004. *Same-Sex Marriage in the United States: Focus on the Facts.* Lanham, MD: Lexington Books.

———. 2005. "Welfare Moms and the Two Grooms: The Concurrent Promotion and Restriction of Marriage in US Public Policy." *Sexualities* 8, No. 2: 169–187.

Cahill, Sean, Juan Battle, and Doug Meyer. 2004. "Partnering, Parenting, and Policy: Family Issues Affecting Black Lesbian, Gay, Bisexual, and Transgender (LGBT) People." *Race & Society* 6: 85–98.

Cahnman, Werner. 1967. "The Interracial Jewish Children," *Reconstructionist*. 33, No. 8: 7–12.

Cain, Madelyn. 2001. *The Childless Revolution: What it Means to Be Childless Today*. Cambridge, MA: Perseus Publishing.

Calhoun, Cheshire. 2000. *Feminism, the Family, and the Politics of the Closet: Lesbian and Gay Displacement*. New York: Oxford University Press.

Carbone, June. 2000. *From Partners to Parents: The Second Revolution in Family Law*. New York: Columbia University Press.

Cardin, Nina Beth. 1998. *Tears of Sorrow, Seeds of Hope : A Jewish Spiritual Companion for Infertility and Pregnancy Loss*. Woodstock, VT: Jewish Lights.

Carp, E. Wayne. 1998. "Orphanages vs. Adoption: The Triumph of Biological Kinship, 1800–1933." In *With Us Always: A History of Private Charity and Public Welfare*. Edited by Donald T. Critchlow and Charles H. Parker, 123–144. Landham, MD: Rowman & Littlefield Publishers, Inc.

———. 1998. *Family Matters: Secrecy and Disclosure in the History of Adoption*. Cambridge, MA: Harvard University Press.

———. 2002. "Introduction: An Historical Overview of American Adoption." In *Adoption in America: Historical Perspectives*. Edited by E. Wayne Carp, 1–26. Ann Arbor, MI: The University of Michigan Press.

———, ed. 2002. *Adoption in America: Historical Perspectives*. Ann Arbor, MI: The University of Michigan Press.

———. 2004. *Adoption Politics: Bastard Nation and Ballot Initiative 58*. Lawrence, KS: University Press of Kansas.

Carroll, Rebecca and Bill Dockery. 1995. "The Debate over Cross-Racial Adoption: An Odd Coalition Takes Aim at a Decades-Old Prejudice Against Transracial Placements." *USA Weekend Magazine* 17–19 (March).

Carter, Bill. 2004a. " 'The Ultimate Reality Show' On Adoption." *The New York Times*, Wednesday, April 28, E1, E8.

———. 2004b. "Walters Defends Show on Adoption." *The New York Times*, Friday, April 30, E5.

CBS News. "Born in USA, Adopted in Canada." 2/19/2005.

Centers for Disease Control and Prevention. 2001. *Marriage Dissolution, Divorce, and Remarriage: United States*. National Center for Health Statistics on the World Wide Web: http://www.cdc.gov/nchs/releases/01newa/firstmarr.htm. Retrieved April 30, 2002.

Chatterjee, Nilanjana and Nancy E. Riley. 2001. "Planning an Indian Modernity: The Gendered Politics of Fertility Control." *Signs: Journal of Women in Culture and Society* 26, No. 3 (Spring): 811–845.

Chau, Jennifer. 2004. "More than Chicken Chow Mein." In Symposium "Tense Dialogues: Speaking (Across) Multicultural Difference in the Jewish Feminist World." Edited by Marla Brettschneider. Of *Nashim: A Journal of Jewish Women's Studies and Gender Issues* 8 (Fall): 136–143.

Chireau, Yvonne and Nathaniel Deutsch, eds. 2000. *Black Zion: African American Religious Encounters with Judaism*. New York: Oxford University Press.

Cohen, Rich. 1998. *Tough Jews*. New York: Simon and Schuster.

Cohen, Steven M. Shifra Bronznick, Didi Goldenhar, Sherry Israel, and Shaul Kelner. 2004. "Creating Gender Equity and Organizational Effectiveness in the Jewish Federation System: A Research-and-Action Project." New York: Advancing Women Professionals and the Jewish Community in partnership with the United Jewish Communities.

Cohen, Tamara, Lead Researcher. 2005. "Listen to Her Voice: The Ma'yan Report, Assessing the Experiences of Women in the Jewish Community and their Relationships to Feminism." New York: Ma'yan: The Jewish Women's Project, a Program of the Jewish Community Center in Manhattan.

Coleman, Alex. 2003. "Variations on a Theme." *Sh'ma* 33, No. 602 (June): 5–6.

Collins, Patricia Hill. 1990. *Black Feminist Thought*. New York: Routledge.

Commission for Women's Equality of the American Jewish Congress. 1993. *Highlights of the Survey of Female Rabbis about Sexual Discrimination and Harassment*. New York: American Jewish Congress.

Conaway, Carol. 2004. "Journey to the Promised Land: How I Became an African-American Jew Rather than a Jewish African-American." In Symposium "Tense Dialogues: Speaking (Across) Multicultural Difference in the Jewish Feminist World." Edited by Marla Brettschneider. Of *Nashim: A Journal of Jewish Women's Studies and Gender Issues* 8 (Fall): 115–128.

Coontz, Stephanie. 1992. *The Way We Never Were: American Families and the Nostalgia Trap*. New York: Basic Books.

———. 2005. *Marriage, a History: From Obedience to Intimacy or How Love Conquered Marriage*. New York: Viking Press.

Cornell, Drucilla. 1998. *At the Heart of Freedom: Feminism, Sex, and Equality*. Princeton, NJ: Princeton University Press.

Cornell University Legal Information Institute. "Marriage Laws of the Fifty States, District of Columbia and Puerto Rico." (7/12/05). http://straylight.law.cornell.edu/topics/Table_Marriage.htm

Cott, Nancy. 1998. "Marriage and Women's Citizenship in the United States, 1830–1934." *American Historical Review* 103, No. 5 (December): 1440–1474.

Council of Jewish Federations Research Department. 1994. "The Status of Women in Lay and Professional Leadership Positions of Federations: Summary Report." New York: Council of Jewish Federations

Courtney, Mark. 1997. "The Politics and Realities of Transracial Adoption." *Child Welfare* 126 (November–December): 749–779.

Cronin, Sheila. 1973. "Marriage." In *Radical Feminism*. Edited by Anne Koedt, Ellen Levine, and Anita Rapone, 213–221. New York: Quadrangle Books.

Cross, June. 1996. *Secret Daughter*. PBS Video.

Crossen, Cynthia. 1989. "Hard Choices: In Today's Adoptions, the Biological Parents Are Calling the Shots." *Wall Street Journal* 14 (September): 1.

Crowley, Jocelyn Elise. 2003. *The Politics of Child Support in America*. Cambridge, U.K.: Cambridge University Press.

Cuddy, Lois A. and Claire M. Roche, eds. 2003. *Evolution and Eugenics in American Literature and Culture, 1880–1940*. Lewisburg, PA: Bucknell University Press.

Curtis, Perry L. 1971. *Apes and Angels: The Irishman in Victorian Caricature*. Washington, DC: Smithsonian Institution.

Dalmage, Heather. 2000. *Tripping on the Color Line: Black-White Multiracial Families in a Racially Divided World*. New Brunswick, NJ: Rutgers University Press.

Daniel, Ruby and Barbara C. Johnson. 1995. *Ruby of Cochin: An Indian Jewish Woman Remembers*. Philadelphia, PA: The Jewish Publication Society.

Daniels, Cynthia. Forthcoming. *Exposing Men: The Science and Politics of Male Reproduction*. New York: Oxford University Press.

Davis, Angela. 1981. *Women, Race, and Class*. New York: Random House.

———. 1998. "An Interview with Angela Davis." By Nina Siegal. *Ms.* (September/October): 73.

Davis, F. James. 1991. *Who Is Black? One Nation's Definition*. University Park, PA: Pennsylvania State University Press.

Davis, Sammy Jr. with Jane and Burt Boyar. 1965. *Yes I Can: The Story of Sammy Davis, Jr.* New York: Farrar, Straus & Giroux.

Dekro, Jeffrey. 1996. "Facilitating Multicultural Progress: Community Economic Development and the American Jewish Community." In *The Narrow Bridge: Jewish Views on Multiculturalism*. Edited by Marla Brettschneider, 27–41. New Brunswick, NJ: Rutgers University Press.

Delgado, Richard and Jean Stefancic, eds. 1997. *Critical White Studies: Looking Behind the Mirror*. Philadelphia: Temple University Press.

Delman, Carmit. 2002. *Burnt Bread and Chutney: Reflections of an Indian Jewish Girl*. New York: One World/Ballantine Books.

Denholtz, Elaine Grudin. 2000. *Balancing Work and Love: Jewish Women Facing the Family-Career Challenge*. Hanover, NH and London: University Press of New England for Brandeis University Press.

Derricotte, Toi. 1997. *The Black Notebooks: An Interior Journey*. New York: W. W. Norton and Co., Inc.

Dickson, Deborah, produced by Donald Goldmacher. 2002. *Ruthie and Connie: Every Room in the House*. Distributed by Women Make Movies.

Dolgoff, Sam, ed. 1972. *Bakunin on Anarchy: Selected Works by the Activist-Founder of World Anarchism*. New York: Alfred A. Knopf.

Du Bois, W. E. B. 1990. *The Souls of Black Folk*. New York: Vintage Books.

Dubowsky, Hadar. 2002. "Jewish Dyke Baby-Making" In *Queer Jews*. Edited by David Shneed and Caryn Aviv, 44–54. New York: Routledge.

Duggan, Lisa. 2004. "Holy Matrimony!" *The Nation* 278, No. 10: 14–19.

Echols, Alice. 1989. *Daring to Be Bad: Radical Feminism in America 1967–1975*. Minneapolis, MN: University of Minnesota Press.

Egan, Patrick and Sherrill, Kenneth. 2005. "Marriage and the Shifting Priorities of a New Generation of Lesbians and Gays." *PS: Political Science and Politics*. 38, No. 2: 229–323.

Ehrenreich, Barbara. 1983. *The Hearts of Men: American Dreams and the Flight From Commitment*. Garden City, New York: Anchor Press/Doubleday.

Eng, David. 2003. "Transnational Adoption and Queer Diasporas." *Social Text* 76, 21, No. 3 (Fall): 1–32.

Engels, Frederick. 1981. *The Origin of the Family, Private Property and the State*. New York: International Publishers.

Epstein, Debbie and Deborah Lynn Steinberg. 1996. "All Het Up! Rescuing Heterosexuality on the *Oprah Winfrey Show*." *Feminist Review* 54 (Autumn): 88–115.

Eskridge, William N., Jr. 1996. *The Case for Same-Sex Marriage*. New York: The Free Press.

Esses, Dianne. 2003. "A Common Language Between East and West." In "Meeting at the Well: Multiculturalism and Jewish Feminism." Edited by Marla Brettschneider and Dawn Rose, Special Section, in the *Journal Of Feminist Studies in Religion* 19, No. 1: 111–118.

Faber, Eli. 1998. *Jews, Slaves, and the Slave Trade*. New York: New York University Press.

Fanshel, David. 1972. *Far from the Reservation: The Transracial Adoption of American Indian Children*. Metuchen, NJ: Scarecrow Press.

Farrell, Warren. 1974. *The Liberated Man: Beyond Masculinity: Freeing Men and Their Relationships with Women*. New York: Random House.

Federal Interagency Forum on Child and Family Statistics. 2001. *America's Children: Key National Indicators of Well-Being*. www.childstats.gov. Retrieved April 30, 2002.

Fein, Esther B. 1998. "Secrecy and Stigma No Longer Clouding Adoption." *New York Times*, October 25, 1: 30–31.

Feinberg, Leslie. 1993. *Stone Butch Blues*. Ithaca, New York: Firebrand Books.

Feld, Merle. 1999. *A Spiritual Life: A Jewish Feminist Journey*. Albany: State University of New York Press.

Ferguson, Kathy. Forthcoming. *Goldman: Political Thinking in the Streets*. Lanham, MD: Rowman and Littlefield.

Fields, Jason and Lynne M. Casper. 2001. *America's Families and Living Arrangements: March 2000. Current Population Reports*. Washington, DC: U.S. Census Bureau.

Fields, Jason and Rose M. Kreider. 2002. *Number, Timing and Duration of Marriages and Divorces: 1996. Current Population Reports*, 70–80. Washington, DC: U.S. Census Bureau.

Fineman, Martha. 1995. *The Neutered Mother, the Sexual Family, and Other Twentieth Century Tragedies*. New York: Routledge.

Fischer, Robert L. 2002. "The Emerging Role of Adoption Reunion Registries: Adoptee and Birthparent Views." *Child Welfare* 81, No. 3 (May/June): 445–470.

Fishman, Sylvia Barack. 1993. *A Breath of Life: Feminism in the American Jewish Community*. New York: The Free Press.

Fogg-Davis, Hawley. 2002. *The Ethics of Transracial Adoption*. Ithaca and London: Cornell University Press.

Fonrobert, Charlotte Elisheva. 2001. "When Women Walk in the Way of Their Fathers: On Gendering the Rabbinic Claim for Authority." *Journal of the History of Sexuality* 10, No. 3/4 (July/October): 398–415.

Foucault, Michel. 1990. *History of Sexuality Volume I*. New York: Vintage Books.

Franklin, V. P., et al., ed. 1998. *African Americans and Jews in the Twentieth Century: Studies in Convergence and Conflict*. Columbia, MO: University of Missouri Press.

Freedberg, Sydney. 1994. *Brother Love: Murder, Money, and a Messiah*. New York: Pantheon Books.

Friedman, Murray. 1995. *What Went Wrong?: The Creation and Collapse of the Black-Jewish Alliance*. New York: Free Press.

Fries, Kenny. 1997. *Body Remember: A Memoir*. New York: Dutton.

Funderburg, Lise. 1994. *Black, White, Other: Biracial Americans Talk about Race and Identity*. New York: William Morrow and Co.

Gager, Kristin Elizabeth. 1996. *Blood Ties and Fictive Ties: Adoption and Family Life in Early Modern France*. Princeton, NJ: Princeton University Press.

Gamson, Joshua. 1998. *Freaks Talk Back: Tabloid Talk Shows and Sexual Nonconformity*. Chicago: The University of Chicago Press.

Geffen, Rela M. 1987. *Jewish Women on the Way Up: The Challenge of Family, Career, and Community*. New York: The American Jewish Committee, Institute of Human Relations.

Gelman, Martin. 1965–1971. *Adat Beyt Moshe, the Colored House of Moses: A Study of A Contemporary Negro Religious Community and Its Leader*. Philadelphia: .s.n.

Gerber, Israel. 1977. *The Heritage Seekers: American Blacks in Search of Jewish Identity*. Middle Village, New York: Jonathan David Publishers.

Gerstmann, Evan. 2005. "Litigating Same-Sex Marriage: Might the Courts Actually Be Bastions of Rationality?." *PS: Political Science and Politics*. 38, No. 2: 217–220.

Gibel, Inge Lederer. 1965. "The Negro-Jewish Scene: A Personal View." *Judaism* 14, No. 1 (Winter): 12–21.

Giddens, Anthony. 1992. *The Transformation of Intimacy: Sexuality, Love, and Erotocism is Modern Societies*. Stanford, CA: Stanford University Press.

Gill, Brian Paul. 2002. "Adoption Agencies and the Search for the Ideal Family, 1918–1965." In *Adoption in America: Historical Perspectives*. Edited by E. Wayne Carp, 160–180. Ann Arbor, MI: The University of Michigan Press.

Gilman, Sander. 1991. *The Jew's Body*. New York and London: Routledge.

———. 1996. *Smart Jews: The Construction of Jewish Superior Intelligence*. Lincoln, NE: University of Nebraska Press.

Gitlitz, David M. 1996. *Secrecy and Deceit: The Religion of the Crypto-Jews*. Philadelphia: Jewish Publication Society.

Gladwell, Malcolm. 2001. "Examined Life." *The New Yorker* 77, No. 40 (December 17): 86.

Glassgold, Peter, ed. 2001. *Anarchy! An Anthology of Emma Goldman's Mother Earth*. Washington, DC: Counterpoint.

Glückel of Hameln. 1977. *The Memoirs of Glückel of Hameln*. Translated by Marvin Lowenthal. New York: Schocken Books.

Gold, Michael. 1998. *And Hannah Wept: Infertility, Adoption, and the Jewish Couple*. Philadelphia, New York, and Jerusalem: The Jewish Publication Society.

Goldberg, Herb. 1976. *The Hazards of Being Male: Surviving the Myth of Masculine Privilege*. New York: A Signet Book.

Golden, Marita. 2004. *Don't Play in the Sun: One Woman's Journey Through the Color Complex*. New York: Doubleday.

Goldman, Emma. 1969. *Anarchism and Other Essays*. New York: Dover Publications, Inc.

Goldman, Karla. 2004. "Who Knew?" In *350 Years of Jewish Women Building Communities in North America*. Brookline, MA: Jewish Women's Archive. Pamphlet.

Goldstein, Richard. 2003. "The Radical Case for Gay Marriage: Why Progressives Must Join this Fight." *The Village Voice* 3–9 (September): 32–34.

Goluboff, Sascha, ed. 2001. Special Issue on Jews, *Identities* 8, No. 2.

Gomez, Laura E. 1997. *Misconceiving Mothers: Legislators, Prosecutors, and the Politics of Prenatal Drug Exposure*. Philadelphia: Temple University Press.

Gonzales, Marti Hope and Sarah A. Meyers. 1993. " 'Your Mother Would Like Me': Self Presentation in the Personal Ads of Heterosexual and Homosexual Men and Women." *Personality and Social Psychology Bulletin* 19: 131–143.

Goode, Erich. 1996. "Gender and Courtship Entitlement: Responses to Personal Ads." *Sex Roles* 34, No. 3–4 (February): 141–169.

Gordon, Albert. 1964. "Negro-Jewish Marriages: Three Interviews." *Judaism* 13, No. 2 (Spring): 164–184.

Gordon, Linda. 1999. *The Great Arizona Orphan Abduction*. Cambridge, MA and London: Harvard University Press.

Gordon, Linda. 2002. *The Moral Property of Women: A History of Birth Control Politics in America*. Urbana and Chicago: University of Illinois Press.

Goslinga-Roy, Gillian M. 2000. "Body Boundaries, Fiction of the Female Self: An Ethnographic Perspective on Power, Feminism, and the Reproductive Technologies." *Feminist Studies* 26, No. 1 (Spring): 113–140.

Gramsci, Antonio. 1971. *Selections from the Prison Notebooks*. New York: International Publishers.

Gray, Ahuvah. 2001. *My Sister, the Jew*. Southfield, MI: Targum Press.

Greenberg, Eric. 2005. "Hip Hop Mogul's Ad Campaign Fuels Feud Between Groups." *Forward* (February 18): 2.

Greer, Germaine. 1971. *The Female Eunuch*. London: Paladin.

Grindstaff, Laura. 2002. *The Money Shot: Trash, Class, and the Making of TV Talk Shows*. Chicago and London: University of Chicago Press.

Gross, Max. 2005. "To Boldly Go Where No Jew Has Gone: Book Features Klingon Intermarriage." *Forward* (March 11): 1–2.

Gross, Robert E. and Mona West, eds. 2000. *Take Back the Word: A Queer Reading of the Bible*. Cleveland, OH: The Pilgrim Press.

Gutman, Herbert G. 1976. *The Black Family in Slavery and Freedom, 1750–1925*. New York: Vintage Books.

Guy-Sheftall, Beverly, ed. 1995. *Words of Fire: An Anthology of African-American Feminist Thought*. New York: New Press.

Hacsi, Timothy A. 1995. "From Indenture to Family Foster Care: A Brief History of Child Placing." *Child Welfare* 74 (January–February): 162–180.

Haider-Markel, Donald and Joslyn, Mark. 2005. "Attributions and the Regulations of Marriage: Considering the Parallels Between Race and Homosexuality." *PS: Political Science and Politics*. 38, No. 2: 233–239.

Hareven, Tamara K. 2000. *Families, History, and Social Change: Life Course and Cross-Cultural Perspectives*. Boulder, CO: Westview Press.

Harper, Frances E. W. 1988. *Iola Leroy, or Shadows Uplifted*. New York and Oxford: Oxford University Press.

Harris, Louis and Bert Swanson. 1970. *Black-Jewish Relations in New York*. New York: Praeger Publishers.

Hart, Sandra Lorraine. 2001. *The Identity of Mixed Race: An Exploratory Study of Multiracial and Multiethnic Identity Development of Black Jews in the United States*. Master's Thesis, Smith College for Social Work, Northampton, MA.

Hartman, Moshe and Harriet Hartman. 1996. *Gender Equality and American Jews*. Albany: State University of New York Press.

Hartmann, Betsy. 1995. *Reproductive Rights and Wrongs: The Global Politics of Population Control*. Boston: South End Press.

Haslanger, Sally and Charlotte Witt, eds. 2005. *Adoption Matters: Philosophical and Feminist Essays*. Ithaca: Cornell University Press.

Heeb: The New Jew Review. 2002. 1, No. 1 (Winter).

Helfand, Judith. 1996. *A Healthy Baby Girl*. New York: Women Make Movies.

Herman, Ellen. 2001. "Families Made by Science: Arnold Gesell and the Technologies of Modern Child Adoption." *Isis* 92, No. 4: 684–715.

Herron, Carolivia. 1997. *Nappy Hair*. New York: Knopf, distributed by Random House.

———. 2003. "Pastel Meetings." In "Meeting at the Well: Multiculturalism and Jewish Feminism." Edited by Marla Brettschneider and Dawn Rose. Special Section in the *Journal Of Feminist Studies in Religion* 19, No. 1: 105–110.

Heschel, Susannah, ed. 1983. *On Being a Jewish Feminist: A Reader*. New York: Schocken Books.

Heyward, Carter. 1989. *Touching Our Strength: The Erotic as Power and the Love of God*. San Francisco: Harper and Row.

Hillygus, D. Sunshine and Todd Shields. 2005. "Moral Issues and Voter Decision Making in the 2004 Presidential Election." *PS: Political Science and Politics* 38, No. 2: 201–209.

Hing, Bill Ong. 1993. *Making and Remaking Asian America through Immigration Policy, 1850–1990*. Stanford, CA: Stanford University Press.

The History Place. 3/30/2005. "World War Two in Europe: The Nuremberg Race Laws." Http://www.historyplace.com/worldwar2/timeline/nurem-laws.htm.

Holmes, Stephen. 1995. "Bitter Racial Dispute Rages over Adoption." *The New York Times*, April 13, A16.

Holzberg, Carol. 1987. *Minorities and Power in a Black Society: The Jewish Community of Jamaica*. Lanham, MD: The North-South Publishing Co.

Horney, Karen. 1967. "The Problem of the Monogamous Ideal." In *Feminine Psychology*, 84–98. New York and London: W. W. Norton and Company.

Horowitz, Bethamie, Pearl Beck, and Charles Kadushin. 1997. *Power and Parity: Women and Men on the Boards of Major American Jewish Organizations: A Research Report*. New York: Ma'yan: The Jewish Women's Project, the Jewish Community Center of the Upper West Side (later Changed to Jewish Community Center of Manhattan).

Howard, Margaret. 1984. "Transracial Adoption: An Analysis of the Best Interests Standard." *Notre Dame Law Review* 59: 503–55.

Howe, Ruth-Arlene. 1997. "Transracial Adoption (TRA): Old Prejudices and Discrimination Float under a New Halo." *Boston University Public Interest Law Journal* 6 (Winter): 409–72.

Hudson, Larry E. Jr. 1997. *To Have and to Hold: Slave Work and Family Life in Antebellum South Carolina*. Athens and London: The University of Georgia Press.

Hull, Gloria T., Patricia Bell Scott, and Barbara Smith. 1982. *All the Women are White, All the Blacks are Men, But Some of us Are Brave*. Old Westbury, NY: Feminist Press.

Hyman, Paula. 1995. *Gender and Assimilation in Modern Jewish History: The Roles and Representation of Women*. Seattle: University of Washington Press.

Ignatiev, Noel. 1995. *How the Irish Became White*. Cambridge, MA: Harvard University Press.

Inhorn, Marcia C. and Frank Van Balen, eds. 2002. *Infertility Around the Globe: New Thinking on Childlessness, Gender, and Reproductive Technologies*. Berkeley, Los Angeles, and London: University of California Press.

Irvine, William B. 2003. *The Politics of Parenting*. St. Paul, MI: Paragon House.

Isaac, Ephriam. 1996. "Hearing the Call: Solidarity with Ethiopian Jews." In *The Narrow Bridge: Jewish Views on Multiculturalism*. Edited by Marla Brettschneider, 219–235. New Brunswick, NJ: Rutgers University Press.

Isserman, Nancy and Lisa Hostein. 1994. *Status of Women in Jewish Organizations*. New York: American Jewish Committee.

Jacobson, Matthew. 1998. *Whiteness of a Different Color: European Immigrants and the Alchemy of Race*. Cambridge, MA: Harvard University Press.

Johnson, Dirk. 1999. "Former Cocaine User Regains Child in Custody Case." *The New York Times*, March 9, A18.

Johnson, Kevin R. 2003. *Mixed Race America and the Law: A Reader*. New York and London: New York University Press.

Johnston, Patricia Irwin. 1996. *Adopting after Fertility*. Indianapolis, IN: Perspectives Press.

Jones, Hettie. 1990. *How I Became Hettie Jones*. New York: Penguin.

Jones, John Calvin. 2004. "What's so Queer about Marriage? It's all in the Family." Paper Presentation to the Annual Foundations of Political Theory

Workshop on Political Myth, Rhetoric, and Symbolism, Annual American Political Science Association Meeting in Chicago.

Jones, Lisa. 1994. *Bulletproof Diva: Tales of Race, Sex and Hair*. New York: Doubleday.

Kahn, Susan Martha. 2000. *Reproducing Jews: A Cultural Account of Assisted Conception in Israel*. Durham, NC and London: Duke University Press.

Kaler, Amy. 2000. " 'Who Has Told You To Do This Thing?': Toward a Feminist Interpretation of Contraceptive Diffusion in Rhodesia, 1790–1980." *Signs: Journal of Women in Culture and Society* 25, No. 3 (Spring): 677–708.

Kandiyoti, Deniz. 1998. "Some Awkward Questions on Women and Modernity in Turkey." In *Re-Making Women: Feminism and Modernity in the Middle East*. Edited by Lila Abu-Lughod, 270–287. Princeton, NJ: Princeton University Press.

Kanegson, Jaron. 2002. "A Young Man From Chelm: or A Nontraditionally Gendered Hebrew School Teacher Tells All." In *Queer Jews*. Edited by Caryn Aviv and David Shneer, 55–69. New York: Routledge.

Kaplan, Elaine Bell. 1997. *Not Our Kind of Girl: Unraveling the Myths of Black Teenage Motherhood*. Berkeley and Los Angeles, CA: University of California Press.

Kaplan, Morris. 1997. *Sexual Justice: Democratic Citizenship and the Politics of Desire*. New York: Routledge.

Katz, Jonathan. 1995. *The Invention of Heterosexuality*. New York: Dutton.

Kaufman, Heidi Nan. 2001. *Semitic Discourse: English Identity and the Nineteenth-century British Novel*. PhD Diss. University of New Hampshire.

Kaufman, Jonathan. 1988. *Broken Alliance: The Turbulent Times Between Blacks and Jews in America*. New York: Scribner.

Kaye, Harvey E. 1974. *Male Survival: Maculinity without Myth*. New York: Grosset and Dunlap Publishers.

Kaye/Kantrowitz, Melanie. 1992. *The Issue is Power: Essays on Women, Jews, Violence and Resistance*. San Francisco: Aunt Lute Books.

Kaye/Kantrowitz, Melanie and I. Klepfisz, eds. 1989. *The Tribe of Dina: a Jewish Women's Anthology*. Boston: Beacon Press.

Kennedy, David M. 1970. *Birth Control in America: The Career of Margaret Sanger*. New Haven and London: Yale University Press.

Kennedy, Elizabeth Lapovsky and Madeline D. Davis, eds. 1993. *Boots of Leather, Slippers of Gold: The History of a Lesbian Community*. New York: Routledge.

Kennedy, Randall. 1994. "Orphans of Separatism: The Painful Politics of Transracial Adoption." *American Prospect* (Spring): 38–45.

———. 2003. *Interracial Intimacies: Sex, Marriage, Identity, and Adoption*. New York: Pantheon Books.

Kertzer, David I. 1997. *The Kidnapping of Edgardo Mortara*. NewYork: Alfred A. Knopf.

Kertzer, David I. and Marzio Barbagli. 2001. *Family Life in Early Modern Times 1500–1789*. New Haven and London: Yale University Press.

———. 2002. *Family Life in the Long Nineteenth Century 1789–1913*. New Haven and London: Yale University Press.

Kessel, Barbara. 2000. *Suddenly Jewish: Jews Raised as Gentiles Discover their Jewish Roots*. Hanover, NH and London: University Press of New England for Brandeis University Press.

Kessler, Gwynn. 2005. "Let's Cross That Body When We Get To It: Gender and Ethnicity in Rabbinic Literature." *Journal of the American Academy of Religion* 73, No. 2 (June): 329–359.

Khazzoom, Loolwa, ed. 2003. *The Flying Camel: Essays on Identity by Women of North African and Middle Eastern Jewish Heritage*. New York: Seal Press Publishers.

Kinda, LoBagola Bata. 1930. *LaBagola: an African Savage's Own Story*. New York: Knopf.

Kitlinski, Tomasz, Pawel Leszkowicz, and Joe Lockard. 2001. "Monica Dreyfus." In *Our Monica Ourselves: the Clinton Affair and the National Interest*. Edited by Lauren Berlant and Lisa Duggan, 203–222. New York and London: New York University Press.

Klepfisz, Irena. 1990a. "Basherte." In *A Few Words in the Mother Tongue: Poems Selected and New (1971–1990)*. By Irena Klepfisz, 183–200. Portland, OR: The Eight Mountain Press.

———. 1990b. *Dreams of an Insomniac: Jewish Feminist Essays, Speeches and Diatribes*. Portland, OR: The Eighth Mountain Press.

Kline, Wendy. 2001. *Building a Better Race: Gender, Sexuality, and Eugenics from Turn of the Century to the Baby Boom*. Berkeley and London: University of California Press.

Knobel, Dale T. 1986. *Paddy and the Republic: Ethnicity and Nationality in Antebellum America*. Middletown, CT: Wesleyan University Press.

Kokhavi, Havah. 1994. *Hakhnasat Orhim*. Tel Aviv: Yaron Golan.

Korgen, Kathleen Odell. 1998. *From Black to Biracial: Transforming Racial Identity Among Americans*. Westport, CT: Praeger.

Kosmin, Barry, Egon Mayer, and Ariela Keysar. 2001. *American Religious Identification Survey*. New York: Graduate Center of the City University of New York. http://www.egonmayer.com/emayer_aris.pdf: 38 (6/18/05).

Krakauer, Hoong Yee Lee. 1991. "Casting Miss Saigon's Baby." *Lilith: The Independent Jewish Women's Magazine* 16, No. 4 (Fall): 5.

Krawitz, Cole. 2004. "A Voice From Within: A Challenge for the Conservative Jewish Movement." In Symposium "Tense Dialogues: Speaking (Across) Multicultural Difference in the Jewish Feminist World." Edited by Marla Brettschneider. Of *Nashim: A Journal of Jewish Women's Studies and Gender Issues* 8 (Fall): 165–174.

Labovitz, Gail. 2000. " 'These Are The Labors': Constructions of the Woman Nursing Her Child in the Mishnah and Tosefta." *Nashim: A Journal of Jewish Women's Studies and Gender Issues* 3 (Spring/Summer): 15–42.

Ladner, Joyce. 1977. *Mixed Families: Adopting Across Racial Boundaries*. New York: Archer Press/Doubleday.

Lampe, Philip E. 1987. *Adultery in the United States: Close Encounters of the Sixth (Or Seventh) Kind*. Buffalo, New York: Prometheus Books.

Lancaster, Roger N. 2003. *The Trouble with Nature: Sex in Science and Popular Culture*. Berkeley and London: University of California Press

Landes, Elisabeth and Richard Posner. 1978. "The Economics of the Baby Short-age." *Journal of Legal Studies* 7: 323–48.

Landing, James, 2001. *Black Judaism: Story of An American Movement*. Durham, NC: Carolina Academic Press.

Larson, Nella. 1986. *Quicksand and Passing*. Edited by Deborah McDowell. New Brunswick, NJ: Rutgers University Press.

Lasch, Christopher. 1975. *Haven in a Heartless World: The Family Besieged*. New York: Basic Books, Inc.

Lazzare, Jane. 1996. *Beyond the Whiteness of Whiteness: Memoir of a White Mother of Black Sons*. Durham, LA: Duke University Press.

Lehr, Valerie. 1999. *Queer Family Values: Debunking the Myth of the Nuclear Family*. Philadelphia: Temple University Press.

Lerner, Gerda. 1997. *Why History Matters: Life and Thought*. New York and Ox-ford: Oxford University Press.

Lerner, Michael. 1992. *The Socialism of Fools: Anti-Semitism on the Left*. Oakland, CA: Tikkun.

Lerner, Michael and Cornel West. 1995. *Jews and Blacks: Let the Healing Begin*. New York: G. P. Putnam's Sons.

——— and Cornel West. 1996. *Jews & Blacks: A Dialogue on Race, Religion, and Culture in America*. New York and London: Plume, Penguin.

Lester, Julius. 1988. *Lovesong: Becoming a Jew*. New York: Arcade Publishers.

Levenson, Bob. 1987. *Bill Bernbach's Book: A History of the Advertising That Changed the History of Advertising*. New York: Villard Books.

Levine, Amy Jill. 2003. "Multiculturalism, Women's Studies, and Anti-Judaism." In Special Section "Meeting at the Well: Multiculturalism and Jewish Femi-nism." Edited by Marla Brettschneider and Dawn Rose in the *Journal of Feminist Studies in Religion* 19, No. 1 (Spring): 119–128.

Levine, Hillel and Lawrence Harmon. 1992. *The Death of an American Jewish Community: A Tragedy of Good Intentions*. New York: The Free Press.

Levinson, Joshua. 2000. "Cultural Androgyny in Rabbinic Literature." In *From Athens to Jerusalem: Medicine in Hellenized Jewish Lore and in Early Christian Literature*. Edited by Samuel Kottek, Manfred Hortsmanshoff, Gerhard Baader, and Gary Ferngren. 119–140. Rotterdam, The Netherlands: Erasmus Publishing.

Lewis, Gregory. 2005. "Same-Sex Marriage and the 2004 Presidential Election." *PS: Political Science and Politics* 38, No. 2: 195–199.

Liem, Deann Borshay. 2000. *First Person, Plural*. San Fransisco: NAATA.

Lilith: The Independent Jewish Women's Magazine. Special Issue on Jewish Hair. 20, No. 1 (Spring 1995).

Lipsitz, George. 1998. *The Possessive Investment in Whiteness: How White People Profit from Identity Politics*. Philadelphia: Temple University Press.

Liss, David. 2003. *The Coffee Trader*. New York: Random House.

Litwoman, Jane. 1990. "Some Thoughts on Bisexuality." *Lesbian Contradictions* (Winter): 4–5.

Liu, Frederick and Stephen Macedo. 2005. "The Federal Marriage Amendment and the Strange Evolution of the Conservative Case Against Gay Marriage." *PS: Political Science and Politics* 38, No. 2: 211–215.

Lorde, Audre. 1984. *Sister Outsider: Essays and Speeches.* Trumansburg, NY: Crossing Press.

———. 1984. "The Erotic as Power," in *Sister Outsider.* Trumansburg, NY: Crossing Press.

Lounds, Morris. 1981. *Israel's Black Hebrews.* Washington, DC: University Press of America.

Mallon, Gerald P. 1998. *We Don't Exactly Get the Welcome Wagon: The Experiences of Gay and Lesbian Adolescents in Child Welfare Systems.* New York: Columbia University Press.

Malone, Ann Patton. 1992. *Sweet Chariot: Slave Family and Household Structure in Nineteenth-Century Louisiana.* Chapel Hill and London: The University of North Carolina Press.

Marks, Ross Kagan, Director. *Twilight of the Golds.* 1997. Fox Lorber Films.

Manga, Julie Engel. 2003. *Talking Trash: The Cultural Politics of Daytime TV Talk Shows.* New York and London: New York University Press.

Marsh, Margaret and Wanda Ronner. 1996. *The Empty Cradle: Infertility in American from Colonial Times to the Present.* Baltimore and London: The John Hopkins University Press.

Marso, Lori Jo. 2003. "A Feminist Search for Love: Emma Goldman on the Politics of Marriage, Love, Sexuality and the Feminine." *Feminist Theory* 4, No. 3 (December): 305–320.

Marquis, Christopher. 2003. "Total of Unmarried Couples Surged in 2000 U.S. Census." *The New York Times,* March 13, A22.

Marx, Karl. 1978. *Contribution to the Critique of Hegel's Philosophy of Right.* In *The Marx-Engels Reader.* 2d ed. Edited by Robert C. Tucker, 53–65. New York: W. W. Norton and Co. Inc.

Massey, Douglas. 1993. *American Apartheid: Segregation and the Making of the Underclass.* Cambridge, MA: Harvard University Press.

Matousek, Mark. 1996. *Sex, Death, Enlightenment.* London: Piatkus.

Matza, Diane. 1997. *Sephardic American Voices: Two Hundred Years of a Literary Legacy.* Hanover, NH and London: University Press of New England for Brandeis University Press.

Ma'yan. 1998. "Power and Parity: Women on the Boards of Major American Jewish Organizations." New York: Ma'yan: The Jewish Women's Project, a Program of the Jewish Community Center in Manhattan.

Mayer, Egon, Barry Kosmin, and Ariela Keysar. 2002. *The American Jewish Identity Survey.* The Graduate Center of the City University of New York. http://www.egonmayer.com/emayer_ajis.pdf : 20 and 25 (6/19/05).

Mays, V. M., L. M Chatters, S. D. Cochran, and J. Mackness. 1998. "African American Families in Diversity: Gay Men and Lesbians as Participants in Family Networks." *Journal of Comparative Families Studies* 29, No. 1: 73–87.

McBride, James. 1996. *The Color of Water: A Black Man's Tribute to His White Mother*. New York: Riverhead Books.

McKinley, Catherine E. 2002. *The Book of Sarahs: A Family in Parts*. Washington, DC and New York: Counterpoint.

McLarin, Kim. 1998. "Primary Colors: The Mother Is Black; Her Interracial Daughter Is Fair-Skinned. Society Has Trouble Seeing Their Connection." *New York Times Magazine* 24 (May): 58.

McMillan, Tracie. 2001. "Down For The Count." *City Limits Monthly*, April. Http: //www.citylimits.org/content/articles/articleView.cfm?articlenumber =159.

Melammed, Reneé Levine. 2002. *Heretics or Daughters of Israel?: The Crypto-Jewish Women of Castille*. New York: Oxford University Press.

———. 2004. *A Question of Identity: Iberian Conversos in Historical Perspective*. New York: Oxford University Press.

Melanson, Yvette. 1999. *Looking for Lost Bird: A Jewish Woman Discovers her Navajo Roots*. New York: Bard.

Melnick, Jeffrey Paul. 1999. *A Right to Sing the Blues: African Americans, Jews, and American Popular Song*. Cambridge, MA: Harvard University Press

———. 2000. *Black-Jewish Relations on Trial: Leo Frank and Jim Conley in the New South*. Jackson: University Press of Mississippi.

Messner, Michael A. 1997. *Politics of Masculinities: Men in Movements*. Thousand Oaks, CA: Sage Publications.

Meyerowitz, Joanne. 2002. *How Sex Changed: A History of Transsexuality in the United States*. Cambridge. MA: Harvard University Press.

Michaels, T. J. and Ali Cannon. 2002. "Which Side Are You On?: Transgender at the Western Wall." In *Queer Jews*. Edited by Caryn Aviv and David Shneer, 84–99. New York: Routledge and Kegan Paul.

Miles, William. 2005. "Carribean Hybridity and the Jews of Martinique. In *The Jewish Diaspora in Latin America and the Carribbean: Fragments of Memory*. Edited by Kristin Ruggiero, 139–162. Portland, OR: Sussex Academic Press.

Millen, Rochelle L. 2004. *Women, Birth, and Death in Jewish Law and Practice*. Hanover, NH and London: University Press of New England for Brandeis University Press.

Miron, Dan. 1996. *A Traveler Disguised: The Rise of Modern Yiddish Fiction in the Nineteenth Century*. Syracuse, NY: Syracuse University Press.

Modell, Judith. 1994. *Kinship with Strangers: Adoption and Interpretations of Kinship in American Culture*. Berkeley, CA: University of California Press.

Modleski, Tania. 1982. *Loving with a Vengeance: Mass-Produced Fantasies for Women*. New York: Methuen.

Moore, Evelyn. 1984. "Black Children Facing Adoption Barriers," *NASW News* (April): 9–10.

Moran, Rachel F. 2001. *Interracial Intimacy: The Regulation of Race and Romance*. Chicago and London: The University of Chicago Press.

Morgan, Lynn M. and Meredith W. Michaels. 1999. *Fetal Subjects, Feminist Positions*. Philadelphia: University of Pennsylvania Press.

Morgan, Robin, ed. 1970. *Sisterhood is Powerful: An Anthology of Writing from the Women's Liberation Movement*. New York: Vintage Books.

Moriel, Liora. 1999. "Dana International: A Self-Made Jewish Diva." In *Race, Gender, and Class: American Jewish Perspectives*. Edited by Marla Brett-schneider, 6, No. 4: 110–124.

Moynihan, Daniel Patrick. March 1965. *The Negro Family: The Case for National Action*. Washington, DC: Office of Policy Planning and Research, United States Department of Labor.

Mumford, Laura Stempel. 1995. *Love and Ideology in the Afternoon: Soap Opera, Women, and Television Genre*. Bloomington and Indianapolis, IN: Indiana University Press.

Nakayama, Thomas K. and Judith N. Martin, eds. 1999. *Whiteness: The Communication of Social Identity*. Thousand Oaks. CA: Sage Publications.

Narayan, Uma. 1998. "Rethinking 'Cultures': a Feminist Critique of Cultural Essentialism and Cultural Relativism." Annual Society of Women in Philosophy Eastern Division Spring Conference Keynote Address. University of New Hampshire, Durham.

Nathanson-Moog, Carol. 1984. "The Psychological Power of Ethnic Images in Advertising." In The Balch Institute For Ethnic Studies, Ethnic Images in Advertising: an Exhibition Co-Sponsored by the Balch Institute for Ethnic Studies and the Anti-Defamation League of B'nai Brith, 19–22. Philadelphia.

National Association of Black Social Workers. 1972. "Position Statement on Trans-Racial Adoption. The Adoption History Project. http://darkwing.uoregon.edu/~adoption/archive/NabswTRA.htm Accessed 11/23/04.

———. 1994. *Position Statement: "Preserving African American Families."* Detroit, MI: National Association of Black Social Workers.

National Jewish Population Survey: Strength, Challenge and Diversity in the American Jewish Population. 2000–2001. A United Jewish Communities Report in Cooperation with the Mandell L. Berman Institute-North American Jewish Data Bank Updated January 2004. New York. http://www.ujc.org/content_display.html?ArticleID=83252 (Accessed 04/19/05).

Nelson, Claudia. 2003. *Little Strangers: Portrayals of Adoption and Foster Care in America, 1850–1929*. Bloomington and Indianapolis, IN: Indiana University Press.

Neufeld, John. 1968. *Edgar Allen*. New York: Signet Press.

Newman, Leslia. 2000. *Heather Has Two Mommies*. Los Angeles: Alyson Wonderland.

Newton, Adam Zachary. 1999. *Facing Black and Jew: Literature as Public Space in Twentieth-Century America*. Cambridge, UK and New York: Cambridge University Press.

Nicolosi, Ann Marie. 2001. " 'We Do Not Want Our Girls to Marry Foreigners': Gender, Race, and American Citizenship." *NWSA Journal* 13, No. 3 (Fall): 1–21.

Nichols, Jack. 1975. *Men's Liberation: A New Definition of Masculinity*. New York: Penguin Books.

Ollman, Bertell. 1971. *Alienation: Marx's Conception of Man in Capitalist Society*. New York and London: Cambridge University Press.

Olyan, Saul. 1994. " 'And with a Male You Shall Not Lie the Lying Down of a Woman': On the Meaning and Significance of Leviticus 18: 22 and 20: 13." *Journal of the History of Sexuality* 5, No. 2.

Oney, Steve. 2003. *And the Dead Shall Rise: The Murder of Mary Phagan and the Lynching of Leo Frank*. New York: Pantheon Books.

Onolemhemhen, Durrenda Nash and Kebede Gessesse. 1998. *The Black Jews of Ethiopia: The Last Exodus*. Lanham, MD: Scarecrow Press.

Ordover, Nancy. 2003. *American Eugenics: Race, Queer Anatomy, and the Science of Nationalism*. Minneapolis and London: University of Minnesota Press.

Osborn, Torie. 1996. *Coming Home to America*. New York: St. Martin's Press.

Ottenheimer, Martin. 1996. *Forbidden Relatives: The Myth of Cousin Marriage*. Urbana and Chicago: University of Illinois Press.

Parfitt, Tudor. 1987. *The Thirteenth Gate: Travels Among the Lost Tribes of Israel*. Bethesda, MD: Adler and Adler.

———. 1993. *Journey to the Vanished City: The Search for a Lost Tribe of Israel*. New York: St. Martin's Press.

Pascoe, Peggy. 2000. "Miscegenation Law, Court Cases, and Ideologies of 'Race' in Twentieth-Century America." In *Unequal Sisters: A Multicultural Reader in U.S. Women's History*. Edited by Vicki L. Ruiz and Ellen Carol BuBois, 161–182. New York and London: Routledge.

Patton, Sandra. 2000. *Birth Marks: Transracial Adoption in Contemporary America*. New York: New York University Press.

Pauly, Philip J. 1987. *Controlling Life: Jacques Loeb and the Engineering Ideal in Biology*. New York and Oxford: Oxford University Press.

Pegueros, Rosa Maria. 2004. "Radical Feminists—No Jews Need Apply." In Symposium "Tense Dialogues: Speaking (Across) Multicultural Difference in the Jewish Feminist World." Edited by Marla Brettschneider of *Nashim: A Journal of Jewish Women's Studies and Gender Issues* 8 (Fall): 174–180.

Peplar, Michael. 2002. *Family Matters: A History of Ideas about Family Since 1945*. London and New York: Longman.

Perry, Twila. 1993/4. "The Transracial Adoption Controversy: An Analysis of Discourse and Subordination." *New York University Review of Law and Social Change* 21: 33–108.

———. 1990–91. "Race and Child Placement: The Best Interests Test and the Cost of Discretion." *Journal of Family Law* 29: 51–127.

Pertman, Adam. 2000a. *Adoption Nation: How the Adoption Revolution is Transforming America*. New York: Basic Books.

———. 2000b. "Senate Ratifies Treaty Setting Global Adoption Standards." *The Boston Globe*, September 21, A4.

Peskowitz, Miriam B. 1997. *Spinning Fantasies: Rabbis, Gender, and History*. Berkeley, CA: University of California Press.

Pfeffer, Paula. 2002. "A Historical Comparison of Catholic and Jewish Adoption Practices in Chicago, 1833–1933." In *Adoption in America: Historical Perspectives*. Edited by E. Wayne Carp, 101–123. Ann Arbor: University of Michigan Press.

Phelan, Shane. 1994. *Getting Specific: Postmodern Lesbian Politics*. Minneapolis, MN: University of Minnesota Press.

———. 1989. *Identity Politics: Lesbian Feminism and the Limits of Community*. Philadelphia: Temple University Press.

Pietrzak, Brooke. 1997. "Marriage Laws and People with Mental Retardation: A Continuing History of Second Class Treatment." *Developments in Mental Health Law*. The Institute of Law, Psychiatry and Public Policy–The University of Virginia. 17, No. 1 and 2 (January–December): 1–3, 33–46.

Plaskow, Judith. 1991. *Standing Again at Sinai: Judaism from a Feminist Perspective*. New York: Harper Collins Publishers.

Platt, Lord and A. S. Parkes, eds. *Social and Genetic Influences on Life and Death*. New York: Plenum Press.

Podhoretz, Norman. 1963. "My Negro Problem—And Ours." *Commentary* 35, No. 2 (February): 93–101.

Pogrebin, Letty Cottin. 1991. *Deborah, Golda, and Me: Being Female and Jewish in America*. New York: Crown Publishers, Inc.

Popper, Nathaniel. 2004. "Nearly a Million Living in Poor Jewish Households." *Forward*, October 8, 1–3.

———. 2005. "Religious Views are Dividing The 'Hidden Jews' of Mexico." *Forward*, July 29, 1–4.

Posner, Richard. 1992. *Sex and Reason*. Cambridge. MA: Harvard University Press.

Porter, Susan L. 2002. "A Good Home: Indenture and Adoption in Nineteenth-century Orphanages." In *Adoption in America: Historical Perspectives*. Edited by E. Wayne Carp, 27–50. Ann Arbor, MI: The University of Michigan Press.

Prager, Karen, Hadar Dubowsky, Robin Beth Schaer, and Alina Sivorinovsky. 1993. "Riddles of Identity: Twentysomething Jewish Feminists Swim in the Crosscurrents of Multiculturalism." *Lilith: The Independent Jewish Women's Magazine* 18, No. 3 (Summer): 13–23.

Prell, Riv Ellen. 1999. *Fighting to Become Americans. Jews, Gender, and the Anxiety of Assimilation*. Boston: Beacon Press.

Presser, Stephen B. 1971–2. "The Historical Background of the American Law of Adoption." *Journal of Family Law* 11: 443–516.

Priest, Patricia Joyner. 1995. *Public Intimacies: Talk Show Participants and the Tell-All TV*. Cresskill, NJ: Hampton Press.

Prinz, Joachim. 1977. *The Secret Jews*. New York: Random House.

Proctor, Robert. 1988. *Racial Hygiene: Medicine Under the Nazis*. Cambridge, MA: Harvard University Press.

Radin, Jessica. 2004. "Better Off Than You Would Have Been: Feminist Legacies for Transnational Adoptive Families in the Jewish Community." In Symposium "Tense Dialogues: Speaking (Across) Multicultural Difference in the Jewish Feminist World." Edited by Marla Brettschneider of *Nashim: A Journal of Jewish Women's Studies and Gender Issues* 8 (Fall): 143–154.

Radin, Margaret Jane. 1987. "Market Inalienability." *Harvard Law Review* 100, No. 8 (June): 1849–1937.

Rapp, Rayna. 1999. *Testing Women, Testing the Fetus: the Social Impact of Amniocentesis in America*. New York and London: Routledge.

Ratcliff, J. D. 1937. "No Father to Guide Them." *Collier's* 99: 19 and 73.

Ratner, Rochelle, ed. 2000. *Bearing Life: Women's Writings on Childlessness*. New York: Feminist Press at the City University of New York.

Rauch, Jonathan. 2004. *Gay Marriage: Why it is Good for Gays, Good for Straights, and Good for America.* New York: Times Books/Holt and Co.

Rawlings, Martha Morse. 1999. "Reconstructing Identities: The Utility of Adolescent Pregnancy." Paper delivered at the Race, Gender and Class Conference October 28–30, New Orleans.

Reddy, Maureen T. 1994. *Crossing the Color Line: Race, Parenting, and Culture.* New Brunswick, NJ: Rutgers University Press.

Reed, James. 1983. *The Birth Control Movement and American Society: From Private Voice to Public Vice.* Princeton, NJ: Princeton University Press.

Reiling, Jennifer, Section Editor. 2000. "Regulation of Marriage." In "JAMA 100 Years Ago." *Journal of the American Medical Association* 283, No. 8 (February 23): 980.

Resnick Levine, Elizabeth, ed. 1991. *A Ceremonies Sampler: New Rites. Celebrations, and Observances of Jewish Women.* San Diego, CA: Women's Institute for Continuing Jewish Education.

Response: Special Issue: Queer Jews. 67 (Winter/Spring 1997).

Rich, Adrienne. 1976. *Of Woman Born: Motherhood as Experience and as Institution.* New York: W. W. Norton and Co., and Bantam.

———. 1979. "Disloyal to Civilization: Feminism, Racism, Gynephobia." In *On Lies, Secrets, and Silence: Selected Prose, 1966–1978,* 275–310. New York: W. W. Norton and Co..

———. 1980. "Compulsory Heterosexuality and Lesbian Existence." *Signs* 5, No. 4 (Summer): 631–660.

Riggle, Ellen, Jerry Thomas, and Sharon Rostosky. 2005. "The Marriage Debate and Minority Stress." *PS: Political Science and Politics* 38, No. 2: 221–224.

Roberts, Dorothy. 1997. *Killing the Black Body: Race, Reproduction, and the Meaning of Liberty.* New York: Pantheon Books.

———. 2002. *Shattered Bonds: The Color of Child Welfare.* New York: Basic Civitas Books.

Roediger, David. 1991 and 1999. *The Wages of Whiteness: Race and the Making of the American Working Class.* London and New York: Verso.

Rogin, Michael. 1996. *Black Face, White Noise: Jewish Immigrants in the Hollywood Melting Pot.* Berkeley, CA: University of California Press.

Rogoff, Leonard. 1997. "Is the Jew White? The Racial Place of the Southern Jew." *American Jewish History* 85, No. 3 (September): 195–230.

Root, Maria, ed. 1996. *The Multiracial Experience: Racial Borders as the New Frontier.* Newbury Park, CA: Sage Publications.

Rose, Dawn. 1999. "Class as Problematic in Jewish Feminist Theology." In *Race, Gender, and Class: American Jewish Perspectives.* Edited by Marla Brettschneider, 6, No. 4: 125–135.

———. 2000. Review of Rachel Adler's *Engendering Judaism: An Inclusive Theology and Ethics* in *Bridges* 8, No. 1 and 2: 60–63.

Rose, Sharon. 1996. "Against Marriage." In *Bisexual Horizons: Politics, Histories, Lives.* Edited by Sharon Rose, Cris Stevens et al., 119–121. Lawrence & Wishart.

Rosenberg, Milla. 2003. "Tans/positioning the (Drag?) King of Comedy: Bisexuality and Queer Jewish Space in the Works of Sandra Bernhard." In *Bisexuality and Transgenderism: InterSEXions of the Others*. Edited by Jonathan Alexander, Karen Yescavage, 171–179. New York: Harrington Park Press.

Rosenberg, Shelley Kapnek. 1998. *Adoption and the Jewish Family: Contemporary Perspectives*. Philadelphia and Jerusalem: The Jewish Publication Society.

Ross, Fran. 1974. *Oreo*. Boston: Northeastern University Press.

Roth, Rachel. 1999. "The Reproductive Rights of Prisoners: Between a Rock and a Hard Place." *Sojourner: The Women's Forum* 24, No. 11 (July 7): 11–.

Rothman, Barbara Katz. 2005. *Weaving a Family: Untangling Race and Adoption*. Boston: Beacon Press.

Ruggiero, Kristin, ed. 2005. *The Jewish Diaspora in Latin America and the Carribbean: Fragments of Memory*. Portland, OR: Sussex Academic Press.

Rush, Sharon. 2000. *Loving Across the Color Line: A White Adoptive Mother Learns About Race*. Lanham, MD: Rowman & Littlefield Publishers, Inc.

Ruttenberg, Danya, ed. 2001. *Yentl's Revenge: The Next Wave of Jewish Feminists*. Seattle: Seal Press.

Sales, Amy, ed. 1995. "Voices for Change: Future Directions for American Jewish Women, The National Commission on American Jewish Women." Waltham, MA: The National Commission on American Jewish Women, Hadassah and Brandeis University.

Salzman, Jack, ed. 1992. *Bridges and Boundaries: African Americans and Jews*. New York: George Braziller, Inc.

Samuels, Elizabeth J. 2001. "The Idea of Adoption: An Inquiry into the History of Adult Adoptee Acess to Birth Records." *Rutgers Law Review* 53: 367–455.

Sandelowski, Margarete. 1993. *With Child in Mind: Studies of the Personal Encounter with Infertility*. Philadelphia: University of Pennsylvania Press.

Sanger, Carol. 1996. "Separating from Children." *Columbia Law Review* 96, No. 2 (March): 375–517.

Sartre, Jean-Paul. 1963. *Black Orpheus*. Translated by S. W. Allen. Paris: Editions Gallimard.

———. 1948. *Anti-Semite and Jew*. Translated by George J. Becker. New York: Schocken Books.

Satlow, Michael L. 1996. " 'Try To Be A Man': The Rabbinic Construction of Masculinity." *Harvard Theological Review* 89, No. 1 (January): 19–40.

Saunders, Anne. 2004. "Lawmakers Consider Unsealing Birth Certificate in Adoptions." The Associated Press State and Local Wire. February 3, BC cycle-Concord, NH.

Scales-Trent, Judy. 1995. *Notes of a White Black Woman*. University Park: Pennsylvania State University Press.

Schiffman, Lisa. 1999. *Generation J*. San Francisco: Harper San Francisco.

Schimel, Lawrence. 1997. "Diaspora, Sweet Diaspora." In *PoMoSexuals: Challenging Assumptions about Gender and Sexuality*. Edited by Carol Queen and Lawrence Schimel, 163–173. San Francisco: Cleis Press.

Schneider, Susan Weidman. 1984. *Jewish and Female: Choices and Changes in our Lives Today*. New York: Simon and Schuster.

Schnur, Susan, ed. 1998. "In Pursuit of Motherhood: Infertility and Adoption" Special Issue *Lilith: The Independent Jewish Women's Magazine* 23, No. 2 (Summer): 19–31.

Schultz, Debra L. 2001. *Going South: Jewish Women in the Civil Rights Movement*. New York and London: New York University Press.

Seccombe, Wally. 1992. *A Millennium of Family Change: Feudalism to Capitalism in Northwestern Europe*. New York: Verso.

Seidman, Naomi. 1997. *A Marriage Made in Heaven: The Sexual Politics of Hebrew and Yiddish*. Berkeley, CA: University of California Press.

Seif, Hinda. 1999. "A 'Most Amazing Borsht:' Multiple Identities in a Jewish Bisexual Community." In *Race, Gender, Class: American Jewish Perspectives*. Edited by Marla Brettschneider, 6, No. 4: 88–109.

Sered, Susan. 1996. *Women as Ritual Experts: The Religious Lives of Elderly Jewish Women in Jerusalem*. New York: Oxford University Press.

———. 2000. *What Makes Women Sick? Maternity, Modesty and Militarism in Israeli Society*. Hanover, NH and London: University Press of New England for Brandeis University Press.

Segura, Gary. 2005. "A Symposium on the Politics of Same-Sex Marriage—An Introduction and Commentary." *PS: Political Science and Politics* 38, No. 2: 189–193.

Shanley, Mary Lyndon. 2001. *Making Babies, Making Families: What Matters Most in an Age of Reproductive Technologies, Surrogacy, Adoption, and Same-Sex and Unwed Parents*. Boston: Beacon Press.

Shapiro, Joseph P. 1993. *No Pity: People with Disabilities Forging a New Civil Rights Movement*. New York: Random House.

Shattuc, Jane M. 1997. *The Talking Cure: TV Talk Shows and Women*. New York and London: Routledge.

Sicular, Eve. 1995–1996. "Gender Rebellion In Yiddish Film." *Lilith: The Independent Jewish Women's Magazine* 20, No. 4 (Winter): 12–17.

Sidel, Ruth. 2000. "The Enemy Within: The Demonization of Poor Women." *Journal of Sociology and Social Welfare* 27, No. 1: 73–84.

Siegal, Nina. 1998. "Women in Prison." *Ms.* (September/October): 65–72.

Sieglitz, Maria. 1991. New Mexico's Secret Jews: Is it Safe to Tell?" *Lilith: The Independent Jewish Women's Magazine* 16, No. 1 (Winter): 8–10, 12.

Silliman, Jael. 2001. *Jewish Portraits, Indian Frames: Women's Narratives from a Diaspora of Hope*. Hannover and London: Brandeis University Press published by the University Press of New England.

Silliman, Jael and Ynestra King. 1999. *Dangerous Intersections: Feminist Perspectives on Population, Environment, and Development*. Cambridge, MA: South End Press.

Simon, Rita J., Howard Altstein, and Marygold S. Melli. 1994. *The Case for Transracial Adoption*. Washington, DC: American University Press.

Simon, Rita J. and Howard Altstein. 2000. *Adoption Across Borders: Serving the Children in Transracial and Intercountry Adoptions*. Lanham, MD: Rowman & Littlefield Publishers, Inc.

Simon, Rita J. and Rhonda M. Roorda. 2000. *In Their Own Voices: Transracial Adoptees Tell Their Stories.* New York: Columbia University Press.

Singer, Ilana Gerard. 1992. "Red-Diaper Daughter." *Lilith: The Independent Jewish Women's Magazine* 17, No. 3 (Summer): 7–10.

Skolnick, Arlene. 1991. *Embattled Paradise: The American Family in an Age of Uncertainty.* New York: Basic Books.

Smith, Barbara. 1979. "Notes For Yet Another Paper on Black Feminism, or Will the Real Enemy Please Stand Up." *Conditions* 5: 123–32.

———, ed. 1983. *Home Girls: A Black Feminist Anthology.* New York: Kitchen Table: Women of Color Press.

Smith, Christine A. and Shannon Stillman. 2003. "Do Butch and Femme Still Attract?" *The Gay and Lesbian Review* 10, No. 4: 17–18.

Smith, Jane, Ann V. Waldorf, and David L. Trembath. 1990. "Single White Male Looking For Thin, Very Attractive . . ." *Sex Roles* 23 (December): 675–685.

Smith, Miriam. 2005. "The Politics of Same-Sex Marriage in Canada and the United States." *PS: Political Science and Politics* 38, No. 2: 225–228.

Smolowe. Jill and Wendy Cole. 1995. "Adoption in Black and White." *Time* 146 (August 14): 7: 50.

Snyder, R. Claire. 1999. *Citizen-Soldiers and Manly Warriors.* Lanham, MD: Rowman & Littlefield Publishers, Inc.

Spiegel, Marcia Cohen. Publication Date: April 11, 2000. Revision Date: January 12, 2004. (6/29/05) *Bibliography of Sexual and Domestic Violence in the Jewish Community.* http://www.mincava.umn.edu/documents/bibs/jewish/jewish.html

Spelman, Elizabeth V. 1988. *Inessential Woman: Problems of Exclusion in Feminist Thought.* Boston: Beacon Press.

Staudenmaier, Peter. 2/26/01. "Slipping the Ties that Bind." www.lipmagazine.org.

Stavans, Ilan. 2003. *The Scroll and the Cross: 1,000 Years of Jewish-Hispanic Literature.* New York and London: Routledge.

Stencel, Sandra, ed. 1999. Special Issue on Adoption Controversies *Congressional Quarterly Researcher* 9, No. 34 (September 10): 777–800.

Steinberg, Stephen. 2001. *The Ethnic Myth: Race, Ethnicity and Class in America.* Boston: Beacon Press.

Stern, Madeleine B., ed. 1974. *The Victoria Woodhull Reader.* Weston, MA: M and S Press.

Stevens, Jacqueline. 1999. *Reproducing the State.* Princeton, NJ: Princeton University Press.

———. 2005. "Methods of Adoption: Eliminating Genetic Privilege." In *Adoption Matters: Philosophical and Feminist Essays.* Edited by Sally Haslanger and Charlotte Witt, 68–94. Ithaca: Cornell University Press.

Stevenson, Brenda E. 1996. *Life in Black and White: Family and Community in the Slave South.* New York and Oxford: Oxford University Press.

Stillman, Jael Miriam and Ynestra King, eds. 1999. *Dangerous Intersections: Feminist Perspectives on Population, Environment, and Development.* Cambridge, MA: South End Press.

Stone, Linda. 2001. *New Directions in Anthropological Kinship.* Lanham, MD: Rowman & Littlefield Publishers, Inc.

Strathern, Marilyn. 1995. "Displacing Knowledge: Technology and the Consequences for Kinship." In *Conceiving the New World Order: The Global Politics of Reproduction*. Edited by Faye D. Ginsburg and Rayna Rapp, 346–363. Berkeley, CA: University of California Press.

Sue, George. 2001. "Making Sense of Bisexual Personal Ads." *Journal of Bisexuality* 1, No. 4: 34–57.

Sullivan, Andrew. 1996. *Virtually Normal: An Argument about Homosexuality*. New York: Vintage Books.

Sullivan, Randall. 2001. "The Bastard Chronicles." *Rolling Stone*, February 15, Issue 862: 53; and March 1, Issue 863: 41.

Svonkin, Stuart. 1997. *Jews Against Prejudice: American Jews and the Fight for Civil Liberties*. New York: Columbia University Press.

Swirl, Inc. 6.22.05. "Everything You Always Wanted to Know about the Census: Gearing up for 2010." http://www.swirlinc.org/CensusFAQs.htm.

Talbot, Margaret. 1998. "Attachment Theory: The Ultimate Experiment." *The New York Times Magazine*. May 24, 24.

Tannenbaum, Frank. 1946. *Slave and Citizen*. New York: Vintage Books.

Taylor, Janelle, Linda Layne, and Danielle Wozniak, eds. 2004. *Consuming Motherhood*. New Brunswick, NJ: Rutgers University Press.

Tessman, Lisa and Bat-Ami Bar On, eds. 2001. *Jewish Locations: Traversing Racialized Landscapes*. Lanham, MD: Rowman & Littlefield Publishers, Inc.

Tevajieh, Kessaye (as told to Penina V. Adelman). 1993. "Out of Africa: A Jewish Woman's Modern Day Exodus." *Lilith: The Independent Jewish Women's Magazine* 18, No. 2 (Spring): 6–11.

Thornton, C. Michael. 1992. "Is Multiracial Status Unique? The Personal and Social Experience." In *Racially Mixed People in America*. Edited by Maria P. P. Root, 321–325. Newbury Park, CA: Sage Publications.

Thornton, Russell. 2001. "What the Census Doesn't Count." *The New York Times*. March 23, A19.

Time Out. 2003. *The New Super Jews* (December–11 2003 Issue): No. 427.

Tobin, Diane, Gary A. Tobin, and Scott Rubin. 2005. "The Growth and Vitality of Jewish Peoplehood: Ethnic and Racial Diversity." See the "In Every Tongue Initiative." San Francisco: Institute for Jewish & Community. Research.http://www.jewishresearch.org/projects_growth. htm (26/18/05)

Tobin, Gary and Groeneman, Sid. 2003. "Surveying the Jewish Population in the United States." San Francisco: Institute for Jewish and Community Research. http://www.jewishresearch.org/PDFs/Population_Report.pdf (6/18/05)

Tucker, Irene. 2000. *A Probable State: The Novel, the Contract, and the Jews*. Chicago: University of Chicago Press.

Tucker, Naomi. 1996. "Passing: Pain or Privilege? What the Bisexual Community Can Learn from the Jewish Experience. In *Bisexual Horizons: Politics, Histories, Lives*. Edited by Sharon Rose, Cris Stevens et al., 32–37. London: Lawrence & Wishart.

Tucker, Robert C., ed. 1978. *The Marx-Engels Reader*. New York: W. W. Norton and Co.

Turner, Jeffrey. 2002. *Families in America: A Reference Handbook*. Santa Barbara, CA: ABC-CLIO.

2003. "Research Shows Sperm Has Egg Locater." *The New York Times*, March 28, A12.

20/20 Special on ABC by Barbara Walters Friday 4/30/04. "Be My Baby: A Unique Look Inside the Open Adoption Process."

UCLA Asian American Studies Center. 1976. "Anti-Miscegenation Laws and the Philipino." In *Letters in Exile: An Introductory Reader on the History of Philipinos in America*, 63–71. Los Angeles: Resource Development and Publications, The Regents of the University of California.

Umansky, Ellen M. and Dianne Ashton, eds. 1992. *Four Centuries of Jewish Women's Spirituality*. Boston: Beacon Press.

Vaid, Urvashi. 1996. *Virtual Equality: the Mainstreaming of Gay and Lesbian Liberation*. New York: Anchor Books.

Vega, Cecilia. 2003. "Sterilization Offer to Addicts Reopens Ethics Issue." *The New York Times*, January 6, B1–2.

Volkman, Toby Alice and Cindi Katz, eds. 2003. Special Issue on Transnational Adoption. *Social Text* 21, No. 1.

Volpp, Leti. 2003. "American Mestizo: Filipinos and Anti-Miscegenation Laws in California." In *Mixed Race America and the Law: A Reader*. Edited by Kevin R. Johnson, 86–93. New York and London: New York University Press.

Wadia-Ells, Susan, ed. 1995. *The Adoption Reader: Birth Mothers, Adoptive Mothers and Adopted Daughters Tell Their Stories*. Seattle: Seal Press.

Walker, Rebecca. 2001. *Black, White, and Jewish: Autobiography of a Shifting Self*. New York: Riverhead Books of Penguin Putnam Inc.

Wall, Richard, Tamara K. Hareven, and Josef Ehmer with the assistance of Markus Cerman, eds. 2001. *Family History Revisited: Comparative Perspectives*. Newark, NJ: University of Delaware Press; London: Associated University Presses.

Walzer, Michael. 1998. "On Involuntary Association." In *Freedom of Association*. Edited by Amy Gutman, 64–74. Princeton, NJ: Princeton University Press.

Warner, Michael, ed. 1993. Introduction to *Fear of a Queer Planet: Queer Politics and Social Theory*, vii–xxxi. Minneapolis, MN: University of Minnesota Press.

Warner, Michael. 1999. *The Trouble with Normal: Sex, Politics, and the Ethics of Queer Life*. New York: Free Press.

Wasserfall, Rahel R., ed. 1999. *Women and Water: Menstruation in Jewish Life and Law*. Hanover, NH and London: University Press of New England for Brandeis University Press.

Weber, Max. 2001. *The Protestant Ethic and the Spirit of Capitalism*. New York and London: Routledge.

Weisbord, Robert and Arthur Stein. 1970. *Bittersweet Encounter: The Afro-American and the American Jew*. Westport, CT: Negro Universities Press.

Weissler, Chava. 1998. *Voices of the Matriarchs: Listening to the Prayers of Early Modern Jewish Women*. Boston: Beacon Press.

West, Cornel and Jack Salzman. 1997. *Struggles in the Promised Land: Towards a History of Black-Jewish Relations in the United States*. New York: Oxford University Press.

West, Robin. 1998. "Universalism, Liberal Theory, and the Problem of Gay Marriage." *Florida State University Law Review* 25, No. 4 (Summer): 705–730.

Weston, Kath. 1991. *Families We Choose: Lesbians, Gays, Kinship*. New York: Columbia University Press.

Will, Thomas E. 1999. "Weddings on Contested Grounds: Slave Marriage in the Antebellum South." *The Historian* 62, No. 1 (Fall): 99–117.

Williams, Gwyneth I. and Rys H. Williams. 1995. " 'All We Want is Equality' " Rhetorical Framing in the Fathers' Rights Movement." In *Images of Issues: Typifying Contemporary Social Problems*. Edited by Joel Best, 191–212. New York: Aldine de Gruyter, Inc.

Williams, Lena. 1995. "Losing Isaiah: Truth in Shades of Gray." *New York Times*, March 23, C1.

Williams, Linda Faye. 2003. *The Constraint of Race: Legacies of White Skin Privilege in America*. University Park: The Pennsylvania State University Press.

Williams, Patricia. 1997a. *Seeing a Color-Blind Future: The Paradox of Race*. New York: The Noonday Press.

———. 1997b. "Spare Parts, Family Values, Old Children, Cheap." In *Critical Race Feminism: A Reader*. Edited by Adrien Wing, 151–158. New York: New York University Press.

Wing, Adrienne, ed. 1997. *Critical Race Feminism*. New York: Routledge.

Wise, Claudia, with Susan Schnur. 1992. "Burned at the Stake: The Rediscovered Case of Isabel Lopez." *Lilith: The Independent Jewish Women's Magazine* 17, No. 3 (Summer): 8–24.

Woods, Karen M. 2003. "A 'Wicked and Mischievous Connnection': The Origins of Indian-White Miscegenation Law. In *Mixed Race America and the Law: A Reader*. Edited by Kevin R. Johnson, 81–85. New York and London: New York University Press.

Wright, Lawrence. 1994. "One Drop of Blood." *New Yorker*, July 25, 46–55.

Wynia, Elly. 1994. *The Church of God and Saints of Christ: The Rise of Black Jews*. New York: Garland Publishing.

Yeskel, Felice. 1996. "Beyond the Taboo: Talking About Class." In *The Narrow Bridge: Jewish Views on Multiculturalism*. Edited by Marla Brettschneider, 27–41. New Brunswick, NJ: Rutgers University Press.

Yeskel, Felice and Chuck Collins. 2000. *Economic Apartheid In America: A Primer on Economic Inequality and Insecurity*. New York: New Press, Distributed by W. W. Norton and Co.

Yngvesson, Barbara and Maureen Mahoney. 2000. " 'As One Should, Ought, and Wants to Be: ' Belonging and Authenticity in Identity Narratives." *Theory, Culture and Society* 17, No. 6 (December): 77–110.

Yolanda Shoshana. 2004. "Am I My Sister's Keeper?" In Symposium "Tense Dialogues: Speaking (Across) Multicultural Difference in the Jewish Feminist World." Edited by Marla Brettschneider of *Nashim: A Journal of Jewish Women's Studies and Gender Issues* 8 (Fall): 154–164.

Zack, Naomi. 1993. *Race and Mixed Race*. Philadelphia: Temple University Press.

———. 1996. "On Being and Not: Being Black and Jewish." In *The Multiracial Experience: Racial Borders as the New Frontier*. Edited by Maria P. P. Root, 140–151. Newbury Park, CA: Sage Publications.

———, ed. 1995. *American Mixed Race: the Culture of Microdiversity*. Lanham, MD: Rowman & Littlefield Publishers, Inc.

Zainaldin, Jamil. 1979. "The Emergence of a Modern American Family Law: Child Custody, Adoption, and the Courts, 1796–1851." *Northwestern University Law Review* 73: 1038–89.

Zerubavel, Yael. 1995. *Recovered Roots: Collective Memory and the Making of Israeli National Tradition*. Chicago: University of Chicago Press.

Zuckerman, Rachel. 2003. "Procedure Offers Hope For Families." *Forward*, August 15, B1–.

Index